Voices from Calcutta

Between 1837 and 1920, 1.3 million indentured labourers migrated from India to sugar plantation colonies in the Indian Ocean and the Caribbean. *Voices from Calcutta* shows how spokesmen from Calcutta – the capital of British India – disrupted this trade and influenced the lives of these migrants. It follows Calcuttans in their journey of debating, investigating and defending indenture, unfolding a complex web of letters, petitions, interviews and investigative reports.

As the indenture debates influenced lived experience on ships and plantations, and shaped the negotiation of subjecthood and labour rights for the British Empire's peripatetic labourers, they became a means by which elite Calcuttans negotiated their own position within the empire. This book locates in Calcutta voices of protest that fundamentally defined the contours of post-slavery labouring across the empire. Instead of simply emanating from Britain, to be dutifully followed in the colonies, labour legislation was informed by voices from those very colonies.

Purba Hossain is Lecturer in Modern History at the University of York. She is a historian of colonial India with an interest in how Indians negotiated life under colonial rule and contributed to imperial processes.

GLOBAL SOUTH ASIANS

Throughout the modern era, South Asia and South Asians have been entangled with global flows of goods, people and ideas. In the context of these globalised conditions, migrants from the subcontinent of India created some of the world's most extensive and influential transnational networks. While operating within the constraints of imperial systems, they nevertheless made distinctive and important contributions to international trade, global cultures and transnational circuits of knowledge. This series seeks to explore these phenomena, placing labourers, traders, thinkers and activists at the centre of the analysis. Beginning with volumes that seek to radically reappraise indenture, the series will continue with books on the mobility of elite actors, including intellectuals, and their contributions to the global circulation of ideas and the evolution of political practice. It will highlight the creativity and agency of diasporic South Asians and illuminate the crucial role they played in the making of global histories. As such it sets out to challenge popular misconceptions and established scholarly narratives that too often cast South Asians as passive observers.

Voices from Calcutta

Indian Indenture in the Age of Abolition

Purba Hossain

CAMBRIDGE
UNIVERSITY PRESS

Shaftesbury Road, Cambridge CB2 8EA, United Kingdom

One Liberty Plaza, 20th Floor, New York, NY 10006, USA

477 Williamstown Road, Port Melbourne, VIC 3207, Australia

314–321, 3rd Floor, Plot 3, Splendor Forum, Jasola District Centre, New Delhi – 110025, India

103 Penang Road, #05–06/07, Visioncrest Commercial, Singapore 238467

Cambridge University Press is part of Cambridge University Press & Assessment, a department of the University of Cambridge.

We share the University's mission to contribute to society through the pursuit of education, learning and research at the highest international levels of excellence.

www.cambridge.org
Information on this title: www.cambridge.org/9781009573009

First published 2025

Printed in India by Avantika Printers Pvt. Ltd.

Cover image: 'Garden Reach', in *Views of Calcutta and Its Environs*, by Sir Charles D'Oyly (London, 1848); shelfmark: X 666, plate 3, British Library Images Online, https://imagesonline.bl.uk/asset/32812.

A catalogue record for this publication is available from the British Library

ISBN 978-1-009-57300-9 Hardback

For EU product safety concerns, contact us at Calle de José Abascal, 56, 1°, 28003 Madrid, Spain, or email eugpsr@cambridge.org.

For ma and baba

Contents

Figures

Acknowledgements

This book was conceived in Kolkata but written in Leeds, Durham and Cambridge. In the process, I have accumulated a wealth of debt. The research was funded by the University of Leeds; the Royal Historical Society, London; and the Economic History Society, London. The School of History (University of Leeds), the Institute of Historical Research and the Institute of Commonwealth Studies (London), St. John's College (University of Durham) and Christ's College (University of Cambridge) provided generous and crucial institutional support. Research for this book took me to the National Archives of India and the Nehru Memorial Museum and Library in New Delhi; the West Bengal State Archives, the National Library, the Sadharon Brahmo Samaj Library, the Town Hall Archives and Library, the Rammohun Library, the Kolkata Port Trust Maritime Archives and Heritage Centre and the Rabindra Bharati Museum in Kolkata; the British Library and the Senate House Library in London; and Gladstone's Library in Hawarden (Wales). I am grateful to the archivists and librarians at these institutions, who have been very patient with my queries.

My initial findings on anti-indenture activism in Calcutta were first discussed in the article 'Protests at the Colonial Capital: Calcutta and the Global Debates on Indenture, 1836–42', *Journal of South Asian Studies*, 33 no. 1 (2017): 37–51.* Chapter 4's discussion of merchant networks and John Gladstone builds upon the article '"A Matter of Doubt and Uncertainty": John Gladstone and the Post-Slavery Framework of Labour in the British Empire', *Journal of Imperial* *and Commonwealth History* 50, no. 1 (2022): 52–80. Some initial findings on the racialisation of indentured labourers as discussed in Chapter 5 were published in '"Docile, Quiet, Orderly": Indian Indenture Trade and the Ideal Labourer', in *Across Colonial Lines: Commodities, Networks, and Empire Building*, ed. Devyani Gupta and Purba Hossain, pp. 179–198 (Bloomsbury Publishing, 2023). I am grateful to Taylor & Francis and Bloomsbury Publishing for allowing me to develop upon them in this monograph.

Writing this book has been a process of learning and unlearning, and I am grateful for my friends, mentors and colleagues who helped me sharpen and develop my ideas. My professors in Kolkata – Soumen Mukherjee, Souvik Mukherjee, Mridu Rai and Shukla Sanyal – were the first to see the potential of this project. My doctoral supervisors, Andrea Major and William Gould, have been exceptional: supportive, generous, patient and kind. My conversations with them shaped how I think through my research. In Leeds, Jonathan Saha, John Gallagher, Sarah Gandee, Catherine Coombs and the late Malcolm Chase were amazingly supportive. Ben, Charlotte, Eilis, Ellie, Emily, George, Jethro, Josh, Laura, Lauren, Owen and Sam kept me sane and grounded over the years, and I could not have asked for a more exciting, welcoming and engaging cohort. Clare Anderson and Elisabeth Leake were supportive and encouraging, and their many helpful suggestions have driven this book. Susan Bayly, Harriet Lyon, Helen Pfeifer, David Reynolds and Sujit Sivasundaram in Cambridge offered their time and advice generously. The anonymous reviewers of this book pushed me to think more broadly and intentionally about agency, voice, empire and resistance. My commissioning editor Anwesha Rana has been an absolute delight to work with, and I am thankful to her and the team at Cambridge University Press for their kind guidance through the publication process.

Closer to home, Andrew has been amazing throughout, and although he has probably heard me talk about indenture one too many times, conversations with him pushed me to interrogate the intersections between indenture history and South Asian history more critically. My parents, Sumita Das and Shah Hossain, from whom I inherited my love for history, travel and books, have shaped this journey in more ways than one. I doubt I would have been a historian without them. To them this book is dedicated.

Abbreviations

APS	Aborigines Protection Society
BFASS	British and Foreign Anti-Slavery Society
BIS	British India Society
BL	British Library, London
BS	Bangla *sambat*, or the Bengali calendar, starting in 593/594 CE
GG-MSS	Glynne-Gladstone Manuscript Collection, Gladstone's Library, Hawarden, Wales
IOR	India Office Records, British Library, London
NAI	National Archives of India, New Delhi
NL	National Library, Kolkata
SAGK	Society for the Acquisition of General Knowledge
WBSA	West Bengal State Archives, Kolkata

Introduction

On the river Ganges in Kolkata (erstwhile Calcutta), there is a small *ghat* (pier) bearing the name of a faraway South American country – the Surinam Ghat.[1] Seemingly out of place in a port city about 15,000 kilometres away from Surinam, it is named after the Surinam Depot, which used to accommodate Indian labourers migrating to the erstwhile Dutch colony as plantation workers. In fact, for a large part of the nineteenth and early twentieth centuries, the port side of Calcutta was dotted with buildings like the Trinidad Depot, Mauritius Depot, British Guiana Depot and Surinam Depot – physical remnants of an 80-year-long trade in Indian labourers. The abolition of slavery in 1833 had prompted the Indian indenture trade, whereby Indian labourers migrated to European plantation colonies to work in the production of sugar.[2] Despite being a key port in the global indenture trade and a site for debating the terms of indenture, Calcutta has remained entirely unexplored in scholarship. This book sets out to insert the British Indian capital of Calcutta into the history of indenture, offering a history of Calcuttans shaping colonial labour on a global stage. Instead of focusing on plantation colonies that labourers migrated *to*, it refocuses indenture literature on a port city that they embarked *from*.

Bringing sugar to the metropolitan plate has a long and complicated history, featuring overseas plantation colonies, absentee planters, lucrative commodity trade, labour migration across continents, slavery and various forms of unfree labour. When slavery was abolished in the British Empire, the empire straddled several plantation colonies. As Abolition deprived planters of their labour base, there was an immediate drive to seek workers to replace enslaved labour, especially since the temporary apprenticeship of ex-slaves had failed to ensure a steady supply of labour for British sugar plantations. Sugar production was a labour-intensive process. Working on the plantations involved sowing, reaping, cutting and processing the sugar cane in sugar boiling units. Moreover, British planters had by this time invested thousands in setting up plantation estates and formed strong parliamentary lobbies to push policies that safeguarded their profits from the sugar trade. After some unsuccessful attempts at using emancipated slaves and European labourers (mainly Portuguese labour from Madeira), Indian indentured labour emerged as the most popular and long-standing post-slavery labour system.

Indian indenture was a decidedly imperial institution set against the backdrop of the British colonial regime in India and colonial plantation regimes spread across the Caribbean and the Indian Ocean. Labourers were recruited from eastern and southern Indian villages, entered into five-year labour contracts (or indentures) with planters and sailed from the three major port cities of Calcutta, Bombay and Madras. Within half a decade of the Slavery Abolition Act of 1833, this had become a standardised, government-sanctioned system of labour migration and a true successor to the slave labour regime. By the end of the nineteenth century, 1.33 million indentured Indians had migrated to work in sugar plantation colonies (Figures I.1 and I.2).[3] Initially emigrating mainly to Mauritius and British Guiana, the Indian

Figure I.1 Map showing Indian ports and plantation colonies that employed indentured Indians

Source: Prepared by the author using a stock image of world map from iStock by Getty Images (stock illustration ID: 1407115316; credit: A. Mokhtari), https://www.istockphoto.com/vector/world-map-drawn-in-outline-gm1407115316-458436202 (accessed in June 2024).

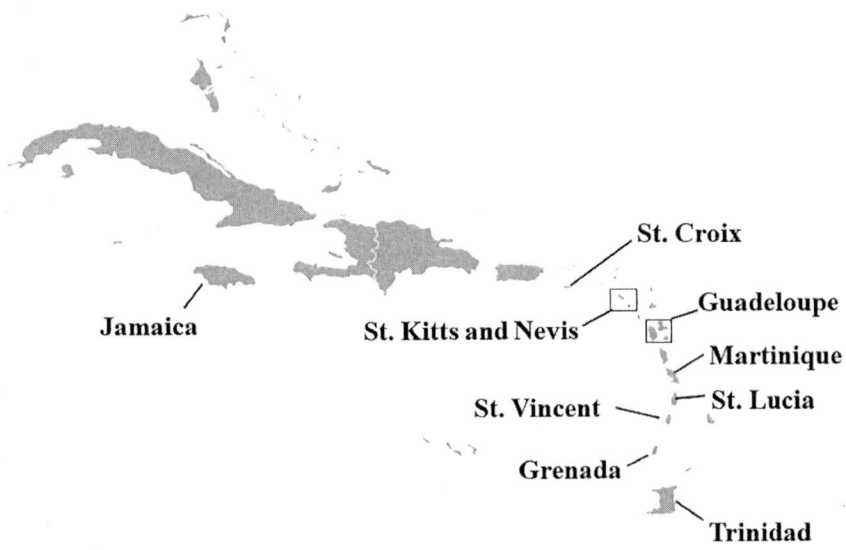

Figure I.2 Caribbean plantation colonies that employed indentured Indians

Source: Prepared by the author using a stock image of Caribbean islands map from iStock by Getty Images (stock illustration ID: 1245676548; credit: Mohamed Rasik), https://www.istockphoto.com/vector/caribbean-island-map-vector-graphics-design-gm1245676548-363096041 (accessed in June 2024).

indenture trade was extended to Jamaica and Trinidad in 1844–1845; Grenada in 1856; Saint Lucia in 1858; Natal (South Africa), Saint Kitts, Saint Vincent and the French colonies of Réunion, Guadeloupe, Martinique and French Guiana in 1860; Danish Saint Croix in 1863; Dutch Surinam in 1873; and Fiji in 1879 (Table I.1).[4]

This migration of indentured Indians provoked an empire-wide debate. Merchants and planters with a direct stake in the continued labour trade argued that Indian indenture was indispensable for continuous sugar production. For an imperial economy heavily dependent on commodity trade, ruination of the sugar trade implied considerable damage to the British economy. Many in Calcutta and Britain, however, saw it as slavery in all but name. Drawing attention to instances of deceptive recruitment, overwork, penal sanction, planter atrocity and mistreatment of labourers during passage and on plantations, they repudiated indenture as a restrictive and exploitative system that needed to be suspended, if not abolished altogether. The indenture trade followed closely on the heels of the abolition debates in Britain, a debate that questioned coerced labour and asked whether certain

Table I.1 Indian indentured emigration to plantation colonies

Plantation colony	Number of Indian indentured migrants
British Guiana	238,861
Dutch Guiana (Surinam)	34,503
East Africa	39,437
Fiji	61,015
French Caribbean	79,089
Jamaica	38,595
Mauritius	455,187
Natal	152,932
Réunion	74,854
Trinidad	149,623
Others (British West Indies)	11,152

Source: Collated by the author based on data from 'Table A.1: Decadal Exports of Indentured Migrants by Origins, Showing Intended Destinations, 1831–1920', in *Indentured Labour in the Age of Imperialism, 1834–1922*, by David Northrup (New York, NY: Cambridge University Press, 1995), pp. 156–157; and 'Table 1: Estimates of Intercontinental Flows of Contract Labor, Gross Movements, Nineteenth and Early Twentieth Centuries', in Stanley L. Engerman, 'Contract Labor, Sugar, and Technology in the Nineteenth Century', *Journal of Economic History* 43, no. 3 (1983): 635–659, p. 642.

labour regimes were immoral, illegitimate or even illegal. Anti-indenture petitioners therefore questioned how far removed the indenture trade was from the recently abolished slave trade, especially as indentured Indians migrated to serve in plantations that until only recently employed enslaved labour.

Indenture has often been relegated to the realm of Caribbean and Indian Ocean histories – seen as a process locally confined to the plantation colonies or as one orchestrated by the British metropole. With renewed focus on Calcutta, this book shows that processes that regulated the lives of indentured migrants were the result of a triangulated conversation between Britain, India and plantation colonies. As the colonial capital of British India, decisions about indenture were often taken in consultation with local officials in Calcutta, and revisions in the system were prompted by petitions from Calcuttans. The negotiation of pro- and anti-indenture arguments in Calcutta contributed directly to emigration legislation and led to post-slavery anxieties being written into law.

Questions around the legal and moral repercussions of the indenture trade brought forth Calcuttans as active participants in discussions within the British Empire, rather than as passive audiences. Decisions on migration, labour rights and contract were debated, criticised and cemented in Calcutta. The basic tenets of the indenture trade – including methods and targeted areas of indenture recruitment, principles of the indenture contract and length of the contract – were decided in consultation with Calcutta. Notions of migrant subjecthood and aspirational citizenship were consolidated in the interstices of these conversations, and racialised stereotypes of migrants were cemented. Indenture regulations, as a result, were not emanating from metropolitan Britain to be dutifully followed in the colonies but were informed by voices from those very colonies. Ultimately, then, this book interrogates how Calcutta and Calcuttans shaped the history of global indenture migration. It braids Calcutta's history into the history of indenture and establishes indenture as an indelible part of the social and spatial history of Calcutta. Focused on the early days of the indenture trade, it also puts a spotlight on the post-slavery empire – exploring its priorities, its moralistic tone and its anxieties around labour shortage.

The City

Established as an urban centre in 1690, Calcutta had grown rapidly from a small riverine market into an imperial port city. One of the most productive areas of the pre-colonial Mughal Empire, the region of Bengal boasted of a strong agricultural and artisanal base supported by financial and communication networks conducive to international trade.[5] The strategic position of Calcutta as a riverine port and as a site frequented by merchants and weavers since the fifteenth century made it favourable for settlement by European traders. In 1690, the English East India Company officially secured permission to establish a mercantile settlement at the site.[6] With the establishment of Fort William by British forces and declaration of the fort as the seat of the Bengal Presidency in 1706, Calcutta was on its way to becoming the colonial capital of British India and a premier commercial port of the empire.[7] By 1773, it had become the administrative seat for the entirety of the East India Company's territories in the Indian subcontinent.[8]

Although central to the indenture experience, Calcutta has remained on the margins of indenture historiography. Scholars like Marina Carter, Dwarka Nath, Richard Allen and Rosemarijn Hoefte have written histories of indenture in individual plantation colonies, analysing how colonies like Mauritius, British Guiana and Surinam moved from the slave labour regime to the indenture regime.[9] Brij Lal and others have focused on the indentured migrant's experience of recruitment, passage, plantation and resistance.[10] Yet others have explored the development of the indenture system and the negotiation of indenture legislation over time.[11] However, besides cursory mentions of Calcutta as a point of embarkation or in scene-setting chapters about the beginning of indenture, most works on Indian indenture have relegated it to the background. This siloed approach to indenture history in disparate colonies fails to recognise Calcutta as a key site within global indenture networks, from where labourers were exported to plantation colonies and where major decisions were taken regarding the regulation of indenture. Similarly, indenture is absent in histories of Calcutta. Even though historians of Calcutta have since the late twentieth century produced several tomes on the urban, social and cultural history of the city, they have overlooked Calcutta's engagement with indenture.[12] This erasure of the history of indenture from the history of Calcutta also reflects on the public memory of the city. Calcutta is mainly remembered as a colonial capital and as the site of nineteenth-century social reforms and twentieth-century anti-colonial resistance, but not as an important theatre in the century-long trade in Indian plantation labourers.

Although neglected in public and academic memory, Indian indenture and colonial Calcutta were intimately linked. Calcutta was connected to a vast agricultural hinterland through a complex network of roads and rivers. This allowed access to labourers who could be persuaded to work in difficult conditions for prospects of a better future. Calcutta also housed shipping companies and merchant houses that helped recruit labourers for the burgeoning trade. When British planter John Gladstone first started negotiating with Indian merchant companies for a steady supply of indentured Indians for his West Indian plantations, it was a merchant company in Calcutta that he contacted. The first two ships carrying indentured labourers to the British West Indies sailed from Calcutta in January 1838. *Hesperus* and *Whitby* carried 165 and 249 Indian labourers respectively and were the first of many indenture voyages sanctioned and governed by the British parliament. John Geoghegan reported that between 1842 and 1870, a total of

342,575 men, women and children emigrated out of the port of Calcutta, as opposed to 31,761 emigrants from Bombay port and 159,259 emigrants from Madras and French ports like Pondicherry.[13] With the exception of Natal, more people immigrated into the various plantation colonies from Calcutta than from any other Indian port, as emigration from Calcutta constituted 64.2 per cent of the total emigration from India in these 28 years.[14] Thus, even though migration also took place from the ports of Bombay, Madras and Pondicherry, early migration laws used Calcutta as the main reference point when setting out provisions for indentured emigration. Indeed, in early emigration legislation, Calcutta was emblematic of port cities that exported indentured Indians.

Calcutta also saw an unparalleled interaction of the colonial and local elite in debating the indenture trade. As Europeans and Indians came together in Calcutta to discuss, defend and criticise indenture, they raised this colonial capital to a position where voices from Calcutta could influence metropolitan labour legislation. The question of how the indenture system should be revised and whether it should continue at all was vigorously debated by merchants, reformers, educationists, philanthropists, officials and missionaries in the city. Particularly between 1838 and 1842, meetings were held, petitions were signed and an investigative committee was instituted in Calcutta in response to the indenture trade. The 'coolie question' appeared 225 times in Calcutta's leading weeklies during these five years.[15] The resultant public sphere was vocal and interacted across racial boundaries, while at the same time being confined to the elites.

The very visualisation of the boundaries of Calcutta and its position within imperial networks was contingent upon its engagement with the indenture trade. Calcutta's physical borders were imagined differently by different stakeholders in the trade. For migrant workers, Calcutta represented the beginning of their journey overseas. It was during their stay at Calcutta, often in 'coolie depots', that they signed their contracts and had emigration agents explain the system to them. Thus, Calcutta became, in migrant imaginings, an extension of the global indenture networks and the site where they first realised their identity as indentured labourers. For indenture officials, the boundaries of Calcutta were more blurred. Calcutta was imagined as intimately linked with the eastern Indian hinterland through rail and road connections. Thus, labourers 'from Calcutta' were more often from eastern Indian villages, connected to Calcutta only through internal networks of migration. For the British colonial state, however, Calcutta was a port city supplying labourers to its plantation colonies – the solution to its post-slavery labour crisis. It was also an important theatre for debates over indentured servitude, inputs from which contributed heavily to emigration regulations and to the post-slavery understanding of labour servitude.

Indenture debates came to have a very real impact on the physical and discursive spaces in Calcutta. As migrants moved from houses of recruiters to 'coolie depots' to ports and finally to ships, they became part of the Calcutta cityscape. Calcuttans recorded sightings of labourers in the city – some saw indentured migrants confined in Calcutta's houses, some wrote to newspapers to report seeing them near the port, while others recorded their domestic servants, horse groomers and gardeners being accosted on the streets by recruiters to convince them to travel to Mauritius. As Britons and Indians in Calcutta met in the Town Hall, signed petitions and helped investigate indenture, spaces of discussion transcended the traditional division between the 'white town' and the 'black town'. Calcuttans joined the conversation on indenture at a time when ideas of servitude and plantation labour were being recast on a global scale.

The Moment

Works on indenture often suffer from a dismissal of the temporal axis of analysis. Seeing the indenture trade not as a continuous system of labour but as one framed by disparate concerns over eight decades helps understand it as a complex system responsive to the changing priorities of colonial society. Proposed in 1836 to replace enslaved labour on British plantations, the Indian indenture system was legalised by an act of parliament in 1837. As it received legal sanction, the number of indentured migrants from India increased from 26,396 in 1831–1840 to 132,738 in 1841–1850 – an increase of about 500 per cent.[16] By the end of the century, indentured Indians had migrated to the British colonies of Mauritius, British Guiana, Jamaica, Trinidad, Fiji, Saint Lucia, Grenada, Saint Vincent, Saint Kitts, Malaya, Seychelles and South Africa, the French colonies of Guadeloupe, Guiana, Réunion and Martinique, Danish Saint Croix and Dutch Surinam. Distinct from spontaneous and private ventures of labour migration from India, Indian indenture operated within a government-sanctioned framework, where labourers were bound by contract to work in sugar plantations for at least five years, and planters were required by law to provide appropriate wages, food supplies, medical supplies and accommodation to the labourers, along with a free return passage to their port of origin. Having spread to multiple plantation colonies, the indenture system was disbanded by an act of government in 1917, finally coming to an end in the 1920s.

The history of Indian indenture thus encompasses distinct plantation geographies with their own unique historical trajectories. In a recent work, Reshaad Durgahee has coined the term 'indentured archipelago' to describe this network of colonies that were not geographically contiguous but connected by their shared experience of indenture.[17] Since its beginning in 1837, the indenture regime was extended to new plantation colonies every few years and newer regulations were introduced periodically in response to changing priorities and labour laws. The complexity of this divergent and oft-changing system of labour can only be understood by teasing out the importance of particular moments in its history. This book thus challenges scholarship that creates a continuous narrative from the beginning of indenture in 1834 to its end in 1920. It focuses on a phase much before indenture entered the political vocabulary of Indian nationalists as nationalist rhetoric began to identify indentured migrants as distinctly 'Indian'. It also exposes the methodological limitations of works that make overarching arguments about who migrated as indentured labourers, whether they were inveigled into the trade or joined of their own accord and whether the indenture trade was a highly regulated system. Indian indenture involved the movement of labourers from different social contexts (across caste, gender and class boundaries) and geographical spaces (across Bengal, Bombay and Madras presidencies) to multiple plantation colonies in the British, French, Dutch and Danish empires. Naturally, its history needs to be broken down by place and time.

Anti-slavery and abolition debates played a vital role in shaping the indenture experience in its early days, as indenture was constantly compared to slavery and framed entirely within the dichotomy of 'free' and 'unfree' labour. Acknowledging this allows for a fuller understanding of how legacies of slavery shaped global ideas of migration, servitude and plantation labour. The term 'post-slavery' is used in literature on plantation colonies to refer to the period after Abolition, but it encompasses a much more complex relationship between slavery and indenture. A post-slavery labour regime is not just one that comes after Abolition but one steeped in the legacies of slavery. As indenture came to be seen as a possible continuation of slavery, the definitions of free and unfree labour were forged in the crucible of the post-slavery indenture debates.

Indenture was discussed in Calcutta at a watershed moment in the history of plantation labour servitude. Slavery was the main rubric against which the indentured labour regime was judged. Anti-indenture activists compared the emergence of indenture to a revival of the slave regime, while merchants and planters continued to posit the difference between the two regimes as their main argument in defence of indenture. The anti-slavery movement, and its eventual culmination into the abolition of slavery, had led to a shift in both the legal definition and public opinion of plantation servitude. British parliamentarians were keen to pass laws that restricted unfree labour practices, British officials across India and the plantation colonies were keen on enforcing them, and the vocal public in Britain and India were eager to ensure that the indenture trade adhered to this post-Abolition moral framework. Thus, instead of visualising Indian indenture as a monolith, it is important to consider its early days as a time in flux – a time when the fate of the system was still being negotiated.

The slavery–indenture dichotomy has received considerable attention in indenture historiography. In *A New System of Slavery*, Hugh Tinker argued that although labourers theoretically entered into indenture freely, the indenture trade replicated conditions of slavery in recruitment, in passage and in the working and living conditions on plantation estates.[18] His work influenced other scholars of Indian indenture to focus on linkages between the two labour regimes. Although not necessarily in agreement with Tinker, scholars like Richard Allen, P. C. Emmer and William Green studied the two labour regimes within the same analytical frame – whether investigating the move from slavery to indenture in Mauritius, the linkages between early modern European indenture in the Americas and Indian indenture migration, or the connections between slavery and indenture in the context of imperial humanitarianism.[19] At the same time, Tinker's thesis faced criticism from scholars emphasising the autonomous agency of indentured labourers. His excessive emphasis on the horrors of the system drew criticism from Brij Lal, Maurits Hassankhan and Doug Munro, who questioned 'the Tinkerian paradigm of docile, non-resisting labour'.[20]

For many scholars, far from being victimised under a 'new system of slavery', indentured migrants were in a position to exercise their autonomous agency and shape their own economic futures. Crispin Bates and Marina Carter showed that indentured migrants used and extended the networks of support created by the migration of plantation labourers, domestic workers, convicts and *sepoys* (Indian soldiers). Thus, Indians increasingly took control of their migratory patterns in the Indian Ocean region, often organising their own repatriation and terms of settlement and even re-emigrating to other colonies.[21] In fact, Bates and Carter argued that the idea of indenture-as-servitude emerged with the twentieth-century nationalists' stigmatisation of 'coolie labour' and their misconceptions or exaggerations about the exploitation of indentured migrants.[22] Many labourers expressed a choice, however limited, to be employed overseas. This allowed them to build their own space within the colonial labour market, take initiative, save money to support their relatives and adapt to their circumstances.[23] Lomarsh Roopnarine showed that migrants resisted and manipulated the indenture system through feigned sickness, strikes and riots, as well as by creating a social space outside the planter-class hegemony and having a meaningful social existence outside of the dominant colonial framework.[24] More recently, Arunima Datta has demonstrated how female indentured migrants in Malayan rubber plantations exercised fleeting moments of agency.[25] Reshaad Durgahee has shown how indentured migrants in Mauritius and Fiji used petitions and the legal system to their advantage, and made their own destinies by choosing re-emigration to newer colonies.[26] For Durgahee, re-emigration, or 'subaltern careering', offered a chance for indentured labourers to move using the very networks created to bind them to plantation colonies.

This book aims to bring Indian indenture out of this slavery-versus-agency narrative, where indentured migrants could only be either mono-dimensional victims of the empire or autonomous agents in control of their movements and economic futures. By interrogating not *whether* indenture was a continuation of slavery but *why* comparison to slavery framed the early indenture debates, it allows for a more nuanced understanding. Clare Anderson rightly recognised that indenture was part of a labour continuum, writing that '[e]nslavement, indenture, apprenticeship, convictism, prison and other kinds of work were not stages in a progressive, teleological move to "abolition" or "freedom"'.[27] Instead, 'slavery was part of a continuum of unfree work practices that spanned empire', and 'empire's variously staggered emancipations were moments that laid the ground for the production of new coerced labour forms'.[28] This book invites us to stop and think about why the 'free' labour–'unfree' labour dichotomy was of importance to discussants in Britain and Calcutta, and how it shaped labour discourse and life on plantations in the age of Abolition.

Abolition had changed the understanding of labour radically and permanently. Priorities of the post-slavery empire manifested as strict indenture regulations (partly in response to petitions and reports from Calcutta), obsession with the signing and upholding of indenture contracts, judging indenture entirely in terms of its similarity to slavery or lack thereof, and framing the indenture question as one of rights, morality and liberty while overshadowing other criticisms of the trade. The legacies of slavery can thus be located not in structural continuities in migrant ships and plantation estates but in the very ways in which indenture was framed, criticised, defended and regulated. This post-slavery context did not merely provide the backdrop to the indenture debates but, indeed, indelibly shaped it.

In Calcutta, this brief period was one of intense debate. Calcuttans asked whether the indenture trade was legally and morally acceptable after a law had been passed in Britain to delegitimise extreme and unfree forms of plantation servitude. In meetings, petitions and news reports, British and Indian residents of Calcutta debated whether indenture represented an exercise in free labour movement or a revival of slave conditions. In response to indenture petitions, the metropolitan government set up investigative committees in Calcutta, Bombay, Madras and Mauritius in 1838, discontinuing the indenture trade in 1839. The trade was only reopened under planter pressure in 1842 with several changes in regulations. The 1842 regulations addressed many of the criticisms of indenture, mainly by increasing surveillance over recruitment and implementing most of the recommendations of the Calcutta investigative committee. This led to a steady decline in public debates on the legitimacy of indenture after 1842 in Calcutta. The discussions that took place within the span of these few years, however, came to have long-lasting effects on indenture over the next eight decades – shaping indenture laws, influencing the experience of indenture and mediating global understandings of plantation servitude.

The beginning of the indenture trade was a time when the contours of the post-slavery empire had started to become apparent. Generally remembered as a time when slavery was abolished, this key moment in the history of imperial labour servitude is less recognised as the time when the idea of free labour was curated and negotiated. Between 1836 and 1842, indenture trade was still only a possibility – a question to be decided. When the trade was resumed in 1842, however, Act XV of 1842 became the ultimate stamp of approval. As indenture came out unscathed from the trial posed by anti-indenture lobbyists and colonial investigative committees, it became the undisputed successor to the colonial plantation regime. Even though specific tenets of the trade would be questioned and negotiated throughout the rest of the nineteenth century, complete abolition of the indenture trade would not be sought till the early twentieth century. By going through the process of negotiation, investigation and parliamentary discussion, this early phase in the history of indenture was thus a time when indenture was not only legitimised but also valorised as the solution to the labour crisis created by Abolition.

The Network

On his way back from the Galápagos Islands on the *HMS Beagle*, Charles Darwin wrote of Port Louis, Mauritius:

> Convicts from India are banished here for life.... Before seeing these people I had no idea that the inhabitants of India were such noble looking men; their skin is extremely dark, & many of the older men had large moustachios [*sic*] & beards of a snow white colour; this, together with the fire of their expressions, gave to them an aspect quite imposing.... Besides such prisoners, large numbers of free people are yearly imported from India; for the planters feared that the negroes, when emancipated, would not work: from these causes the Indian population is very considerable.[29]

Although this came as a surprise to Darwin, Indians had been migrating to Mauritius since the beginning of the nineteenth century, mostly as convicts or labourers for public works projects. Between 1789 and 1939, the British transported around 108,000 Indian, Burmese, Malay and Chinese convicts to penal settlements around the Bay of Bengal and the Indian Ocean, with convicts emerging as a 'highly mobile workforce that was vital to British imperial ambitions'.[30] Their labour was used for land clearance, infrastructural development, mining, agriculture and cultivation, as well as to settle lands and establish villages.[31] Labourers also moved to Europe at this time to work in domestic spaces: records from the West Bengal State Archives (WBSA) attest to the migration of several 'native servants', *ayah*s and 'Portuguese servants'.[32] Besides, there was a demand for skilled Indian workers such as wood workers and gardeners in Europe, as well as a steady stream of maritime workers, *lascar*s (sailors or ship crew) and military labourers migrating overseas.[33] Thus, it was not uncommon to find Indian workers abroad even before the indenture trade was introduced.

The agrarian nature of pre-colonial and early colonial Indian economy necessitated seasonal migrations in search of employment. Warfare, economic contingencies, forest enclosures and increased rent also pushed villagers to migrate.[34] The colonial state and its large economic projects, on the other hand, provided opportunities for employment in tune with the agrarian calendar.[35] It was thus common for villagers to migrate outside harvesting seasons – often moving overseas and often supplying men for public works, military labour, domestic labour and indigo plantation labour within India.[36] Indenture migration needs to be seen as part of this broader network of soldiers, convicts, artisans, *lascars* and servants who emigrated from India.[37]

The indenture trade was far from a standalone system. The prevalence of South Asian migrant workforces in international labour markets since the seventeenth century made India an obvious choice for planters in the first place. Recruiters for the indenture trade tapped into existing networks of internal and external migration, and discussions about indenture in Calcutta often viewed migrant labourers as a composite group. One testimony for the Calcutta investigative committee (1838–1839) used the example of indigo workers who could never be persuaded to stay on for longer than a year on plantations to argue that Indian villagers would never knowingly leave the country for five years, and hence indentured migrants must have been deceived into joining the trade.[38] A nuanced history of indenture is only possible by repudiating siloed studies and privileging scholarship that is cognisant of the position of indenture within wider networks of colonial labour migration.

In 'Rereading the Archive', Tony Ballantyne argued for visualising the British Empire not as 'a spoked wheel with London as the "hub"' but as a 'complex web consisting of horizontal filaments that run among various colonies in addition to the "vertical" connections between the metropole and individual colonies'.[39] Calcutta was, to use Ballantyne's words, a nodal point in the global web of indenture, rather than part of a binary, hierarchical relationship where the colony existed only in relation to the metropole. By analysing how Calcuttans continually negotiated with the colonial state, this book consolidates the importance of the 'periphery' in the British Empire. The indenture debates gave voice to common Calcuttans, and as a result, sweeping new regulations were drafted in the metropole, and novel understandings of contracts, labour rights, subjecthood and imperial citizenship emerged in these debates. This challenges the traditional image of empires consisting of a unilinear flow of ideas – decisions taken in the metropole (core) and dutifully followed in the colonies (periphery) with no space for colonised voices.[40] In reality, voices from South Asia played a crucial role in shaping labour laws in the empire and codifying the empire's relationship with its migrating labour population.

As the chapters unfold a complex web of letters, petitions, committee reports and news articles that made the colony–metropole conversation possible, they shed light on the role of the colonial state as the purveyor of laws – often as a benevolent paternal presence – who was expected to be responsive to feedback from its subjects in Calcutta. They also historicise the role of investigative committees of the empire, seeing colonial commissions of inquiry as techniques of colonial knowledge production. On the part of the state, the repeated use of commissions of inquiry and periodically revised regulations suggested their overarching official commitment to the potential of colonial law to eradicate abuses and make indenture a legitimate post-slavery system of labour. In a nutshell, then, this book is as much a history of indenture and Calcutta as it is a history of the British Empire.

Whose Voices?

Voices from Calcutta necessarily begs the question: whose voices? The early indenture debates in Calcutta were a negotiation between merchants and planters' representatives in the city, on the one hand, and British and Indian reformers, philanthropists, officials, entrepreneurs and missionaries, on the other. Together, they engaged in open debates in the Calcutta Town Hall, participated in colonial investigative practices, signed petitions to the colonial government and wrote to periodicals about the indenture question. While the 1830s and 1840s are remembered as a time of social reform in Bengal, it is rarely remembered as a time when imperial ideas of labour migration and servitude were being negotiated in Calcutta. By focusing on this vocal space, repudiating scholarship that assumes a strict division between the white town and the black town of Calcutta, and nuancing scholarly understanding of why Calcuttans participated in debating indenture, this book sheds light on the social life of Calcutta. By emphasising the development of a vocal discursive public in Calcutta that included both British and Indian inhabitants and cultivated links across the empire, this book locates in Calcutta voices of protest that fundamentally changed post-Abolition rhetoric in the empire.

The migrant was conspicuous in his absence from this discursive space, appearing only in spaces fixed and curated for him by elite Calcuttans. Through the Calcutta investigative committee or similar investigative interviews at the port, a limited space had been created for the migrant to speak to his experience of indenture. Where migrant voices did appear, they were regulated and limited according to the needs of the discourse. Instead of open questions about their experience, testimonies of indentured labourers were guided by interview questions intended to restrict discussion to themes relevant to the investigating bodies. Migrants were also considered unreliable witnesses – their testimonies being given different weightage according to race, occupation and social position. In navigating the early indenture debates, this book thus also introduces the challenge of recovering the voices of early indentured migrants from sources not written to showcase their voices.

As this book reveals, the Calcutta debates critically shaped the experience of indenture as it saw the cementing of a racialised trope of the migrant labourer, the negotiation of subjecthood rights and the realisation of vocal, participatory and aspirational citizenship. In many ways, the Calcutta debates forged the identities of the migrant-subject and the citizen-spokesman in juxtaposition to one another. The migrant was a South Asian labourer moving through the city, but the petitioner was decidedly Calcuttan; the migrant was a mobile subject of the empire, while the petitioner from Calcutta was an aspiring citizen. Voices from Calcutta remained elite and close to the ruling structure but were punctuated, even if momentarily, by migrant voices.

The ruling authority of the home government in British India was maintained through a complex system of writing, documenting and reporting emblematic of the *kaghazi raj*.[41] It is these very documents – colonial correspondences, petitions and reports – that, when used alongside periodicals, publications and institutional records, help reconstruct the history of the indenture debates in Calcutta. As historians are increasingly pointing out, archives are neither neutral repositories of unquestionable facts nor complete in their information. Scholars of empire have long questioned the objectivity of archival records and pointed to the importance of exploring archival provenance, power structures and authorship to interrogate how archives affect the writing of history.[42] As Antoinette Burton argues, 'archives do not simply arrive or emerge fully formed; nor are they innocent of struggles for power in either their creation or their interpretive applications'.[43] Archives have the power to shape *how* history is written and *whose* history is written. The historian thus has to be cognisant of whose voices exist in the archives and recover the histories of people who are absent in the archives as subjects, authors or both.

For Calcutta, the history of early indenture debates has to be constructed without records from the migrants themselves. Many of the record-keeping systems that characterised the indenture trade during its heyday were still being constructed in the 1830s and 1840s. Records of the Protector of Emigrants and the Protector of Immigrants from Indian ports and plantation colonies respectively remain a key source on the indenture trade, offering detailed accounts of the labourers, their backgrounds and the emigration process itself. These, however, are not available for the early days of indenture when information on the trade and the labourers is scarcer and more piecemeal. It is difficult to find personal letters, memoirs and depositions from indentured migrants in the period between 1836 and 1842, and the Dead Letters' Office in Kolkata does not hold any letters from this period either. The Gillander House archive, if it ever held records on individual migrants, is no longer accessible under the current administration, even though its office continues to stand in central Calcutta. Similarly, the Maritime Archives and Heritage Centre in Kolkata does not hold any emigration records or passenger lists from before the 1860s – records that would have been useful for exploring the language used to describe indentured migrants in official records. This paucity of sources in the early years of indenture creates an undue dependence on the colonial archives. At the same time, it is precisely this paucity that was emblematic of the early stages of indenture as it gradually moved from being examined, negotiated and repudiated to being enshrined into law.

*   *   *

This book follows Calcuttans in their journey of debating, investigating and defending the indenture trade. Chapter 1 establishes the historical link between indenture and Calcutta. By discussing Calcutta's connections with an agricultural hinterland from where labour could be procured, by analysing John Gladstone's negotiations over the establishment of the Indian indenture scheme to prop up sugar production and by describing the emergence of 'coolie depots' across the portside of Calcutta, the chapter shows how indenture became part of the very fabric of the city. Chapter 2 moves attention to the Calcutta Town Hall as one of the main theatres of debate. Discussions and petitions emerging from the Town Hall threw up some of the earliest concerns with indenture, including the accusation that the indenture trade was 'a new system of slavery'. Chapter 3 shifts focus to the activities of the Calcutta investigative committee of 1838–1839. This regime of investigation was predicated on what Ann Laura Stoler calls 'hierarchies of credibility' – migrants offered the main evidence base for the quotidian abuses of the indenture trade but were considered unreliable witnesses at the same time.[44] Coupled with the Town Hall meeting and petitions from Calcutta, the investigative committee catapulted Calcutta to a key decision-making space in the British Empire.

Chapter 4 explores the vastly understudied merchant and planter arguments in defence of indenture, demonstrating that pro-indenture voices were more nuanced than previously imagined. Instead of a simplistic argument focused on personal profits, the pro-indenture argument that arose in the aftermath of Abolition brought together questions of commerce, justice, rights and free labour. West India planters worked hand in hand with pro-indenture petitioners from Calcutta to maintain a constant pressure on parliament, which made it possible for this much-criticised labour system to continue for almost a century.

The very trope that considered Indian indentured migrants as primitive, ignorant and undifferentiated in terms of race and religion also celebrated them as ideal labourers. Chapter 5 disentangles this complex process of racialisation of indentured Indians, which saw the coming together of nineteenth-century ideas of race, caste and primitivism. Problematising the concept of race itself, this chapter contributes to scholarship on social division in South Asia. Chapter 6 explores how ideas of rights, subjecthood and citizenship were negotiated in the Calcutta debates. It establishes the twin persons of the migrant-subject and the citizen-spokesman, who emerged through the Calcutta debates as key global actors. In discussing aspirational and performative citizenship, the chapter engages closely with notions of citizenship and subjecthood in colonial South Asia.

Taken together, these chapters insert South Asia into the narrative as an active space of negotiation rather than a passive procurer of labourers. As discussions in its first six years shaped indenture for the next eight decades, the resultant empire was one inhabited by those who implemented its various systems and regulations (such as colonial officials and parliamentarians), those who negotiated it (such as merchants, planters, citizen-spokesmen and anti-indenture petitioners) and those who were bound by it (such as the migrants). As will become clear through the course of this book, the histories of indenture in plantation colonies cannot be read bereft of the histories of Calcutta and South Asia.

Notes

1. Throughout this book, historical spellings have been retained: 'Calcutta' instead of 'Kolkata', 'Coomar' rather than the conventional 'Kumar', and 'Guiana' and 'Surinam' for the Caribbean colonies.

2. Historically, the term 'indenture' has been used in reference to several intercontinental streams of bonded labour, including English, French, Irish and German indentured servants in the seventeenth and eighteenth centuries; Chinese plantation workers; and Indian migrants contractually bound to plantations producing commodities like sugar, rubber and tea. This book confines itself to the history of Indian contract-bound labourers emigrating to European sugar plantation colonies in the nineteenth and early twentieth centuries. For the rest, see P. C. Emmer, *Colonialism and Migration: Indentured Labour Before and After Slavery* (Leiden: Martinus Nijhoff Publishers, 1986).

3. Between 1831 and 1920, more than two million indentured labourers emigrated from China, Africa, Europe, South Asia and other geographies. Of them, 1,336,030 were Indians, as opposed to 386,901 Chinese labourers, 96,032 African labourers and 56,027 Europeans. 'Table A.1. Decadal Exports of Indentured Migrants by Origins, Showing Intended Destinations, 1831–1920', in *Indentured Labour in the Age of Imperialism, 1834–1922*, by David Northrup (New York, NY: Cambridge University Press, 1995), pp. 156–157.

4. John Geoghegan, *Note on Emigration from India* (Calcutta: Superintendent of Government Printing, 1873). For the smaller West Indian islands and French colonies, the dates given indicate when the emigration law was passed to allow emigration to said colonies, which may differ from the date of actual commencement of emigration.

5. Swati Chattopadhyay, *Representing Calcutta: Modernity, Nationalism and the Colonial Uncanny* (London: Routledge, 2005), p. 8.

6. John Archer, 'Paras, Palaces, Pathogens: Frameworks for the Growth of Calcutta, 1800–1850', *City and Society* 12, no. 1 (2000): 19–54.

7. Farhat Hasan, 'Indigenous Cooperation and the Birth of a Colonial City: Calcutta, c. 1698–1750', *Modern Asian Studies* 26, no. 1 (1992): 65–82, p. 70.

8. Meera Kosambi and John E. Brush, 'Three Colonial Port Cities in India', *Geographical Review* 78, no. 1 (1988): 32–47, p. 43. Calcutta remained the capital city of British India till 1911, when the seat was moved to Delhi.

9. Dwarka Nath, *A History of Indians in British Guyana* (London: Thomas Nelson & Sons, 1950); Marina Carter, *Servants, Sirdars and Settlers: Indians in Mauritius, 1834–1874* (New Delhi and New York: Oxford University Press, 1995); Rosemarijn Hoefte, *In Place of Slavery: A Social History of British Indian and Javanese Laborers in Suriname* (Gainesville, FL: University Press of Florida, 1998); Richard Allen, *Slaves, Freedmen and Indentured Laborers in Colonial Mauritius* (Cambridge, UK: Cambridge University Press, 1999). See also S. B. Mookherji, *The Indenture System in Mauritius, 1837–1915* (Calcutta: Firma KLM, 1962); Adrian C. Mayer, *Indians in Fiji* (London: Oxford University Press, 1963); Surendra Bhana, *Indentured Indian Emigrants to Natal, 1860–1902: A Study Based on Ships' Lists* (New Delhi: Promilla & Co., 1991); Walton Look Lai, *Indentured Labor, Caribbean Sugar: Chinese and Indian Migrants to the British West Indies, 1838–1918* (Baltimore, MD: Johns Hopkins Press, 1993); K. O. Laurence, *A Question of Labour: Indentured Immigration into Trinidad and British Guiana, 1875–1917* (London: Ian Randle Publishers, 1994); Lomarsh Roopnarine, 'The First and Only Crossing: Indian Indentured Servitude on Danish St. Croix, 1863–1868', *South Asian Diaspora* 1, no. 2 (2009): 113–140; Margriet Fokken, *Beyond Being Koelies and Kantráki: Constructing Hindostani Identities in Suriname in the Era of Indenture, 1873–1921* (Hilversum: Verloren, 2018).

10. Brij V. Lal, *Chalo Jahaji: On a Journey through Indenture in Fiji* (Acton: Australian National University Press, 2012); Crispin Bates and Marina Carter, 'Tribal and Indentured Migrants in Colonial India: Modes of Recruitment and Forms of Incorporation', in *Dalit Movements and the Meanings of Labour in India*, ed. Peter Robb, pp. 159–185 (New Delhi: Oxford University Press, 1993); Marina Carter, *Voices from Indenture: Experiences of Indian Migrants in the British Empire* (London: Burns & Oates, 1996); Lomarsh Roopnarine, *Indo-Caribbean Indenture: Resistance and Accommodation, 1838–1920* (Kingston: University of the West Indies Press, 2007); Rattan Lal Hangloo, *Indian Diaspora in the Caribbean: History, Culture, and Identity* (New Delhi: Primus Books, 2012); Maurits Hassankhan, Brij V. Lal and Doug Munro (eds.), *Resistance and the Indian*

Indenture Experience: Comparative Perspectives (New Delhi: Manohar Publishers, 2014).

11. Panchanan Saha, *Emigration of Indian Labour 1834–1900* (New Delhi: People's Publishing House, 1970); David Northrup, *Indentured Labour in the Age of Imperialism, 1834–1922* (New York, NY: Cambridge University Press, 1995); Hugh Tinker, *A New System of Slavery: The Export of Indian Labour Overseas 1830–1920* (London: Oxford University Press, 1974).

12. Key works on the history of Calcutta include S. N. Mukherjee, *Calcutta, Myths and History* (Calcutta: Subarnarekha, 1977); Pradip Sinha, *Calcutta in Urban History* (Calcutta: Firma KLM, 1978); P. T. Nair, *Calcutta in the 18th Century: Impressions of Travellers* (Calcutta: Firma KLM, 1984); Peter J. Marshall, 'Eighteenth Century Calcutta', in *Colonial Cities: Essays on Urbanism in a Colonial Context*, ed. R. J. Ross and G. Telkamp, pp. 87–104 (Dordrecht: Martinus Nijhoff Publishers, 1985); Pradip Sinha (ed.), *The Urban Experience: Calcutta, Essays in Honour of N. R. Ray* (Calcutta: Riddhi-India, 1986); Nisith Ranjan Ray, *Calcutta: Profile of a City* (Calcutta: K. P. Bagchi & Company, 1986); P. T. Nair (ed.), *Calcutta in the 19th Century: Company's Days* (Calcutta: Firma KLM, 1989); Jeremiah P. Losty, *Calcutta: City of Palaces: A Survey of the City in the Days of the East India Company (1690–1858)* (London: British Library, 1990); Sukanta Chaudhuri, *Calcutta, the Living City*, vol. 1: *The Past* (Calcutta: Oxford University Press, 1990); J. S. Grewal (ed.), *Calcutta: Foundation and Development of a Colonial Metropolis* (Chandigarh: Urban History Association of India, 1991); Sukanta Chaudhuri, *Calcutta, The Living City*, vol. 2: *The Present and Future* (Calcutta: Oxford University Press, 1995); S. Chattopadhyay, *Representing Calcutta*; Partho Datta, *Planning the City: Urbanization and Reform in Calcutta, c. 1800–1940* (New Delhi: Tulika Books, 2012); and Michael Mann, *A British Rome in India: Calcutta – Capital for an Empire* (Worms: Wernersche Verlagsgesellschaft, 2022).

13. Geoghegan, *Note on Emigration from India*, p. 70.

14. Ibid.

15. The term 'coolie' is problematic because it bears a history of colonialism, stigmatisation and prejudice. It has been used in this book within quotes to reflect the complex, historically specific identity that the term invokes and to stay true to its use in nineteenth-century records. See Chapter 5 for how this term was used to flatten the diverse social identities of indentured migrants.

16. Northrup, *Indentured Labour*, pp. 156–157.

17. Reshaad Durgahee, *The Indentured Archipelago: Experiences of Indian Labour in Mauritius and Fiji, 1871–1916* (Cambridge, UK: Cambridge University Press, 2022).

18. Tinker, *A New System of Slavery*.

19. Allen, *Slaves, Freedmen and Indentured Laborers*; Richard Allen, 'Slaves, Convicts, Abolitionism and the Global Origins of the Post-Emancipation Indentured Labor System', *Slavery and Abolition* 35, no. 2 (2014): 328–348; Emmer, *Colonialism and Migration*; William A. Green, 'Emancipation to Indenture: A Question of Imperial Morality', *Journal of British Studies* 22, no. 2 (1983): 98–121.

20. Hassankhan, Lal and Munro (eds.), *Resistance and the Indian Indenture Experience*, foreword.

21. Crispin Bates and Marina Carter, 'Enslaved Lives, Enslaving Labels: A New Approach to the Colonial Indian Labor Diaspora', in *New Routes for Diaspora Studies*, ed. Sukanya Banerjee, Aims McGuinness and Steven McKay, 67–92 (Bloomington, IN: Indiana University Press, 2012). See also Crispin Bates, 'Some Thoughts on the Representation and Misrepresentation of the Colonial South Asian Labour Diaspora', *South Asian Studies* 33, no. 1 (2017): 7–22.

22. Bates and Carter, 'Enslaved Lives, Enslaving Labels'.

23. Crispin Bates, 'Coerced and Migrant Labourers in India: The Colonial Experience', *Edinburgh Papers in South Asian Studies* 13 (2000): 1–33; Bates and Carter, 'Enslaved Lives, Enslaving Labels'.

24. Roopnarine, *Indo-Caribbean Indenture*.

25. Arunima Datta, *Fleeting Agencies: A Social History of Indian Coolie Women in British Malaya* (Cambridge, UK: Cambridge University Press, 2021).

26. Durgahee, *The Indentured Archipelago*.

27. Clare Anderson, 'After Emancipation: Empires and Imperial Formations', in *Emancipation and the Remaking of the British Imperial World*, ed. Catherine Hall, Nicholas Draper and Keith McClelland, pp. 113–127 (Manchester: Manchester University Press, 2014), p. 125.

28. Ibid., p. 113.

29. Diary entry of 30 April 1836, in *Charles Darwin's Diary of the Voyage of H.M.S. 'Beagle'*, ed. Nora Barlow (New York: Macmillan Company; Cambridge, UK: Cambridge University Press, 1933 [1845]), pp. 401–402.

30. Clare Anderson (ed.), *A Global History of Convicts and Penal Colonies* (London: Bloomsbury Publishing, 2018), p. 211. See also Clare Anderson, 'Transnational Histories of Penal Transportation: Punishment, Labour and Governance in the British Imperial World, 1788–1939', *Australian Historical Studies* 47, no. 3 (2016): 381–397; Clare Anderson, *Convicts in the Indian Ocean: Transportation from South Asia to Mauritius, 1815–53* (London: Palgrave Macmillan, 2000).

31. Anderson, *A Global History of Convicts*, p. 211.

32. General Department (General) Proceedings, West Bengal State Archives, Kolkata (WBSA).

33. See, for instance, Letter to Captain F. W. Birch, Superintendent of Police, requesting 10 native gardeners to Mauritius, 5 December 1838, no. 30, General Department (General) Proceedings, WBSA; Letter on Labour Migrating for Public Works, 24 May 1837, nos. 14–15, General Department (General) Proceedings, WBSA. For overseas military labour, see 'Projecting Power: The Indian Army Overseas' and 'Recruiting Sikhs for Colonial Police and Military', in *Imperial Connections: India in the Indian Ocean Arena, 1860–1920*, by Thomas Metcalf (Berkeley, CA: University of California Press, 2007). Maritime labour has been studied in Gopalan Balachandran, 'Conflicts in the International Maritime Labour Market: British and Indian Seamen, Employers, and the State, 1890–1939', *Indian Economic and Social History Review* 39, no. 1 (2002): 71–100; Michael Fisher, 'Working Across the Seas: Indian Maritime Labourers in India, Britain, and in between, 1600–1857', *International Review of Social History* 51, no. S14 (2006): 21–45; Michael Fisher, *Counterflows to Colonialism: Indian Travellers and Settlers in Britain, 1600–1857* (New Delhi: Permanent Black, 2004); Ravi Ahuja, 'Networks of Subordination: Networks of the Subordinated – The Ordered Spaces of South Asian Maritime Labour in an Age of Imperialism (c. 1890–1947)', in *The Limits of British Colonial Control in South Asia: Spaces of Disorder in the Indian Ocean Region*, ed. Ashwini Tambe and Harald Fischer Tiné, 23–58 (London: Routledge, 2008).

34. Bates, 'Coerced and Migrant Labourers', pp. 6–8.

35. For labour mobility and agrarian conditions in South Asia, see Gyan Prakash, *Bonded Histories: Genealogies of Labor Servitude in Colonial India* (Cambridge, UK: Cambridge University Press, 2003); Sugata Bose, *Peasant Labour and Colonial Capital: Rural Bengal since 1770* (Cambridge, UK: Cambridge University Press, 1993); Anand Yang, *The Limited Raj: Agrarian*

Relations in Colonial India, Saran District, 1793–1920 (Berkeley, CA: University of California Press, 1989); Anand Yang, 'Peasants on the Move: A Study of Internal Migration in India', *Journal of Interdisciplinary History* 10, no. 1 (1979): 37–58; Ian Kerr, 'On the Move: Circulating Labor in Pre-Colonial, Colonial, and Post-Colonial India', *International Review of Social History* 51, no. S14 (2006): 85–109.

36. For labour-use in public works, see Peter J. Marshall, 'The Company and the Coolies: Labour in Early Calcutta', in *The Urban Experience, Calcutta: Essays in Honour of Professor Nisith R. Ray*, ed. Pradip Sinha, pp. 23–38 (Calcutta: Riddhi-India, 1987). The military labour market within India has been explored in Gavin Rand and Kim Wagner, 'Recruiting the "Martial Races": Identities and Military Service in Colonial India', *Patterns of Prejudice* 46, nos. 3–4 (2012): 232–254; D. H. A. Kolff, *Naukar, Rajput and Sepoy: The Ethnohistory of the Military Labour Market in Hindustan, 1450–1850* (Cambridge, UK: Cambridge University Press, 1990). Key works on domestic labour include Nitin Sinha, Nitin Varma and Pankaj Jha (eds.), *Servants' Pasts: Sixteenth to Eighteenth Century South Asia*, vol. 1 (New Delhi: Orient Blackswan, 2019); Nitin Sinha and Nitin Varma (eds.), *Servants' Pasts: Late-Eighteenth to Twentieth Century South Asia*, vol. 2 (New Delhi: Orient Blackswan, 2019).

37. See Sunil Amrith, *Crossing the Bay of Bengal: The Furies of Nature and the Fortunes of Migrants* (Cambridge, MA: Harvard University Press, 2013); Clare Anderson, 'Convicts and Coolies: Rethinking Indentured Labour in the Nineteenth Century', *Slavery and Abolition* 30, no. 1 (2009): 93–109; Crispin Bates, 'Courts, Ship-Rolls and Letters: Reflections on the Indian Labour Diaspora', in *Creating an Archive Today*, ed. Toshie Awaya, pp. 131–158 (Tokyo: Centre for Documentation and Area-Transcultural Studies, Tokyo University of Foreign Studies, 2005).

38. 'Testimony of Dwarkanath Tagore', 9 November 1838, in 'Proceedings of the [Calcutta Investigative] Committee, from 22 August 1838 to 14 January 1839', in *Letter from Secretary to Government of India, to Committee on Exportation of Hill Coolies: Report of Committee and Evidence* (East India House: Ordered by the House of Commons to be printed, 12 February 1841), Parliamentary Papers (House of Commons) 16, No. 45 (henceforth 'Proceedings of the Calcutta Committee').

39. Tony Ballantyne, 'Rereading the Archive and Opening Up the Nation-State: Colonial Knowledge in South Asia (and Beyond)', in *After the*

Imperial Turn: Thinking with and through the Nation, ed. Antoinette Burton, pp. 102–121 (Durham, NC: Duke University Press, 2003), pp. 112-13.

40. For a historiographical discussion of the core-periphery argument and its limitations, see Alan Lester, 'Imperial Circuits and Networks: Geographies of the British Empire', *History Compass* 4, no. 1 (2006): 124–141.

41. See Martin Moir, 'Kaghazi Raj: Notes on the Documentary Basis of Company Rule – 1783–1858', *Indo-British Review* 21, no. 2 (1993): 185–193. Here *kaghazi* refers to the obsession with paper-documents, or *kagaz*.

42. See Ann Laura Stoler, '"In Cold Blood": Hierarchies of Credibility and the Politics of Colonial Narratives', *Representations* 37 (January 1992): 151–189; Ann Laura Stoler, 'Colonial Archives and the Arts of Governance', *Archival Science* 2, nos. 1–2 (2002): 87–109; Joan Schwartz and Terry Cook, 'Archives, Records, and Power: The Making of Modern Memory', *Archival Science* 2, no. 2 (2002): 1–19; Antoinette Burton, 'Introduction: Archive Fever, Archive Stories', in *Archive Stories: Facts, Fictions, and the Writing of History*, ed. Antoinette Burton, pp. 1–24 (Durham, NC: Duke University Press, 2006); Ann Laura Stoler, *Along the Archival Grain: Epistemic Anxieties and Colonial Common Sense* (Princeton, NJ: Princeton University Press, 2009); Gyanendra Pandey (ed.), *Unarchived Histories: The 'Mad' and the 'Trifling' in the Colonial and Postcolonial World* (Oxon and New York: Routledge, 2013).

43. Burton, 'Introduction', p. 6.

44. Stoler, '"In Cold Blood"'.

1

Calcutta and Indenture

A Historical Connection

On a warm September afternoon of 1838, prominent Scottish watchmaker and philanthropist David Hare was passing through the streets of north Calcutta when he came upon a group of men shouting for help. In a later statement, he recounted:

> I have frequently passed along ... Tuntunniah-street, and observed a number of men always on the top of one of the houses on that street ... I believe it was about the 11th of September last I was passing, between three and four o'clock in the afternoon, and there was a much larger number than I had seen before.... The people on the top of the house were crying out, 'Dohye Sahib' – 'Dohye Company'. I asked what was the matter, and the people around my palanquin told me they were a parcel of Coolies confined there, who were to be sent to the Mauritius.[1]

On entering the building, he saw more than a hundred men confined behind bolted doors, guarded by police watchmen. The men had been kidnapped on their way to Calcutta and to nearby pilgrimage sites and were to be sent to Mauritius to work on sugar plantations. They complained of being held against their will, locked up, beaten and mistreated, and urged that they would sooner die than go to Mauritius.[2] After a prolonged negotiation with the watchmen and the Calcutta police, Hare was able to help release the confined men. With detailed reports in newspapers, this incident – and the image of labourers being migrated overseas against their will – soon became the popular image of Calcutta's encounter with indenture migration.

A walk through Calcutta in the nineteenth century was likely to bring citizens into contact with indentured labourers, whether confined in the houses of north Calcutta or living in the various 'coolie depots' (warehouses) that dotted the riverbank. As migrants moved from villages to Calcutta to port-side depots to ships and, finally, to plantation estates, Calcutta represented the beginning of their journey, where migrants first realised their identities as indentured labourers. Through Calcutta's connections with the agricultural hinterland, planter negotiations over the establishment of indenture and the emergence of 'coolie depots', indenture became part of the very fabric of the city.

Slavery to Indenture: A New Labour Regime

As the Slavery Abolition Act of 1833 caused labour shortage on colonial plantations, British planters were prompted to look for alternative sources of labour. In spite of monetary compensation to planters and the apprenticeship system, Abolition had led to severe economic problems like trade depression, rising costs of commodities like sugar and rum and the immediate need for migrant labourers to replace enslaved labour on plantations. Indian indenture quickly emerged as a viable solution to this labour crisis.

India boasted of a labour pool that was already experienced in migrating for labour. Records from the time mention that Indian migrants were employed in military labour in India, domestic work in Europe and Britain, skilled labour across the empire, and convict labour in Burma (Moulmein and Arracan) and the Australian colonies (New South Wales and Van Diemen's Land). In many places, indenture followed on from experimental and short-lived schemes for the transportation of agricultural and convict labour to plantation colonies. This included the employment of Indian convict labour in public works projects in Mauritius (1815–1817), the emigration of Indian labourers from Pondicherry and Karikal (both French colonies) to French Bourbon in 1826 and the transportation of 150 labourers from Bengal to Bourbon in September 1830.[3]

One of the earliest proponents of indenture was British planter John Gladstone (father of four-time prime minister William Gladstone), whose negotiations with the British government resulted in a lasting indentured labour regime. A trader of sugar and cotton, and owner of plantation estates in Jamaica and British Guiana, John Gladstone actively represented planter

Figure 1.1 Plaque outside Gillander House, Kolkata

Source: Photograph by the author, August 2017, Kolkata.

Note: In 1935, Gillanders Arbuthnot & Company was incorporated as a limited company under the Indian Companies Act (Act VII) and is now part of the Kothari Group of Companies.

interests in public discussions on Abolition and emancipation.[4] He recognised the threat that Abolition posed to planters and traders and started negotiating with British parliamentarians to allow for the procurement of plantation labourers from India. On 4 January 1836, Gladstone wrote a letter to the Calcutta-based merchant firm Gillanders Arbuthnot & Company asking about the possibility of employing migrants from Bengal in his West Indian estates (Figure 1.1). Gladstone asked for a hundred 'young, active, [and] able-bodied' labourers to be exported to his estates Vreedenhoop and Vriedenstein, offering in exchange wages according to contract, comfortable housing, medical assistance and a free passage to British Guiana. He explained:

> You will probably be aware that we are very particularly situated with our negro apprentices in the West Indies, and that is [a] matter of doubt and uncertainty how far they may be induced to continue their services on the plantations after their apprenticeship expires in 1840.… We are, therefore, most desirous to obtain and introduce labourers from other quarters, and particularly from climates similar in their nature … it has occurred to us that a moderate number of Bengalees, such as you were

sending to the Isle of France [Mauritius], might be very suitable for our purpose.[5]

Established in 1819, Gillanders Arbuthnot & Company had long been involved in the emigration of Indians as servants and labourers to England, South Africa and plantation colonies.[6] The firm had arranged for the emigration of 39 labourers from India to Mauritius in 1834 and a further 50 labourers in 1835.[7] They had also served as procurers of labourers to Mauritian sugar planters such as Edward Worthington, Robert Edie, Captain Harvey, Mr Sanders and Mr Griffens in 1835.[8]

Gillanders Arbuthnot & Company were keen on Gladstone's proposal and soon replied:

[W]ithin the last two years, upwards of 2000 natives have been sent from [Calcutta] to the Mauritius. [W]e are not aware that any great difficulty would present itself in sending men to the West Indies, the natives being perfectly ignorant of the place they go to or the length of the voyage they are undertaking.[9]

Gladstone's communication with this Calcutta-based firm represented the beginning of a journey towards establishing a legal, systematic network of indentured labour migration that could replace enslaved and emancipated labourers on colonial plantations. The back-and-forth over Gladstone's proposal came to determine the primary principles of the indenture contract and passage, including ship size, food, clothing and medical provisions, the proportion of male and female labourers, and the provision of five years of contract-bound labour.[10]

Merchant demand for labourers and the willingness of Calcutta-based firms to procure them were not enough to initiate a continuous trade in indentured labourers – it was important to win the support of the British government. To that end, in February 1837, Gladstone wrote to the president of the Board of Control for India to ask permission for 'moving workers, under agreed indentures, from India to the West Indies'.[11] Highlighting the uncertainty of labour procurement under the temporary apprenticeship system, Gladstone argued in this letter that Indian workers offered the best chance of saving the sugar trade. For Gladstone, Indian labourers were not only a better fit for plantation labour than Europeans, but also supposed to create competition for local labour and thus induce the apprentices to meet the wishes of the employer more readily.[12] Many of the main provisions of the indenture trade were negotiated and finalised in these letters, and the standard term of contract was established as five years, since Gladstone argued that the trade would only become commercially viable if labourers could get accustomed to the labouring conditions in Guiana for five years rather than the three years initially proposed.[13]

This was not an easy question for the British parliament because of accusations that the indenture scheme was a 'new system of slavery'. Even as the anti-slavery lobby pushed the parliament for the abolition of any form of unfree labour remotely akin to slavery, the British parliament ultimately gave its nod to the scheme. Although opposed within the House of Lords, an Order in Council was issued in 1836, agreeing to the introduction of Indian labourers in British Guiana under five-year contracts. In the next year, the parliament passed Act V of 1837, which came to govern the principles of recruitment and passage.

This was a pivotal moment in the history of Indian indenture. The correspondence with officials not only recognised the planters' need for labour as an official problem but also introduced Indian migrants as a viable replacement for enslaved labour. Indians had long been involved in long-distance migration for labour, but Gladstone's intervention aided the transformation of this private and often spontaneous system of labour migration into an organised scheme of contractual labour migration, legally sanctioned by the colonial government and regulated by imperial policies. Gladstone's plantation estates in Demerara and Jamaica, his presidency of the Liverpool West India Association and membership of the British Guiana Association, and his close familial links to merchant houses in Calcutta made him exemplary of merchant voices during the change from slavery to indenture. Gladstone used his relationship with parliamentarians and other planters to become one of the most prominent voices in favour of Indian indenture – negotiating the provisions of the trade through letters, publishing his views by writing to the British press and pushing for emigration laws to make the regime official.[14]

The *Hesperus* and the *Whitby* were the first ships to carry indentured labourers under the Order in Council of 1837. The *Hesperus* sailed from Calcutta on 29 January 1838 to British Guiana with 165 Indian indentured workers on board, arriving in British Guiana on 5 May and Georgetown on 8 May.[15] The *Hesperus*'s captain wrote of the journey:

> I left Calcutta on Tuesday January 29th … for Demerara, with 253
> bags of rice, 150 bags cullyes, 9 bales clothing, 150 coolies, 6 women, 11
> children and 2 interpreters, which are all well with the exception of two
> and they have nothing serious the matter with them…. Myself and crew
> are all quite well.[16]

However, he had spoken too soon as cholera broke out onboard only a few days later, taking several lives. The ship's doctor wrote of a victim: 'The virulence of the disease in this man may be judged from the duration of his illness: at 8 o'clock he was in good health … and at 1 o'clock he was a corpse, a lapse of scarcely 5 hours.'[17] The other ship, *Whitby*, was provided by a second planter, Andrew Colville, to procure labourers for the estates of Colville in Demerara and Davidson, Barclay & Company in Berbice.[18] It sailed from Calcutta on 13 January with 249 Indian labourers onboard and arrived in British Guiana on 5 May with 244 workers who survived the journey.[19]

The questioning of unfree labour systems that had been introduced with the abolition debates continued with the passing of the Slave Trade Act of 1807 (which prohibited slave trade within the British Empire) and the Slavery Abolition Act of 1833 (which prohibited the use of slave labour within the British Empire).[20] By 1837, about half a decade after Abolition, negotiations between sugar planters and the metropolitan government had created a government-sanctioned system of labour migration based on five-year labour contracts or indentures. True to its trans-imperial nature, the new labour regime was established through negotiations between a West India planter, a Calcutta-based merchant firm and the British parliament.

Migration Networks and the Hinterland

Calcutta was ideally suited for the establishment of the indenture trade. As a major port on the eastern coast, Calcutta was central to Indian trade – about half of India's exports of cotton, silk, sugar, jute, saltpetre and indigo were shipped through Calcutta during the colonial period.[21] The city's links to river channels and oceanic routes across the Bay of Bengal not only attracted migrant labour but also made it easier to transport them within the subcontinent and abroad. The bay was a maritime thoroughfare traversed by numerous overseas labour movements – including convict labour, domestic and skilled labour, slave labour, indentured labour and maritime labour.[22]

It also formed a common space for movement from different Indian ports such as Calcutta, Madras and Pondicherry. Although situated at different locations and maintaining separate identities, all three ports made use of Bay of Bengal networks and the littoral of the bay to maintain connections and to transport indentured Indians. The development of this 'transcontinental regime of labour' was facilitated by the political and economic contexts of imperialism and the expansion of shipping in the nineteenth century.[23]

Within the subcontinent, Calcutta was connected to a vast agricultural hinterland through a complex network of roads, rivers and channels and situated within existing networks of migration, employment and pilgrimage. As Brij Lal has shown, in the nineteenth century, 'migration [did] not appear as an aberration or an unnatural phenomenon, but as a rational and conscious act'.[24] It was common for villagers to migrate outside harvesting seasons and be temporarily employed in agricultural plantations, public works or factories. In fact, the local agricultural calendar allowed for extensive labour during June to November, but December to May was a slack period.[25] Often, labourers were attracted by new employment opportunities in the burgeoning city, such as the construction of roads, houses and the new Fort William (c. 1757–1775), while others were employed as menial workers who swept streets, cleaned canals and performed similar public works.[26] Calcutta's position as a port and colonial capital made it possible for indenture recruiters to tap into such networks of mobile labour within the subcontinent – whether of public workers, plantation labourers or domestic workers in Calcutta homes. Merchants like Gillanders Arbuthnot & Company used these labour networks to actively argue for the migration of indentured Indians from Calcutta to plantation colonies.

It is now well documented that seasonal migration routes intersected with indenture migration. In fact, the agrarian situation – including rising rents, the seasonal nature of agricultural work and the position of peasants as low-paid agricultural labourers rather than landowners – remained key to determining the migration patterns of indentured Indians. The series of annual reports on 'emigration from the port of Calcutta to British and foreign colonies', which began to be published in 1843, show that most indentured labourers from Calcutta hailed from modern-day Bihar, Uttar Pradesh, Jharkhand and West Bengal.[27] John Geoghegan's *Note on Emigration from India* (1873) reported that half of all emigrants from the Calcutta port hailed from Bihar, closely followed by North-Western Provinces and Oudh (Awadh) and western Bengal.[28]

In the 1830s and 1840s, the main recruiting grounds were Bihar and Chhotanagpur; but over the years, this gradually shifted westwards. By the 1860s, indentured Indians were drawn mostly from Arrah, Gyah, Patna, Allahabad, Ghazipur, Oudh, Cawnpore (Kanpur), Jaunpur, Gorakhpur and other places in eastern India.[29] Anand Yang's study on Bihar corroborates this. By retracing the steps of inhabitants of Saran (Bihar), Yang shows that many early indentured emigrants hailed from Chhotanagpur, but in the 1840s and 1850s labourers were increasingly drawn from modern-day Uttar Pradesh and Bihar.[30] Not all migrants, however, were agricultural labourers: some were artisans, petty tradesmen, barbers or servicemen. For instance, the Royal Commissioners who visited the Mauritius immigration depot in 1837 reported that of the 207 immigrants who arrived on the *Hindoostan*, 156 had worked as agricultural labourers and the rest were artisans, servicemen, clerks and *sepoys*.[31] The Indian Rebellion of 1857 provided further impetus for emigration. A minute from the Calcutta emigration department pointed out that '[p]rior to the Mutiny the monthly average of Mauritius Emigration was about 700, ... but suddenly shot up to two times and then three times by the end of 1859'.[32] There was a strong coincidence between the major areas of the rebellion and the main recruiting areas.[33]

Intermediary recruiters acted as middlemen between planters and this hinterland. Variously referred to as *sirdar*s, *arkatti*s and *duffadar*s in eastern India, their services were solicited by Calcutta-based merchant houses to procure migrant labourers from Indian villages.[34] They formed the vital link between the port city and the hinterland, facilitating a smooth and continuous process of recruitment by appropriating and making use of pre-existing networks of migration. Referring to them as 'in part a foreman, in part a headman, and in part a recruiting contractor', Tirthankar Roy showed that the middlemen recruiters were an indispensable part of labour organisation in mills, mines, ports and plantations.[35] The role of labour intermediaries evolved significantly between the 1820s and 1860s, with returnees increasingly replacing *arkatti*s and *duffadar*s.[36] Returned migrants, who had already spent some time in overseas plantation colonies, made use of kinship networks to recruit from within their extended family or from their villages. Intermediary recruiters were remunerated according to the number of labourers recruited or from a cut of the wage advance given to labourers before sailing, which provided scope for misusing their power.[37] Often seen as a deceptive figure who tempted ignorant Indians into the indenture trade with false promises, the public image of the labour intermediary is apparent in this report from the *Bengal Hurkaru*:

> The Duffadar … may be termed the grand decoy of the Indian coolies and the main-spring of the kidnapping system, he need bring with him no other qualification but that of being an accomplished scoundrel; and he will be certain of employment by the agents of the shippers to kidnap coolies. Educated in the school of roguery, he knows the value of deception … it was no wonder [the migrants] fell a ready prey to the allurement of these devils in human form.[38]

John Archer argues that one of the central problems of urban history is its conceptualisation of the city as 'wholly differentiated from the hinterland'.[39] For Calcutta, it was its links to the hinterland that allowed for the indenture trade by encouraging access to a vast migrant labour pool. Connections with the hinterland coincided with available networks of trade, army recruitment and occupational migration (including for public works, railways, plantations, ports and agriculture). Ultimately, these connections put Calcutta at the centre of the indenture trade, and consequently at the centre of the indenture debates.

Spaces of Indenture: The 'Coolie Depots'

Several urban spaces in Calcutta bear testimony to the indenture trade. The term 'coolie' appears often in place names, such as Coolie Darwaza and Coolie Ghat near Fort William and Coolie Bazaar near Hastings, although in some cases this term was a reference to manual labourers more broadly.[40] Places like Surinam Ghat, named after the Surinam Depot situated on the river Ganges, betray a more obvious connection to the indenture trade.[41] Like most colonial port cities in the subcontinent, Calcutta was composed of a central fort adjacent to the commercial waterfront, residential areas generally divided across race and class lines, a peripheral manufacturing zone and an outlying military zone.[42] While the indenture debates happened in central spaces of the city, such as the Town Hall, indentured Indians occupied more peripheral spaces near the port.

For the indentured migrants, one of their earliest interactions with the city was in the emigration depots, where they were accommodated before being shipped to plantation colonies. Indentured migrants living in the depots met agents of their future employers, as well as emigration agents, surgeon superintendents and other government officials that the prevailing regulations demanded. Such interactions became more regulated with changing emigration policies (especially with the need for certificates to attest to the labourers' good health and willingness to emigrate), but functioned within limitations imposed by the large number of potential emigrants and the limited time that the agents could accord to each. Labour contracts were also discussed and signed in the depots. Migrants were issued standard clothing in these depots: for Mauritius, the kit included a cap and a 'Guernsey frock', while for the West Indies and Fiji, warm clothes were issued for the journey. Women received flannel jackets, woollen petticoats, stockings, shoes and sarees.[43] Ultimately, these 'coolie depots' represented the beginning of the labourer's journey overseas – the site where migrants first realised their identity as indentured labourers.[44]

In the 1830s, migrants were mainly kept at the homes of recruiters until the ship's departure, with nominal, and at times non-existent, inspection.[45] In 1842, one of the first emigration depots was opened in Bhowanipore, Calcutta, while recruits in Madras and Bombay were still accommodated in warehouses. The Bhowanipore Depot was initially meant to accommodate emigrants to Mauritius, but soon came to serve as the emigration depot for Trinidad, Jamaica and Demerara as well. Besides living spaces for migrants, the Bhowanipore Depot included a hospital, a dispensary, cooking sheds and a water tank.[46] Later, separate depots for men and women destined for Trinidad, Fiji, Saint Lucia, Saint Kitts, Saint Helena and British Guiana were opened closer to the port in Garden Reach. Migrants moving to Demerara, Natal and the Caribbean island of Nevis were accommodated at a depot at 25 Garden Reach, those moving to Surinam at 20 Garden Reach, and those migrating to Cayenne, Guadeloupe and Martinique at 76 Garden Reach.[47] The last two were managed by the Dutch and French governments respectively. As a report from 1883–1884 shows, the riverbanks of Garden Reach 'afford[ed] great conveniences for the establishment of depots, as most of the houses in that locality was suitable for residence and office in one; and, having extensive garden grounds attached, [were] admirably adapted for depots'.[48] In fact, it was the view of Garden Reach observable to people first arriving into Calcutta by boat, complete with its Palladian residences and garden houses, that won Calcutta the epithet 'City of Palaces'.[49] Besides being close to the port, Garden Reach also afforded proximity to jute mills, cotton mills, coal sheds and dock yards. Depots were later opened in more interior parts of Bengal, including modern-day Orissa, Assam, Bangladesh, Bihar and Jharkhand. Often referred to as 'coolie sheds', these regional depots served to accommodate labourers proceeding to Calcutta.

Official maps have rarely recorded names of places eked out to accommodate the indenture trade – places demonstrative of the tangible impact of the indenture trade on the city space. Urban cartography was selective in its focus, homing in on military strategy and defence in the late eighteenth and early nineteenth centuries and land use and sanitation in the late nineteenth century.[50] Only in the late nineteenth century did maps start recording spaces frequented by indentured migrants, a prime example of which was the map titled 'Detail of Garden Reach' (1887). This map highlighted six 'coolie depots' (including the Trinidad, British Guiana and Jamaica depots) and a 'coolie line' temple (Figure 1.2). Such emigration depots continued to be present throughout the nineteenth and early twentieth centuries, dotting the landscape in and around the Calcutta port.

Similarly important was the placement of merchant houses. Managing agency houses, originally founded as British merchant enterprises that worked on commission, acted as labour contractors and agents for planters.[51] The managing agency system began in the 1830s, when the East India Company lost its trading monopoly, allowing for private trading.[52] Merchant houses had since been involved in coal mining, indigo plantations and shipping enterprises, as well as in procuring migrant labourers. Mercantile groups such as Henley, Dowson & Bestel, Gillanders Arbuthnot & Company, and Lyall Matheson & Company find mention in early indenture contracts as mediators between emigrants and plantation owners, who signed the contracts on behalf of the planters. They played a key role in appointing recruiters to procure a suitable emigrant labour force, overseeing the process of embarkation and the signing of indenture contracts, as well as arranging travel to plantation colonies. The presence of several such merchant houses in Calcutta, with commercial and personal links to merchants in metropolitan Britain and planters in British plantation colonies, made Calcutta the centre of a continued and reliable trade in indentured labourers. Although some historians have claimed that agency houses were unique to colonial Calcutta, S. D. Chapman convincingly argues that they were active in different parts of the world, such as Mathesons and Swires in China; Wallace Brothers and Steel Brothers in Burma; Hendersons in Borneo, Siam and Java; Mackinnon

Figure 1.2 'Coolie depots' on the bank of the river Ganges

Source: Part of R. B. Smart, 'Detail of Garden Reach', Sheet 7 [Garden Reach] of the Hooghly Survey, 1887, IOR/X/9126/7, British Library, London.

Mackenzie in East Africa; Finlay Muir in South Africa; and Guthries, Bousteads and Symes in Malaya.[53]

Regulating a Trade in 'Coolies'

As the indenture trade became legalised in 1837, it drew significant official and public attention. Early negotiations over Indian indenture facilitated a constantly changing labour regime, which responded to inputs from Calcutta and other parts of the empire. West India merchants residing in Britain were in a position to exert economic and political pressure to support merchant interests, while planters based in the colonies could promote their interests through petitions, memoranda and pressure groups in Britain. At the same time, anti-indenture pressure groups in Britain and petitions from Calcutta maintained constant pressure on parliament to regulate the indenture trade and enforce strict restrictions on travel and work conditions. They alleged that instead of acting as a replacement for slave labour, indenture migration perpetuated the actual conditions of slavery through forceful recruitment, a lack of information about living and working conditions prior to reaching the plantation colonies, conditions of passage synonymous with the middle passage, the use of penal sanction and the continuation of service under overseers who previously employed enslaved labourers. The establishment of the Indian indenture trade thus became a long-drawn process of negotiation between pro- and anti-indenture voices in Britain and the colonies.

Act V of 1837 was the cornerstone of the indenture trade. Passed on 1 May 1837, it provided a detailed schema for indenture migration from India. Even though emigration laws underwent changes over time in response to feedback from parliamentarians, the anti-slavery lobby, the British public and voices from the colonies, the central tenets of this act continued to define the trade. This act made contracts the central focus of indenture legislation. It became legally binding for the labourer and a representative of the planter to be examined in person by an appointed official. The indenture officer would then produce copies of the contract in English and in the mother tongue of the emigrant (or any other language they understood), and the labourer was to be examined to ensure that he understood the terms of the contract. The act further regulated the provisions of food, water and medical supplies, and made it legally binding for appointed officials to inspect ships and their provisions before allowing embarkation.[54] Act V of 1837 thus provided the baseline for indentured emigration. In no uncertain terms, it stated that emigration under the indenture scheme could only continue with a legal contract of service ratified by an authorising officer and with the labourer's right of repatriation at the end of five years.

However, the British parliament remained divided over the issue. Prominent abolitionist Henry Brougham vehemently opposed 'this infernal trade' on grounds that it replicated slave conditions.[55] In a meeting on 16 July, he showed indignation at the fact that 'these poor and ignorant creatures, the hill coolies, were smuggled away under the idea that Mauritius … was a village belonging to the East India Company'.[56] Under increasing censure – not least from Calcutta – the indenture trade was suspended, and investigative committees were formed across India and plantation colonies to enquire into its alleged abuses.[57] With the passing of Act XIV on 29 May

1839, indenture migration to Mauritius, Demerara, Réunion, Ceylon and the Australian colonies (New South Wales and Van Diemen's Land) was prohibited, with a fine of 200 rupees or three months' imprisonment for flouting the ruling.[58] Despite such opposition to indenture, however, many British planters maintained that the migration of indentured labourers was central to the economies of both the sugar colonies and metropolitan Britain and that, in fact, the abuses alleged to exist in the trade could be remedied by further regulations. In light of increasing pressure from such interest groups, and the publicisation of the results of the investigative committees, the parliament declared the resumption of indentured emigration, but under stricter regulations.

In December 1842, Act XV was passed, which removed previous restrictions on the trade and resumed emigration from Calcutta, Bombay and Madras. However, it included several regulatory measures to ensure protection from some of the abuses alleged to exist in the trade. The act introduced stricter shipping regulations, made it legally binding on the colony to grant return passage to each labourer and proposed that officers be appointed at each port to supervise the trade. It declared that water and food provisions should be specified and surveyed by the emigration agent, the duration of the voyage determined by ordinances and the details of indentured emigration kept on record, with penalties for non-compliance, fraud or export by false imprisonment or intoxication.[59] The Marine Surgeon was made responsible for producing fitness and vaccination certificates for emigrants. Act XV of 1842 represented the ultimate legal sanctioning of indentured labour migration. Its regulatory measures undercut the need for prohibition of indenture, and, in fact, resumption was proof that the imperial government had no immediate plans of discontinuing the programme. Besides marking the resumption of the indenture trade, this act also opened the door for the system to be extended to around 20 colonies.

Calcutta was deeply involved in this process of negotiation. Gladstone's detailed conversation with the Calcutta-based Gillanders Arbuthnot & Company helped establish some of the central features of the indenture system – including the contract, the labour pool and the system of labour recruitment. Petitions and public resolutions from Calcutta that criticised the indenture trade added to the growing pressure against its continuance. The report of the Calcutta committee of 1838–1839 was used by the anti-indenture lobby to point to the problems of the trade, and its recommendations were incorporated in future acts. Many of the revisions in regulations in 1842 – such as the creation of the posts of emigration agent and protector of emigrants and the institution of penalties for those who flouted emigration rules – followed directly from the recommendations of the Calcutta investigative committee.[60]

Moreover, early legislation prioritised Calcutta: Act V of 1837 governed emigration through the port of Calcutta, and it was only with the passing of Act XXXII of 1837 that the scheme was extended to Madras and Bombay.[61] Similarly, when indentured emigration was resumed after its brief suspension, Act XXI of 1843 initially restricted emigration to the port of Calcutta, till Act XX of 1844 allowed for the provision of emigration to Jamaica, British Guiana, Trinidad and other West Indian colonies from all three ports: Calcutta, Bombay and Madras.[62] The decline of anti-indenture voices after 1842 was also reflected in Calcutta. As the 1842 regulation addressed, and in many ways answered, the concerns raised in the debates over indenture, there was a gradual decline in anti-indenture arguments from Calcutta in both public spaces and newspapers. The 1843 editions of the *Friend of India* showed a distinct move away from news of indentured labour (which tended to be first-page news in 1838–1842), losing prominence by 1844 as indentureship was gradually extended to other colonies.

The Calcutta of Migrants

Even as the indenture question moved away from the public discursive sphere after 1842, indenture and Calcutta remained intimately linked as migrants moving through Calcutta experienced, inhabited and remembered the city. As migrants lived in 'coolie depots' at the bank of the Ganges, they inhabited the space of Garden Reach near the Calcutta port. Being close to the port made it easier to carry migrants to the Bay of Bengal in the south and eventually out into the open sea. Indentured migrants, however, were not confined to the port area. David Hare saw labourers confined in a house on Tuntunniah street in northern Calcutta.[63] Even before the Bhowanipore Depot was opened in 1842, migrants testified to being lodged in houses in Bhowanipore and to embarking on ships from Baboo Ghat, a few miles north of the Calcutta port.[64] Despite their transient presence in the city, as the administrative and commercial districts in the centre of Calcutta housed offices of shipping companies like Gillanders Arbuthnot & Company, and as indentured migrants went up to the Calcutta Town Hall to testify for the investigative committee, the history of indenture was woven into the very social fabric of this nineteenth-century city.

In the migrants' universe, Calcutta was at once the site of work, of separation and of return. Many migrants who joined the indenture trade and testified to the Calcutta investigative committee originally came to Calcutta in search of work: Sheik Manick was recruited in Calcutta while looking for work, Boodoo Khan joined on his way to Calcutta in search of employment and Karoo was convinced to travel to Calcutta with the promise of a road-repairing job.[65] Others like Bhurossee had travelled to Calcutta 'to get occasional employment' in the houses of Indian elites.[66] For other migrants, Calcutta was one of many stops in their journey from the village to the plantation, as they were recruited in the districts and brought to Calcutta accompanied by sub-agents from local depots.[67]

Calcutta was, in many ways, the gateway to plantation colonies, which were themselves not very well known to Indian villagers. Duncan Pitcher reported that, as late as 1883, plantation colonies were imagined to be a cluster of colonies located in a singular direction: 'The voyage to Fiji is 18 weeks, and to Jamaica 20 weeks. In the coolie's imagination, you go past Fiji to Jamaica.'[68] George Grierson wrote that the plantation colony was 'a kind of *Limbo* where every one goes who is lost sight of'.[69] In parts of Bihar, if someone's son or brother went missing after a family quarrel, 'it is at once concluded that he has gone to the *Tapu* [island], and nothing more is thought about it'.[70] Grierson spoke to the father of an indentured migrant in Gaya, who believed that '"Chíní Dád" (Trinidad) and "Damra" (Demerara) are zillahs [districts] in Mirich [Mauritius]'.[71] As 'Mirich', 'Damra' and 'Chinidad' entered the Indian vocabulary, they were also distorted to relate to the indenture experience: Chinidad contained the word *chini* for sugar, upon whose production the entire indenture trade rested.

Many saw Calcutta as geographically contiguous to the plantation colonies. Life in a land criss-crossed by rivers had given rise to migrants who were new to the concept of open seas. Boodoo Khan expected a land journey to Mauritius; and as late as 1898, Munshi Rahman Khan expected that land would be visible throughout the journey.[72] Emigration reports abounded in instances of migrants jumping off ships, which some saw as suicide attempts, but others recognised as attempts to swim back to the shores of Calcutta. James Smart of the Bengal Pilot Service testified to the Calcutta investigative committee that before his ship joined the sea at the mouth of the Ganges, 'every night almost some went overboard; I saw two men myself jump overboard, and I don't think they reached the shore.'[73] Captain Alexander Mackenzie stated that one of the migrants on his ship jumped overboard 'with the intention of proceeding to Calcutta', even though the ship was 'within two days' sail of Mauritius'.[74] These ideas did not disappear with increased emigration. During their investigation of emigration to Fiji in 1916, C. F. Andrews and W. W. Pearson interviewed a migrant who thought that Fiji was 'about two hundred *kos* from Muttra [north-Indian city of Mathura]'.[75] Recruiters sometimes deceived migrants by referring to Fiji 'as a district near to Calcutta', and many migrants remained unaware of their real destination 'until they found themselves tossing and sea-sick in the Bay of Bengal'.[76]

Finally, Calcutta was intimately connected to the *kala pani* – the dark waters of the ocean, which, once traversed, severed one's caste and community ties. Pitcher reported that as the term had come to connote transportation and exile, 'if, when talking of the voyage, the words *kala pani* are used, the coolie is apt to lose all self-possession'.[77] Grierson's 1883 report stated that when explaining to migrants about their destinations, 'the word "Tapu" [island] is always used, and never "Kalapani", the use of which would be quite sufficient to prevent many from enlisting'.[78]

Saurabh Mishra has recently argued that 'life on ships was both a microcosm of, as well as a precursor to, the life on plantations' since it was on ships that migrants were 'tutored' into the ways of living that mirrored life in the plantations.[79] However, their transformation into 'coolies' of the British Empire had already begun in the depots of Calcutta, where migrants were initiated into indenture and into their new role as indentured labourers. As purpose-built barracks, depots introduced new norms of living, eating and daily routines that mimicked the supervised, routinised and regulated life on plantation estates. Depots instituted official hierarchies between colonial officers, recruiters and *duffadar*s that mirrored plantation hierarchies. The late-nineteenth-century memoirs of Totaram Sanadhya and Munshi Rahman Khan detailed the breaking down of caste-based restrictions on commensality in depots, much before migrants boarded their ships and crossed the *kala pani*. Khan wrote that before reaching the Calcutta depot, migrants were allowed to cook their own meals and wear markers of their caste (like the *janau*), but once they reached Calcutta, they had to wear 'government uniform', eat without caste-based separation, and consume food cooked and served by men of unknown caste backgrounds.[80] Once everyone donned their new clothes, '[n]o Hindu wore the sacred thread or had put *tilak* on their foreheads.... All Hindus had become *sudras*.'[81] Sanadhya wrote: 'I saw that Chamar, Koli, Brahman and so forth were all seated in one place and forced to have their meal together.'[82] Thus, for many migrants, depots also represented the point where family, kinship and community ties were first severed as Indians of different castes lived, cooked and ate together, defying strict observance of caste rules and symbolising their break from their motherland.

Reflecting on port cities and their relation to the hinterland, Tai-Yong Tan defines them as places of contact that serve as transit points for the movement of goods, labour and capital and as nodal centres for the reception and transmission of culture, knowledge and information. As a result, the urban, social, cultural and political identity of the port city is determined by the relationship between the port city, the dominant hinterland and the external economic space it serves.[83] Calcutta was this and more. Albeit not the only port, Calcutta remained at the centre of the vast networks of indenture and was unique in the extent of interaction the city and its inhabitants enjoyed with the indenture system. The indenture question thrived in the city, as it came to be debated, investigated and defended.

Notes

1. Testimony of David Hare, 8 October 1838, in 'Proceedings of the [Calcutta Investigative] Committee, from 22 August 1838 to 14 January 1839', in *Letter from Secretary to Government of India, to Committee on Exportation of Hill Coolies: Report of Committee and Evidence* (East India House, ordered by the House of Commons to be printed, 12 February 1841), Parliamentary Papers (House of Commons) 16, No. 45, p. 53 (henceforth 'Proceedings of the Calcutta Committee'). 'Dohye sahib, dohye Company' is a plea for help, literally translated as 'Please have mercy Sir, please have mercy, [the East India] Company'.

2. Quoted in ibid.

3. Clare Anderson, *Convicts in the Indian Ocean: Transportation from South Asia to Mauritius, 1815–53* (London: Palgrave Macmillan, 2000), p. 6; Hugh Tinker, *A New System of Slavery: The Export of Indian Labour Overseas 1830–1920* (London: Oxford University Press, 1974), p. 61; Panchanan Saha, *Emigration of Indian Labour 1834–1900* (New Delhi: People's Publishing House, 1970), p. 22.

4. For more on John Gladstone, see Sydney George Checkland, *The Gladstones: A Family Biography 1764–1851* (London: Cambridge University Press, 1971); Richard Sheridan, 'The Condition of the Slaves on the Sugar Plantations of Sir John Gladstone in the Colony of Demerara, 1812–49', *New West Indian*

Guide 76, nos. 3–4 (2002): 243–269; Trevor Burnard and Kit Candlin, 'Sir John Gladstone and the Debate over the Amelioration of Slavery in the British West Indies in the 1820s', *Journal of British Studies* 57, no. 4 (2018): 760–782.

5. Letter from John Gladstone to Gillanders Arbuthnot & Company, dated 4 January 1836. Enclosure No. 1 to Gladstone's letters to Lord Glenelg, dated 28 February 1838, in *Copies of All Orders in Council, or Colonial Ordinances, for the Better Regulations and Enforcement of the Relative Duties of Masters and Employers, and Articled Servants, Tradesmen and Labourers, in the Colonies of British Guiana and Mauritius and of Correspondence Relating Thereof* (ordered by the House of Commons to be printed, 2 March 1838) (henceforth *Masters and Employers*).

6. See Letter from G. C. Arbuthnot requesting return of a deposit on account of a native female servant who proceeded to England, 21 October 1835, no. 3; letter from G. C. Arbuthnot, dated 9 September 1835, nos. 38–40; letter from Mr. Gillanders and Arbuthnot and Co. requests return of a deposit on account of a native servant named Chand Khan, who proceeded to Europe with Mr W. T. Robertson on board the *Duke of Argyle*, dated 22 January 1835; and letter from Messers Gillanders Arbuthnot and Co. requests return of deposit made on account of a native female servant named [Mohum Hinghun], who had accompanied Mrs Minchin to England, dated 18 December 1837, 20 December 1837, nos. 46–47, in General Department (General) Proceedings, WBSA.

7. Letter from the Chief Magistrate of Calcutta D. McFarlan to H. T. Prinsep, dated 30 March 1835, 1 April 1835, no. 18, in General Department (General) Proceedings, WBSA.

8. Letter from D. McFarlan to H. T. Prinsep, Secretary to the Government of Bengal, dated 12 February 1835, 21 February 1835, no. 12; letter from D. McFarlan to G. A. Bushby, Secretary to the Government, General Department, dated 23 July 1835, 29 July 1835, no. 54, in General Department (General) Proceedings, WBSA.

9. Letter from Gillanders Arbuthnot & Company to John Gladstone, dated 6 June 1836, in Enclosure No. 1 to Gladstone's letters to Lord Glenelg, dated 28 February 1838, in *Masters and Employers*.

10. Letter from John Gladstone to Gillanders Arbuthnot & Company, dated 10 March 1837 and 20 May 1837, in Enclosure No. 1 to Gladstone's letters to Lord Glenelg, dated 28 February 1838, in *Masters and Employers*.

11. Letter from John Gladstone to Sir John Cain Hobhouse, President of the Board of Control, London, dated 23 February 1837, 6 December 1837, no. 54, General Department (General) Proceedings, WBSA.

12. Ibid.

13. Letter from John Gladstone to Lord Glenelg, dated 29 April 1837, GG/348. Glynne-Gladstone MSS, Gladstone's Library, Hawarden, Wales (henceforth 'GG-MSS'). See also letter from John Gladstone to Sir George Grey, 23 March 1837, in *Papers Respecting the East-India Labourers Bill* (London: printed by order of the General Court by J. L. Cox & Sons, 1838), pp. 27–28.

14. For Gladstone's role at this pivotal juncture, see Purba Hossain, "'A Matter of Doubt and Uncertainty': John Gladstone and the Post-Slavery Framework of Labour in the British Empire', *Journal of Imperial and Commonwealth History* 50, no. 1 (2022): 52–80.

15. David Dabydeen, Jonathan Morley, Brinsley Samaroo, Amar Wahab and Brigid Wells (eds.), *The First Crossing Being the Diary of Theophilus Richmond, Ship's Surgeon Aboard the Hesperus, 1837–8* (Guyana: Caribbean Press, 2010), p. xviii.

16. Letter from Captain Baxter to John Gladstone, 2 February 1838, quoted in Dabydeen et al. (eds.), *The First Crossing*, pp. xix–xx.

17. Diary entry of Theophilus Richmond, dated 18 February 1838, in Dabydeen et al. (eds.), *The First Crossing*, p. 90.

18. Dabydeen et al. (eds.), *The First Crossing*, p. xviii.

19. Dwarka Nath, *A History of Indians in Guyana* (London: Thomas Nelson & Sons, 1950), pp. 11–12.

20. Notably, India was excluded from the 1833 legislation since it fell under the jurisdiction of the East India Company rather than the British government. Slavery in India was not de-legalised until 1843.

21. Tai-Yong Tan, 'Port Cities and Hinterlands: A Comparative Study of Singapore and Calcutta', *Political Geography* 26, no. 7 (2007): 851–865. For movements and commerce along the Hooghly River, see Robert Ivermee, *Hooghly: The Global History of a River* (London: Hurst Publishers, 2020).

22. For the importance of the Bay of Bengal, see Sunil Amrith, *Crossing the Bay of Bengal: The Furies of Nature and the Fortunes of Migrants* (Cambridge, MA: Harvard University Press, 2013).

23. Ravi Ahuja, 'Mobility and Containment: The Voyages of South Asian Seamen, c. 1900–1960', *International Review of Social History* 51, no. 14 (2006): 111–141, p. 111.

24. Brij V. Lal, *Chalo Jahaji: On a Journey through Indenture in Fiji* (Acton: Australian National University Press, 2012), p. 112.

25. Anand Yang, *The Limited Raj: Agrarian Relations in Colonial India, Saran District, 1793–1920* (Berkeley, CA: University of California Press, 1989), p. 199.

26. See Kaustubh Mani Sengupta, 'The New Fort William and the Dockyard: Constructing Company's Calcutta in the Late Eighteenth Century', *Studies in History* 32, no. 2 (2016): 231–256; Sangeeta Dasgupta, '"Heathen Aboriginals", "Christian Tribes", and "Animistic Races": Missionary Narratives on the Oraons of Chhotanagpur in Colonial India', *Modern Asian Studies* 50, no. 2 (2016): 437–478.

27. Leela Gujadhur Sarup, *Colonial Emigration, 19th–20th Century: Annual Reports from the Port of Calcutta to British and Foreign Colonies* (Kolkata: Aldrich International, 2007).

28. John Geoghegan, *Note on Emigration from India* (Calcutta: Superintendent of Government Printing, 1873), p. 67.

29. Ibid.

30. Yang, *The Limited Raj*, p. 191. See also Anand Yang, 'Peasants on the Move: A Study of Internal Migration in India', *Journal of Interdisciplinary History* 10, no. 1 (1979): 37–58.

31. Cited in Marina Carter, *Servants, Sirdars, and Settlers: Indians in Mauritius, 1834–1874* (New Delhi and New York: Oxford University Press, 1995), pp. 108–109.

32. Quoted in Brinsley Samaroo, 'The Caribbean Consequences of the Indian Revolt of 1857', in *Indian Diaspora in the Caribbean: History, Culture, and Identity*, ed. Rattan Lal Hangloo, pp. 71–93 (New Delhi: Primus Books, 2012), p. 79.

33. Samaroo, 'The Caribbean Consequences'.

34. For details on the recruiter, see Crispin Bates and Marina Carter, 'Sirdars as Intermediaries in Nineteenth-Century Indian Ocean Indentured Labour Migration', *Modern Asian Studies* 51, no. 2 (2017): 462–484; Tirthankar Roy, 'Sardars, Jobbers, Kanganies: The Labour Contractor and Indian Economic History', *Modern Asian Studies* 42, no. 5 (2008): 971–998; Amit Kumar Mishra, 'Sardars, Kanganies and Maistries: Intermediaries in the Indian Labour Diaspora During the Colonial Period', in *The History of Labour Intermediation: Institutions and Finding Employment in the Nineteenth and Early Twentieth Centuries*, ed. Sigrid Wadauer, Thomas Buchner and

Alexander Mejstrik, pp. 368–387 (New York and Oxford: Berghahn Books, 2015).

35. Roy, 'Sardars, Jobbers, Kanganies', p. 972.

36. Bates and Carter, 'Sirdars as Intermediaries', p. 467. Carter argues that this system of labour recruitment became more popular after renewed government controls in 1842. Marina Carter, 'Strategies of Labour Mobilisation in Colonial India: The Recruitment of Indentured Workers for Mauritius', *The Journal of Peasant Studies* 19, nos. 3–4 (1992): 229–245.

37. Testimony of John Hughes, 10 September 1838, and testimony of J. J. McCann, 6 September 1838, in 'Proceedings of the Calcutta Committee'.

38. *Bengal Hurkaru*, 21 December 1838, p. 4.

39. John Archer, 'Paras, Palaces, Pathogens: Frameworks for the Growth of Calcutta, 1800-1850', *City and Society* 12, no. 1 (2000): 19–54, p. 19.

40. According to P. T. Nair, Coolie Bazar was named after the large influx of manual labourers to the area during the building of the new Fort William. P. Thankappan Nair, *A History of Calcutta's Streets* (Calcutta: Firma KLM, 1987).

41. Technically, the river flowing through Calcutta is the Hooghly, a western distributary of the Ganges. It is locally known as Ganga/Ganges as well as Hooghly/Hugli.

42. Meera Kosambi and John E. Brush, 'Three Colonial Port Cities in India', *Geographical Review* 78, no. 1 (1988): 32–47, p. 33.

43. Tinker, *A New System of Slavery*, p. 140.

44. For detailed accounts of emigration depots in late-nineteenth-century Calcutta, see Carter, *Servants, Sirdars and Settlers*, ch. 3; Margriet Fokken, *Beyond Being Koelies and Kantráki: Constructing Hindostani Identities in Suriname in the Era of Indenture, 1873–1921* (Hilversum: Verloren, 2018), ch. 2.2.

45. Carter, *Servants, Sirdars and Settlers*, p. 78.

46. 'Plan of the Mauritius Emigration Depot, Bhowanipore, 1861', reproduced in Tinker, *A New System of Slavery*, p. 136.

47. Captain C. Burbank, *Annual Report on Emigration from the Port of Calcutta to British and Foreign Colonies for 1864–1865*, dated 23 May 1865, no. 299 (Calcutta: Bengal Secretariat Press, 1865); J. G. Grant, *Annual Report on Emigration from the Port of Calcutta to British and Foreign Colonies for 1873–1874*, no. 609/A (Calcutta: Bengal Secretariat Press, 1874).

48. Report of J. G. G. Grant (1883–1884), quoted in Fokken, *Beyond Being Koelies*, pp. 90–91.

49. On his way into Calcutta to accompany indentured migrants on the *Hesperus* to British Guiana, the ship's surgeon Theophilus Richmond wrote:

> At last we have arrived at Calcutta, the Metropolis of the East, the far famed City of Palaces, the Emporium of wealth, the chosen habitation of luxury! The last few miles of the approach from the river is a succession of beautiful villas, belonging to persons who either reside there altogether or go after the business of the day from the city; it is named Garden Reach…. Few things can be more striking than this approach to Calcutta.

Diary entry of Theophilus Richmond, dated 8 December 1837, in Dabydeen et al. (eds.), *The First Crossing*, pp. 55–56.

50. Keya Dasgupta, *Mapping Calcutta: The Collection of Maps at the Visual Archives of the Centre for Studies in Social Sciences* (Kolkata: Centre for Studies in Social Sciences, 2009).

51. For the managing agency system in India, see Blair Kling, 'The Origin of the Managing Agency System in India', *Journal of Asian Studies* 26, no. 1 (1966): 37–47; Blair Kling, *Partner in Empire: Dwarkanath Tagore and the Age of Enterprise in Eastern India* (Berkeley, CA: University of California Press, 1976); Maria Misra, *Business, Race, and Politics in British India, c. 1850–1960* (Wotton: Clarendon Press, 1999); Stephanie Jones, *Merchants of the Raj: British Managing Agency Houses in Calcutta Yesterday and Today* (London: Macmillan Press, 1992).

52. Jones, *Merchants of the Raj*, p. 1.

53. S. D. Chapman, 'The Agency Houses: British Mercantile Enterprise in the Far East c. 1780–1920', *Textile History* 19, no. 2 (1988): 239–254, p. 239.

54. Emigration Act V of 1837, passed by the Governor-General in Council on 1 May 1837, Home Department, Public Branch, Annex Building, National Library, Kolkata (NL).

55. Geoghegan, *Note on Emigration from India*, p. 9.

56. Quoted in ibid.

57. Extract from Proceedings of the President in Council, dated 11 July 1838, in letter from the Government of Bengal, dated 6 June, August 1838, no. 5, General Department (General) Proceedings, WBSA.

58. Emigration Act XIV of 1839, passed by the Honourable President of the Council of India in Council on 27 May 1839, Home Department, Public Branch, Annex Building, NL.

59. Act XV of 1842, Colonial Emigration Acts (Bombay Education Society Press, 1842), Home Department, Public Branch, Annex Building, NL.

60. Ibid.

61. Emigration Act XXXII of 1837, passed by the President of the Council of India in Council on 15 December 1837, Home Department, Public Branch, Annex Building, NL.

62. Tinker, *A New System of Slavery*, p. 77.

63. Testimony of David Hare, 8 October 1838, in 'Proceedings of the Calcutta Committee'.

64. Testimony of Boodoo Khan, 1 October 1838, and testimony of Sheik Manick, 1 October 1838, in 'Proceedings of the Calcutta Committee'.

65. Testimony of Boodoo Khan, 1 October 1838, testimony of Sheik Manick, 1 October 1838, and testimony of Karoo, 16 November 1838, in 'Proceedings of the Calcutta Committee'. For details, see Chapter 3.

66. 'No. 2 Statement of Bhurossee', in Attachment to letter from the Chief Magistrate of Calcutta, Home Department, Public Branch Consultations, dated 26 May 1841, no. 48, National Archives of India, New Delhi (NAI).

67. Grierson and Pitcher's 1883 reports on recruiting operations in the Bengal Presidency and the North-Western Provinces and Oudh respectively offered detailed discussions on district-based sub-depots. See George Abraham Grierson, *Report on Colonial Emigration from the Bengal Presidency* (with diary) (Calcutta: n.p., 1883); Duncan J. Pitcher, 'Report on the System of Recruiting Labourers for the Colonies', in 'Major Pitcher's Report on the Result of His Inquiry into the System of Recruiting Labourers for the Colonies', Proceedings of the Revenue and Agricultural Department, February 1883, Proceedings no. 2, IOR/P/2057, British Library, London (BL).

68. Pitcher, 'Report on the System of Recruiting Labourers for the Colonies', p. 32.

69. Grierson, *Report on Colonial Emigration from the Bengal Presidency*, p. 18 (emphasis in original).

70. Ibid.

71. Ibid., p. 52.

72. Testimony of Boodoo Khan, 1 October 1838, in 'Proceedings of the Calcutta Committee'; *Autobiography of an Indian Indentured Labourer Munshi Rahman Khan (1874–1972), Jeevan Prakash*, trans. Kathinka

Sinha-Kerkhoff, Ellen Bal and Alok Deo Singh (New Delhi: Shipra Publications, 2005), p. 83.

73. Testimony of James Smart, 15 October 1838, in 'Proceedings of the Calcutta Committee'. Similar reports of jumping overboard can be seen in the testimony of Captain F. W. Birch, dated 30 August 1838, and the testimony of Captain A. G. Mackenzie, dated 6 September 1838, in 'Proceedings of the Calcutta Committee'; letter between Colonial Secretary George Dick and the Chief Secretary of Bengal Government, dated 18 August 1838 (Port Louis), and letter between H. T. Prinsep and T. Dickens, dated 3 October 1838, in 3 October 1838, no. 7A, 7B and 7C, General Department Proceedings, WBSA; and C. F. Andrews and W. W. Pearson, *Report on Indentured Labour in Fiji: An Independent Enquiry* (Calcutta: Star Printing Works, 1916), p. 19.

74. Testimony of Captain A. G. Mackenzie, 6 September 1838, in 'Proceedings of the Calcutta Committee'.

75. Andrews and Pearson, *Report on Indentured Labour in Fiji*, p. 7. *Kos*, or *coss*, is a unit of distance that varied based on time period and region. In this context, one *kos* is between 1.25 and 2 miles. Henry Yule, *Hobson-Jobson: A Glossary of Colloquial Anglo-Indian Words and Phrases, and of Kindred Terms, Etymological, Historical, Geographical and Discursive* (new edition edited by William Crooke) (London: J. Murray, 1903 [1886]), p. 262.

76. Andrews and Pearson, *Report on Indentured Labour in Fiji*, p. 9.

77. Pitcher, 'Report on the System of Recruiting Labourers for the Colonies', p. 18.

78. Diary entry of December 22, in Grierson, *Report on Colonial Emigration from the Bengal Presidency*, p. 5.

79. Saurabh Mishra, 'Violence, Resilience and the "Coolie" Identity: Life and Survival on Ships to the Caribbean, 1834–1917', *Journal of Imperial and Commonwealth History* 50, no. 2 (2022): 241–263, pp. 242, 253.

80. *Autobiography of an Indian Indentured Labourer*, pp. 77–80.

81. Ibid., p. 78.

82. Totaram Sanadhya, *My Twenty-One Years in the Fiji Islands and The Story of the Haunted Line*, ed. John D. Kelly and Uttra Kumari Singh (Suva: Fiji Museum, 1991). Chamar, Koli and Brahman/Brahmin are caste epithets.

83. Tan, 'Port Cities and Hinterlands', pp. 853, 862.

2

Debating Indenture

The beginning of the indenture trade was a pivotal moment in the history of colonial labour servitude. With the abolition debates of the early nineteenth century, and the subsequent outlawing of slavery in the British Empire, the assessment of labour movements was based on a complete and immediate revocation of the slave trade. Naturally, the labour regime created to replace slave labour was evaluated along the rubric of the recently condemned slave trade. Discussions around Abolition had created a new dichotomy of acceptable and unacceptable (exploitative) forms of labour regimes. Thus, provisions that had been discarded as unacceptable within the slave labour regime – such as the use of coercive and deceptive practices in the procurement of labour, mistreatment of labourers during passage and on plantations and the detention of labourers against their will – also had to be discarded in the labour systems that followed. Calcutta took centre stage in these unfree labour debates. By playing a vocal role in negotiating the indenture trade, Calcuttans contributed significantly to the rhetoric that christened the indenture trade 'a new system of slavery'.

The implementation of Act V of 1837 had created a new emigration policy applicable exclusively to the indenture trade, in the process defining the indenture trade as separate from other migratory labour regimes. One of the provisions of the act stated that it did not apply to 'native seamen' (such as *lascars*) or domestic servants, thus implying a newly emerged legal status for indentured plantation workers that separated them from other workers in the eyes of the colonial state.[1] The indenture debates in Calcutta thus not only negotiated specific provisions for recruitment, accommodation and passage of migrant labourers, but indeed questioned the very legitimacy of the indenture trade in the age of Abolition.

'A Vigilant Public'

Early nineteenth-century Calcutta housed a mix of European and Indian inhabitants. Records from 1837 counted 3,138 'British-born subjects and their legitimate descendants', 137,651 'Hindoos' and 58,744 'Mussulmans'.[2] As British public employment opportunities expanded with colonial expansion, British society in Calcutta came to include people from all walks of life: Company and civil officials, merchants, clerks, craftsmen, soldiers and missionaries. The Indian society in Calcutta, on the other hand, was variegated and divided along lines of class, caste and gender. The vocal Indian community tended to be English-educated – landholders, merchants, reformers, educationists and philanthropists – many of whom were close to the ruling structure or to Europeans by virtue of their trade. Together, they were vocal in political campaigns and actively participated in debating sociopolitical issues, one of the earliest of which was the migration of indentured Indians from Calcutta.

The *Friend of India* wrote in 1842 that Calcutta boasted of 'a vigilant public, fully alive to the danger of the new system, and a free and almost mistrustful press'.[3] Indenture petitions, reports and news out of Calcutta revealed a closed, collaborative and elite circle of Calcuttans – the main social and economic movers of Calcutta society – making decisions on behalf of the city and discussing an issue that expanded beyond the geographical limits of South Asia. Looking at Calcutta of the 1830s and 1840s through the lens of indenture helps lay bare the structures of power, influence and communication that characterised this colonial capital. The indenture debates emerged in a space where Indo-British relationships were cultivated through commercial partnerships, shared political interests and membership in associations. As migrants passed through the city and as the city discussed the merits of indenture, the debates revealed a vocal, active and engaging public sphere in Calcutta that operated across racial boundaries.

Like other colonial cities, Calcutta was nominally divided into a 'white' town and a 'black' town. The white town consisted of European settlements within and around Fort William, with well-planned residential, administrative and mercantile hubs, European-influenced architecture, broad thoroughfares and discrete city blocks. By contrast, the black town was made up of Indian neighbourhoods with densely packed houses organised along caste, religious and occupational lines. It was characterised by its narrow streets and traditional *paras* (neighbourhoods) and *haats* (temporary markets).[4] Peter J. Marshall argues that in cities like Calcutta, the British maintained 'an almost exclusively British community', and any Indian who penetrated this social veneer had to be 'willing to participate on British terms'.[5] Such a conceptualisation of the city as inhabited by an undifferentiated Indian urban class that maintained their distance from the colonial ruling class reinforces the idea of Calcutta as divided along racial lines.

The indenture debates reveal, however, that Indian merchants, educationists and commercial agents constantly frequented the so-called white town. British officials often lived in areas of north Calcutta considered to be within the black town, while Indian settlements could be found in the heart of the white town.[6] Swati Chattopadhyay argues that the notion of Calcutta as a British city was disseminated through maps, paintings and historical narratives that depicted the coloniser and the colonised as occupying disparate physical spaces.[7] In the historical representation of Calcutta, a singular narrative was created, which moved seamlessly from the founding of the city by Job Charnock, to the Battle of Plassey in 1757, to the granting of the Diwani of Bengal to the East India Company in 1765, while denying Indians any agency or representation in the development of Calcutta. The indenture debates reveal a similar blurring of the boundaries between the white town and the black town, since the debates could only have taken place in an urban space where the white town was punctuated by Indian presence.

Theatres of Debate: The Town Hall of Calcutta

In the nineteenth century, the Calcutta public were actively involved in the creation and use of new public spaces. Although early public meetings were held in taverns and amusement halls such as Wright's New Tavern, Moore's Assembly Rooms, Le Gallais Tavern, the Harmonic Tavern, the Exchange and Public Rooms, and the Old Court House, Calcuttans soon felt the need for a designated space for meetings.[8] James Long recounted in 1852 that as the Old Court House fell into a 'ruinous condition' at the turn of the century, the decision was taken to erect a new town hall.[9] In February 1804, the inhabitants of Calcutta formally petitioned to have a town hall erected; and with finances from the public lottery, it was opened in 1813.[10] Within the next few years, the Town Hall became the cornerstone of the public sphere (Figure 2.1). In the 1820s and 1830s, it housed meetings on the abolition of the stamp regulation, the abolition of extra duties on Indian goods, the erection of memorials, the establishment of the Calcutta School Society and the gathering of aid for victims of the Irish Famine (1822).[11] It is thus no surprise that when indentured emigration began in the 1830s, the Town Hall became the space for debating indenture and for petitioning the colonial government to suspend the trade. It became one of the first spaces in Calcutta where the anti-indenture argument was publicly discussed.

On 15 June 1838, 152 inhabitants of Calcutta petitioned the sheriff James Young to hold a public meeting to discuss indentured emigration. Consequently, a Town Hall meeting was held on 10 July to discuss criticisms against the indenture trade and its alleged resemblance to slavery. This meeting was attended by British and Indian inhabitants of Calcutta from diverse walks of life, including merchants and entrepreneurs like Dwarkanath

Figure 2.1 The Town Hall of Calcutta

Source: Photograph by Rabirashmi Roy, Wikimedia Commons, https://commons.wikimedia.org/wiki/File:Town_Hall_-_Kolkata_-_West_Bengal.jpg (accessed in April 2024). Licensed under the Creative Commons Attribution-Share Alike 4.0 International licence.

Tagore, clergymen such as Reverend James Charles and Reverend Thomas Boaz, marine officers like A. G. Mackenzie and barrister and social reformer Longueville Clarke.[12] An equally diverse group of entrepreneurs, merchants, government officials and missionaries had petitioned the Calcutta sheriff to call the meeting, including T. Dealtry (archdeacon), Roger Dias (court pleader), Krishnamohan Banerjee (educationist and missionary), Rustomjee Cowasjee (merchant and entrepreneur), Manick Chunder Sein, Govindo Haldar and Woopendey Mohun Tagore.[13]

The Town Hall meeting of 1838 commenced with an absolute condemnation of the prevailing system of indenture and the passing of the following resolution:

> Resolved, that this meeting having heard of the commencement, continuance, and extension of a system of exporting the natives of India to the British slave and other colonies, expresses its deepest regret that such a traffic should exist, and, more especially, that it should have originated in this port, believing the system to be fraught with unmixed evils to the so called 'free emigrants'.[14]

The outright rejection of the trade as 'fraught with unmixed evils' was at least partially based on the understanding that conditions of slavery were pervasive and shaped the indenture experience. In particular, the attendees were concerned that indentured migrants were migrating to work in 'British slave colonies' – plantations that had employed slave labour for decades and where indentured migrants could expect to encounter similar working and living conditions. Bishop Daniel Wilson argued in the meeting that indentured labourers were likely to face similar treatment to the enslaved labourers preceding them, their freedom being similarly restricted.[15] He asked: 'Where were the laws to protect them in an old slave colony and from the tyranny of task-masters who had spent a whole life in driving slaves?'[16] Longueville Clarke summed up this sentiment to loud cheers from the audience: 'It were better to trust their property with the common thief, their characters with the common slanderer, their lives with the cut-throat, the honor of their daughters with the bawd, than the liberty of man with the slave-owner.'[17]

There was also concern that indentured migrants would be subject to similar penal sanctions and regulatory measures as the enslaved labourers before them. Mr Dickens argued that in plantation colonies, the only relation that had existed up to then had been that of 'master and slave; where labour (in itself honourable) has always been stigmatized as the portion of slavery; where the late masters of slaves are the lawgivers; where the prejudices of color are entertained and produce a degree of hatred, and scorn of fellow men'.[18] Reverend Charles asserted that the indenture trade was similar to the slave trade because both reduced man into 'an article of merchandize'.[19] These concerns led the attendees to petition the colonial government for a full enquiry into the indenture trade and to suspend the trade pending the decision of this inquiry. Confident in their criticism of the indenture trade, the Town Hall resolution held that the enquiry would 'necessarily lead to prompt and total suppression' of the trade.[20]

Most speeches admonishing indenture and arguing its similarity to the slave trade were greeted with cheers from the audience. However, the decision to suspend the indenture trade was not unanimous: some favoured continued emigration. Major Archer, for instance, found the comparison to slavery tenuous, arguing that labourers in Mauritius were well treated and received better wages than in India.[21] He maintained that laws in Mauritius were 'leaning towards the coolies and against the planters' and that offences were rare.[22] Captain Mackenzie used his considerable experience as a ship's captain to argue that the indenture trade was not as inhumane as made out to be.[23] Petitions for abolition of the indenture trade without a thorough and impartial inquiry, he argued, would undermine colonial policy and be an acknowledgement that the British government permitted 'a Slave Trade to grow and flourish under [their] eyes'.[24] Mr Osborne argued that the comparison to slavery was not fair, pointing specifically to the lack of evidence about the alleged atrocities perpetrated in the indenture system.[25] As for the accounts of kidnapping and abuse appearing in the papers, he considered them inaccurate.[26]

Although divergent in their views of indenture, all attendees agreed to opening an inquiry into the trade and, to that effect, presented a petition to the President in Council. This petition characterised indenture as a system that deceived unwilling labourers to migrate overseas and left thousands of families without the protection of an earning member. Indentured emigrants, it argued, were 'neither aware of their destination [,] the real nature of their engagement [n]or of the extent of their future labor and reward' and were in fact transferred from one planter to another in Mauritius and reshipped to West Indian plantations.[27] The petitioners demanded a full enquiry into the indenture trade and measures for its speedy and complete suppression. Instead of discussing specific incidences of abuse, the petition asserted that cases of abuse and fraudulence were not isolated incidents but part of a systemic problem. Thus, only drastic measures such as changed emigration policies or a complete suspension of the trade could remedy the situation. Regulations already in place, including the vigilance of emigration officials, were not deemed sufficient to suppress abuses.

The Town Hall meeting remains one of the first spaces where pro- and anti-indenture arguments were made together, and the resultant petition was the first to articulate Calcutta's opinions on indenture to the metropole. At the same time, petitions offered only momentary snapshots into the indenture debates in Calcutta, a fuller view of which was apparent in news reports and periodicals.

Print and Protest: The Indenture Question in Periodicals

As the site of the first vernacular press and one of the earliest printing and publishing industries in British India, Bengal had been at the forefront of printing. The coming of print impacted indigenous scholarship, literacy and access to learning, and it was this rise in the literate public that encouraged the emergence of periodicals and the discussion of social issues within them.[28] Starting with the publication of *Hicky's Bengal Gazette* in 1780, periodicals became more widely published and read by the beginning of the nineteenth century. By the 1840s, there were several English periodicals in Calcutta, including the *Calcutta Gazette*, *Bengal Hurkaru*, *Calcutta Monthly Journal*, *Calcutta Journal*, *John Bull*, *Bengal Herald*, *Calcutta Courier*, *Friend of India* and *Calcutta Christian Observer*.[29] Vernacular newspapers soon followed. The first newspaper in Bengali emerged in 1818, and by 1842 there were at least 44 Bengali newspapers, such as *Sambad Koumudi*, *Samachar Chundrika*, *Bangadut* and *Sambad Bhaskar*.[30]

Although operating within constraints of class, caste and access to English education, the movement for free press invited the participation of several inhabitants of Calcutta in issues of wider public interest. The indenture trade was one of them. Extensive coverage of the indenture debates in periodicals brought the issues to the attention of the public and allowed for further public commentary through letters to editors. Thus, even in the absence of physical meetings, the indenture debates could flourish within Calcutta with inputs from its citizens and be disseminated across the empire. In this, the indenture debates had parallels with the anti-slavery movement. Some of the techniques

of organisation (like the use of petitions and public meetings) and methods of
information dissemination (through publications, periodicals and pamphlets)
were common to both movements.[31]

Between 1837 and 1844, periodicals such as the *Friend of India*, *Calcutta
Courier*, *Bengal Hurkaru*, *The Englishman*, *Calcutta Review*, *Samachar
Chundrika*, *Calcutta Star* and *Bengal Spectator* offered detailed reportage on
Indian indenture. Frequently referring to 'the coolie question', periodicals
kept a close eye on changing regulations, on meetings and petitions from
Calcutta, as well as on reports of deceitful recruitment and imprisonment of
labourers. The indenture trade was frequently mentioned at least once a week
in reports or letters to the editor, often appearing as first-page news.

Most periodicals, like the *Friend of India*, *Bengal Hurkaru* and *The
Englishman*, favoured increased regulation or complete suspension of the trade.
Resonating the anti-indenture sentiments of the city, they critiqued both the
manner in which the trade operated and the policies behind it. News reports
highlighted miseries of the voyage overseas, number of deaths on board and
miserable living and working conditions on plantations, many suspecting that
due to the fresh memory of the slave trade, indentured labourers were subjected
to harsher treatment in passage and on estates.[32] Reports often pointed
to abduction techniques used to procure indentured labourers, including
eyewitness accounts of kidnapping and unlawful detention, and relatives
complaining about the loss of loved ones to indenture.[33] An official from the
district of Purulia complained in the *Friend of India* about the procurement of
labourers on false pretences, stating: 'a few persons are occasionally taken away
by men, who I have reason to believe, represent themselves to be servants of the
Government'.[34] Many reporters were convinced that indentured emigration was
based on 'the wants of the Colonies, rather than the wants of the labourers'.[35]

By contrast, newspapers like the *Calcutta Courier* were decidedly pro-
indenture. They countered the claims of anti-indenture reports and
condemned the attack on indenture as an unfair and undeserved vilification of
planters, merchants and recruitment agents. The *Calcutta Courier* urged that
stopping the indenture trade will 'injure the interests of the whole population
of the Mauritius who are innocent, and will moreover, ... cast a stigma most
undeserved upon the Mauritius Planters and their Agents here'.[36] An 1838
report summed up the anti-indenture position thus:

> [D]ust has been thrown in the eyes of the public, and they have been
> illogically asked to jump to the conclusion, that because the *duffadars*

and crimps of Bengal are great villains; therefore, the planters at the Mauritius and the government authorities there, and in other colonies, are equally bad.[37]

Reports in pro-indenture periodicals claimed that there was no kidnapping or confinement involved, and that the numbers for kidnapping and deaths on passage had been greatly exaggerated by rival newspapers.[38]

The argument over Indian indenture played out publicly in the print media, mirroring the polarity of opinions in Calcutta. Most periodicals that reported on the indenture trade were in English, with the exception of *Samachar Chundrika* and the bilingual *Bengal Spectator* – possibly a result of Indo-British collaboration on the issue. News reports questioned and challenged rival reportage, quoted their reports while undermining them and printed letters to the editor that offered alternative views. Notably, the editor of the *Bengal Hurkaru* called the *Calcutta Courier*'s editor 'the solitary champion of the trade in coolies' while undermining their reports as biased against the labourers.[39] Similarly, the *Calcutta Courier* frequently challenged the *Bengal Hurkaru*'s reports, saying of its editor: 'He is all for the Cooley, and careth not a button for the Agent....'[40] Pro- and anti-indenture arguments are often treated separately in academic scholarship, but periodicals allowed for a more interactive public sphere by allowing regular back-and-forth between the two camps and offering increased public access to indenture discussions.

Indenture petitions from Calcutta were loyal and non-subversive, highlighting their confidence in the benevolence of the colonial state. News reports, however, challenged government decisions more firmly. Many reports questioned government acts and asked for the immediate redressal of problems in the trade. This reached its apogee in an 1838 news report that warned:

If England, deaf to the voice of humanity, should determine to perpetuate the system [and] allow the exportation to be extended from the East India to the West India Islands, it will only remain to enquire, whether Britain is any longer worthy of being entrusted with the improvement of India.[41]

This attitude was not confined to news reports but extended to letters from the public, possibly emboldened by the anonymity that such publications offered. A letter to the editor of the *Bengal Hurkaru* defiantly signed off as 'no trader in human beings', others signed off as 'an enemy to slavery' and 'Justus', while yet another called the indenture trade 'a trade of human flesh', thus defining themselves by their moral abhorrence of the indenture system.[42]

Detailed reportage kept the indenture question in public memory throughout the period between 1837 and 1843. The *Friend of India* argued that the indenture trade epitomised that iniquity which characterised the African slave trade and could only be prevented from becoming an instrument of oppression through the 'utmost vigilance of the public authorities'.[43] Periodicals made this vigilance practicable. The indenture question entered public memory through meetings, changed regulations or petitions only at particular junctures, but news was ubiquitous and frequent. It was possible for any reader of English periodicals to gain a good understanding of the indenture debates in Calcutta, stay updated on changes in regulation or incidents of kidnapping, formulate their opinion on the debates and weigh in on them through letters to the editors. It was not uncommon for many of the periodicals to write on the 'coolie question' every week – commenting on where labourers had been sighted in Calcutta, reporting on meetings and petitions on indenture and consistently repeating their views on recruitment, regulations, conditions of work and whether the trade should be allowed to continue.

As we saw in Chapter 1, David Hare came across a group of labourers confined in a building in north Calcutta in 1838, who claimed to have been kidnapped and held against their will. Hare's discovery and his subsequent complaint to the police received wide coverage in periodicals. The *Bengal Hurkaru* and the *Asiatic Journal and Monthly Miscellany* used this incident as an example of the inefficiency and apathy of the Calcutta police, pointing especially to the police magistrate's remark that the confined labourers 'were unworthy of sympathy, as they had broken their contracts'.[44] While the police continued to point to the legitimacy of the indenture contracts and the problems of breaching them, periodicals countered it with accusations of illegal confinement and the use of police forces to imprison labourers.[45] As this incident became widely publicised, the colonial state's accountability to public demands became increasingly apparent. The news reports not only made the problems of the indenture trade public but also made the police and other wings of the state aware of the ramifications of public scandals around indenture. The initial reports on the Hare incident were thus followed by frequent assurances from the government, as well as multiple reports from the police to senior members of government explaining their decisions.[46] Through periodicals, the indenture question thus spread from the administrative sphere to the public sphere, emerging as a subject of public attention and a point of public pressure.

Even if preserved in colonial archives today, periodicals operated outside the official record-keeping processes of the colonial Indian state. Although still influenced by the power relations within colonial Calcutta and the pro- or anti-indenture stance of their owners, periodicals provided spaces of interaction outside the confines of more formal associations and meetings. As it allowed for opinions from the common public – often anonymously – periodicals were key to disseminating information on the trade, moulding public opinion, encouraging wider participation and keeping a constant vigilance over the indenture question in a way that meetings and petitions could not. They gave rise to a body of evidence that offered multiple narratives of key events in the city, acted as eyes of the city, gave voice to members of the public through 'letters to the editors' and helped the indenture discussion cross geographical boundaries. Janette Martin has shown that newspaper reports on public meetings can be unreliable due to bad acoustics, cramped accommodation, mumbling speakers and noisy venues.[47] Thus, in a way, periodicals were not just repeating speeches made in public meetings but creating a narrative of the indenture trade of their own – becoming the mouthpiece, however unreliable, of those who were vocal about indenture.

The Indenture Contract

The indenture trade, as the name suggests, was characterised by an agreement of indenture signed between the labourer and the employer. As the key thing that separated indentured labour from slave labour regimes, the contract remained central to the indenture debates. Questioning or invalidating the legitimacy of contracts was tantamount to invalidating the indenture trade itself. A typical contract signed between the legal representative of the planter and the labourer at the port of origin was overseen by government-appointed officials and stated unambiguously that the labourer was voluntarily engaging to be employed in the plantation for five years. It covered wages, food and medical provisions and the respective duties of the labourer and the planter. Besides making sure that migration was legal, contracts were supposed to make recruiters and planters accountable. The indenture contract thus represented the legal basis of the arrangement while also being testament to post-slavery anxieties around unfree labour systems.

Contracts were sporadic but prevalent in the migratory labour systems that preceded indenture. The transportation of labourers from Calcutta to Réunion in 1830 involved contracts that allowed for five years of service against a promise of rations and a monthly salary of 8 rupees.[48] In 1834, contracts were signed for the engagement of 151 Indian labourers in the sugar plantations of John Shaw Sampson in Mauritius and 48 labourers in W. West's plantations.[49] In the following year, the Chief Magistrate of Calcutta reported the emigration of 270 labourers to serve in Mauritian sugar plantations under similar contracts.[50] A circular from 1836 stated that the house of Henley, Dowson & Bestel of Calcutta had shipped more than 5,000 'free agricultural labourers' to Mauritius under similar contractual obligations.[51] In many ways, these contracts set the tone for the indenture trade by determining conditions of employment. The five-year contract signed with John Sampson, for instance, specified wages, food and clothing provisions that were reiterated in indenture contracts that followed. Sampson was to provide each labourer with 'Fourteen Chittacks of Rice [,] two Chittacks of Dal [,] one and a half a Chittack of Ghee and two Chittacks of Fish', 'one Blanket [,] two Dhooties [,] one Chintz Jacket [,] one Lascar Cap [,] one Wooden Bowl for each man and one Brass Lota or Cup for every four men', as well as an advance payment of six months' wages.[52] Since these early labour migrations, and more prominently since the emigration act of 1837, contracts became compulsory and written with meticulous detail.

The contract was one of the first things discussed between John Gladstone and Gillanders Arbuthnot & Company. The firm confirmed that they had previously arranged for the emigration of 800 Indians to Mauritius under five-year contracts, saying: 'Our letters from the isle of France speak very favourably of the men hitherto sent, many of whom … have their task completed by two o'clock, and go home.'[53] They advised Gladstone to model future labour contracts on these Mauritian ones. The contract was also one of the first things negotiated with parliamentarians, as Gladstone convinced Lord Glenelg to sign off on five years of indentureship, as opposed to three years.[54] Gladstone's conversation with Lord Glenelg further cemented the provision for return voyages at the expense of the planter, since the latter was convinced that Indians would never see the British transatlantic colonies as a permanent home and could only be persuaded to migrate 'by the hope of returning thither [to India] with whatever they may be able to save by labour in a distant land'.[55]

Contracts, however, suffered from critical fallacies, not least of which was the use of ambiguous, nebulous terms to refer to the indentured migrant in the absence of a well-established category of employment. In these early contracts, the migrant was often termed a 'free labourer' or a 'general agricultural labourer'.[56] In Peroo's contract from November 1837, the English permit used the term *khidmutgar*, which normally refers to a domestic servant like a butler (Figure 2.2).[57] The Bengali translation of Peroo's contract mentioned the same conditions in rudimentary Bengali legalese, using both *khidmutgar* and *mojurgiri* to refer to the migrant – the latter a reference to wage labour, from *mojuri* (wages).[58] Slippages between domestic, agricultural and professional labour terms were more common in Bengali translations, where 'labourer' was often translated as *mojur* (wage labourer) or *chakor* (domestic servant).[59] The Bengali version of a labourer's permit for Mauritius stated the object of emigration as *chakri korite* – that is, to do a job or work in a professional capacity.[60] These slippages obfuscated the purpose of emigration, often leading migrants to believe that they were to be employed in domestic labour rather than plantation work outdoors.

Even as steps were taken to make the indenture system separate from the slave regime in legal terms, there were continuities between the two. This included similarities in the process of labour procurement, the lack of transparency during passage and the oft-used provision for punishment or

---

INDIAN LABOURER'S PERMIT.

Duffadar Bhuwanny.   No. 152.

I, PEROO, engage to proceed to Mauritius to serve E. Antard, père, or such other person as I may be transferred to (such transfer being made by mutual consent, to be declared before a public officer), as a khidmutgar, for the space of five years from the date of this agreement, on consideration of receiving a remuneration of Company's rupees ten (10) per month, and food and clothing as follows ; viz.

14 chittacks rice, ⎫
 2   „   dholl, ⎬ daily ;
- ⅜   „   ghee, ⎪
- ¼   „   salt, ⎭

1 blanket   - ⎫
2 dhooties   - ⎪
1 chintz mirjaee ⎬ yearly ;
1 lascar's cap   - ⎪
1 wooden bowl   ⎭

also one lotah or brass cup between four persons, and medicine and medical attendance when required ; also to be sent back to Calcutta at the expiration of my period of service, free of all expense to myself, should such be my wish, subject to the terms of my general agreement. Executed this   day of November 1837.

Peroo, his + mark.

Figure 2.2 Indian labourer's permit for Mauritius

Source: Indian Labourer's Permit for Peroo, dated November 1837, in Appendix No. 3 to *Letter from Secretary to Government of India, to Committee on Exportation of Hill Coolies: Report of Committee and Evidence* (East India House, ordered by the House of Commons to be printed, 12 February 1841), p. 106.

non-payment of wages in case of the labourer's refusal or inability to work. It was these caveats that made contracts central to the indenture regime. A lot of the discourse around indenture was therefore centred on whether certain aspects had been written into contract. Many anti-indenture petitioners in Calcutta argued that the tenets of contract could be circumvented to suit the needs of the employer, whether by transferring labourers to plantation estates they did not sign up for or by retaining part of their wages. In the Town Hall meeting, for instance, Mr Dickens showed that out of the pay of 5 rupees per month, 1 rupee was retained by the employer as insurance against the labourer becoming a burden to the colony after the end of the contract. Thus, the labourer was at the mercy of the planter, who could discharge him at the last minute to avoid paying for his return passage.[61]

'A New System of Slavery'

Why did so much of the debate in Calcutta revolve around contracts and enslavement? The early nineteenth century saw the rise of strong voices against unfree systems of labour, most prominent of which was the movement condemning transatlantic slavery. Anti-slavery organisations like the British and Foreign Anti-Slavery Society (BFASS) saw in Indian indenture the continuation of slave conditions.[62] Instead of visualising Indian indenture as a solution to the post-Abolition labour deficit and an exercise in 'free labour', they considered it as slavery in all but name. This created anti-indenture pressure groups in the British Empire, which argued that the indenture trade recruited labourers through misinformation and was a new form of unfree labour not so different from the recently disbanded slavery. Consequently, criticisms of the indenture trade were publicised in many periodicals. In July 1838, the Anti-Slavery Society of Kendal petitioned the House of Commons to prevent the passing of a bill to allow for indenture migration from India.[63] The *Taunton Courier* reported that indentured emigration 'organizes no peculiar superintendence to watch over [the migrants'] interests and to guard them from slave-holding oppression'.[64] Drawing reference to slavery, it exclaimed: 'In the dark and tyrant days of Elizabeth, it was by a similar pretext that Sir John Hawkins ... obtained a similar license, that gave rise to the nefarious African slave-trade.'[65]

In the British parliament, similarity to slavery remained the primary criticism of the indenture trade; and even with the temporary prohibition of indenture migration in 1839, the question of deception and mistreatment loomed large. Lord Auckland argued that strict regulations and increased vigilance were not sufficient to 'prevent the frequent infliction of grievous oppressions and deceits upon large numbers of persons helpless from their poverty and from their utter ignorance and inexperience'.[66] In a July 1839 meeting, Lords Brougham and Ellenborough argued that the 'mortality and massacre of the voyage far exceeded the African middle passage itself'.[67] In the context of Gladstone's selling of his estate in Demerara along with his labourers in 1841, Her Majesty's Attorney and Solicitor General declared: '[S]uch transactions, certainly, have very much the aspect of a sale of the services of the coolies, as if they were slaves for a limited time....'[68] This juxtaposition of slavery and indenture continued to be a common refrain in the indenture debates – circulated in Britain by parliamentary discussions, periodicals, pamphlets and publications, but also evident in meetings, petitions and reports from Calcutta. As a result, the phrase 'new system of slavery' became synonymous with indenture.

The Calcutta Town Hall petition of 1838 pointed out that the professedly benevolent intentions of the indenture trade will not prevent it from becoming an oppressive system – much as it did not for the slave trade. The right of labourers to choose their employment worked only with the caveat that they were aware of their rights and the terms of employment they entered into. Referring to a speech made by Lord Brougham in the House of Lords, the Town Hall petition argued: '[I]t would appear that the slave trade which it has cost the British people twenty millions to suppress – commence[d] with as professedly benevolent intentions as this trade.'[69] In fact, petitioners pointed to the irony of designating indentured labourers as 'free labourers' when the same term had previously been employed by those 'engaged in the exportation of the unhappy sons of Africa to other countries'.[70]

The petition apprehended that if the indenture trade continued, 'the Coast Ports of India will soon resemble the slavemarts of Africa and the Mauritius become a slave emporium for the world ... and that the evils so long inflicted on the Negro race will be transferred to the inhabitants of British India'.[71] Their apprehensions about the trade drew from three main contentions: that the merchants and planters involved in the indenture trade were previously involved in the slave trade, that the trade was expanding rapidly to previously enslaved colonies and that the men who employed labourers entertained 'inhumanizing views' about them.[72] Ultimately, the petition insisted that cases of mistreatment and deception were not isolated instances but a systemic problem, arguing that 'the system [of indenture] was radically bad and contained in itself the elements of a new species of slavery'.[73]

The similarity-to-slavery argument was made even more forcefully in periodicals. The *Bengal Hurkaru* considered indentured emigration a cruel and unjust process and expressed concern that planters who were accustomed 'to look upon their slaves in no better light than the beasts of the field' cannot be expected to treat the indentured labourers any better.[74] The *Friend of India* argued that the indenture system was one of fraud and injustice, which employed teenage boys to do the work of full-grown men on plantations and falsely advertised the advance payment of six months' wages that many labourers never received.[75] Some pointed out that precautions taken at the port of embarkation did not prevent abuses in the plantation colonies. *The Englishman* wrote that the Indian government had no control over plantation colonies like Mauritius and the West Indies and thus had no authority to enforce regulations there.[76] Moreover, many indentured migrants moved from British India to non-British colonies. *The Englishman* maintained that the issue of emigration to foreign ports was most serious: '[T]here is no guarantee that once the coolies leave the ports, ... they would be sent to those same ports. There is no way of tracing or regulating it.'[77]

Another report argued that distance from their homelands would create more opportunities for abuse 'because helpless men of a servile class and colour are often committed to the charge of unscrupulous Europeans at an impassable distance from their native home'.[78] Articles in the *Bengal Hurkaru* pointed out that a system that depended on the 'shipment of coolies, delivered to order' was likely to be abusive.[79] It further alleged that labourers were often recruited by false propaganda, where participation in the trade was advertised as a government order (*kompanie ka hukum*) rather than a voluntary act.[80] As the *Friend of India* reported in August 1838, this was not a temporary but a perpetual arrangement, whereby 'the free labourer of India is to replace the slave; and the Cooly Trade to be substituted for the slave trade'.[81] In fact, it considered the indenture trade 'a wanton, unnecessary, immitigable evil' that could not be resolved by regulations alone.[82] The periodical was also a space where residents of Calcutta could raise their concerns through letters to the editors. A letter to the *Bengal Hurkaru* complained: 'Obtaining possession of a man's person, and sending him out of the country is kidnapping.... Is it not slave trading?'[83]

Some very important tenets of free labour were being espoused in these news reports, including the idea that contracts only held meaning if signatories knew what they were signing, that erstwhile slaveowners could not be expected to treat labourers well overnight just because slavery had been abolished, and that lawmakers needed to be cognisant of the limitations of indenture regulations in preventing abuse in faraway, and especially non-British, colonies. The constant comparison between slavery and indenture and the importance given to the upholding of contracts were hallmarks of the post-slavery empire.

The Post-Slavery Empire

The term 'post-slavery' has often been used to mean the period following slavery. Post-slavery Mauritius, for instance, refers simply to Mauritius after Abolition. This book, however, shows that instead of being a simple marker of time, post-slavery is a description of how permanently Abolition had changed the understanding of labour servitude in the empire. Akin to the 'post' in postcolonialism, the post-slavery empire was one haunted by the image of slavery. Labour systems that emerged after Abolition were continuously mapped, negotiated and compared against slavery. Both legally and morally, anything similar to slavery had become unacceptable. As it followed a vibrant debate in Britain about slave labour, anti-slavery activism framed how indenture was questioned, debated and defended.

The contractual nature of indenture, the finiteness of the scheme and its image as the solution to the post-Abolition labour shortage were crucial in accepting the indenture trade as a post-slavery labour regime. In this immediately post-Abolition environment, contracts became the basis for differentiating between slavery and post-slavery labour regimes. Planters and merchants used the presence of contracts to argue that indenture represented an exercise in 'free' labour. The very presence of contracts was seen as security against exploitation or 'unfree' labour systems. Those petitioning against the indenture trade, on the other hand, used the inadequacies of the contracts to criticise the regime and consider it a continuation of slavery.

Focusing on the post-slavery moment also allows for a more nuanced approach to the slavery–indenture dichotomy that Hugh Tinker and others have discussed. It helps us locate the legacies of slavery not just in the structures but in the very ways in which the indenture trade was framed, debated, investigated and regulated. As the indenture trade operated over 80 years and extended to multiple plantation colonies in the British, French and Dutch empires, its priorities changed with time. As the slave labour system laid the foundations upon which indentured labour was erected, slavery became the natural reference point for understanding and discussing indenture in its early years. As a result, early discussions on indenture framed the debate *entirely* within the dichotomy of 'free' and 'unfree': anti-indenture petitioners criticised indenture by pointing out its similarity to slavery, and merchants and planters continued to posit the difference between the two regimes as their main defence of indenture. The idea of 'free labour' developed in juxtaposition to unfree labour by determining what forms of unfree labour were deemed acceptable after slavery had been declared as morally and legally reprehensible. This was a key moment in the history of imperial labour servitude when the idea of free labour itself was curated and negotiated.[84]

The effects of the anti-slavery movement were still palpable in the 1830s and 1840s, but as the urgency of the slavery question was lost over the years, other issues came to supersede this argument. By the turn of the century, abuses within the indenture trade were framed by Indian abolitionists and nationalist leaders as a question of national honour, with female labourers becoming subjects and symbols of collective protest.[85] Time frame is thus key for understanding the global indenture debates and, indeed, for recognising Calcutta's place within them. Focusing on changes over time allows us to see the early indenture debates as an exercise in post-slavery anxieties being written into law.

Legislating Servitude

The Town Hall of Calcutta enjoyed concentric spheres of influence. Located about 10 kilometres away from the Calcutta port and Garden Reach, where labourers were accommodated, the Town Hall was central to the city. Limits of servitude were shaped and negotiated in this forum as it gave voice to the Calcutta public sphere. One year later, it would become the base for a trenchant investigation into the indenture trade led by prominent Calcuttans. Its influence, however, spread far beyond the city as debates in the Town Hall shaped recruitment patterns and the indenture experience across the hinterland. Beyond India, Calcutta was part of a broader sphere of influence that extended across the empire. The Town Hall meeting signalled the beginning of a sustained discourse in Calcutta that compared indentured servitude to the slave trade. One of the earliest and most publicised records of the Calcutta public's opinion of indenture, it brought to light the importance of petitioning the colonial government to institute changes in emigration regulations.

The idea of servitude had undergone a radical transformation in the anti-slavery and indenture debates as free labour came to be distinguished from unfree labour. The focus on contracts and enslavement as evident in the Calcutta debates was part of a larger trend and needs to be seen in the context of labour legislation in the metropole. The early nineteenth century saw a pivotal change in British labour legislation with the passing of the Masters and Servants Act. Since the fourteenth century, several acts in Britain had governed the relationship between employers and employees, including the Master and Servant Act of 1823 (which codified the general use of penal sanctions for contract breach), the Master and Servant Act Reform of 1844 and the Trade Union Act of 1871 (which clarified the legality of trade unions).[86] For more than 500 years, the master and servant laws had 'fixed the boundaries of "free labor" in Britain and throughout the British Empire'.[87] In fact, these laws were one of the many legal ligaments that helped make the British Empire a conceivable whole.[88]

Indentured labour in the colonies was partly shaped by wage labour in Europe.[89] Although labour use in English factories and colonial plantations varied vastly, many defining characteristics of the master and servant laws mirrored that of Indian indenture. Under these laws, employment relationship was governed by private contracts between individual employers and employees, the contract could be summarily enforced by magistrates, and its breach by uncooperative workers could be punished by whipping, imprisonment, forced labour, fines or forfeiture of all wages.[90] As Douglas Hay and Paul Craven argue in *Masters, Servants and Magistrates*, master and servant legislation was 'a catalog of constraints and incentives'.[91] They determined constraints on 'freedom' across the empire while also framing contractual relationship and penal sanctions. Even though statute law was often ignored or misapplied in the colonies, the tenets of the master and servant laws governed colonial employment relations.[92] These laws determined punishments for breach of contract, including mobility-related offences (such as absenteeism and desertion) and breach of workplace discipline (such as misdemeanour, disobedience and neglect of duty) – tenets that were central to the indenture system as well. As indenture legislation often used the terms 'master' and 'servant' to denote the employer and employee, there were also significant verbal slippages between the two forms of legislation.

By the 1830s and 1840s, provisions such as imprisonment for breach of contract and use of the law to crush trade union activity came to be challenged in Britain.[93] It was in this context that the indenture debates brewed. Debates around Abolition and the master and servant laws provided an opportune moment for challenging prevailing notions of servitude and employer–employee relationship. The post-slavery debates in Britain and Calcutta thus need to be seen in this historical context, where the limits of servitude and the understanding of contractual obligations between employer and employee were being challenged and negotiated. A key aspect of the indenture trade that makes its relation to slavery and anxieties around its revival clear is the emphasis on contracts, itself a remnant of English labour legislation.

Notes

1. Emigration Act V of 1837, passed by the Governor-General in Council on 1 May 1837, Home Department, Public Branch, Annex Building, NL.
2. Walker Graham Blackie (ed.), *The Imperial Gazetteer; a General Dictionary of Geography, Physical, Political, Statistical and Descriptive*, vol. 1 (Edinburgh and London: Blackie & Son, 1856), p. 561.
3. *Friend of India*, 29 September 1842, p. 610.
4. John Archer, 'Paras, Palaces, Pathogens: Frameworks for the Growth of Calcutta, 1800–1850', *City and Society* 12, no. 1 (2000): 19–54.
5. Peter J. Marshall, 'British Society in India under the East India Company', *Modern Asian Studies* 31, no. 1 (1997): 89–108, pp. 101–102.
6. Partho Datta writes:

> Clive lived in Dum Dum, Charles Perrin had a garden house in Bag Bazar (the heart of north Calcutta), and there was a European settlement in Chitpur. Similarly, Indian settlements were found south of the fort in Hastings (Cooly Bazar), in Garden Reach and in Bhowanipur. Nor was town planning restricted to European initiatives. The deposed Awadh monarch, Wajid Ali Shah, laid out an elegant garden township in Garden Reach ... which at its peak accommodated 40,000 inhabitants.

Partho Datta, 'Review Essay: Celebrating Calcutta', *Urban History* 19, no. 1 (1992): 84–98, p. 89.

7. Swati Chattopadhyay, *Representing Calcutta: Modernity, Nationalism, and the Colonial Uncanny* (London: Routledge, 2005), introduction.

8. Basudeb Chattopadhyay, *The Town Hall of Calcutta: A Brief History* (Calcutta: Homage Trust, 1998), p. 12.

9. James Long, 'Calcutta in the Olden Time: Its Localities', *Calcutta Review* 18 (July–December 1852).

10. Bhabani Bhattacharya, *Socio-Political Currents in Bengal: A Nineteenth Century Perspective* (New Delhi: Vikas Publications, 1980), pp. 27–28.

11. Anil Chandra Das Gupta (ed.), *The Days of John Company: Selections from Calcutta Gazette, 1824–1832* (Calcutta: Superintendent Government Printing, 1959); Benoy Ghose, *Selections from English Periodicals of Nineteenth Century Bengal, 1815–33* (Calcutta: Papyrus, 1978); B. Chattopadhyay, *Town Hall of Calcutta*; 'Coolee Trade Petition', *Calcutta Review* 44 (July 1838), p. 304.

12. 'Meeting for Preventing the Exportation of Coolies', *Calcutta Review* 44 (July 1838), p. 311.

13. Letter to Alexander Ross (President of the Council of India and Deputy Governor of the President of Fort William) from James Young (Sheriff of Calcutta), [Petition] on Behalf of Those Assembled at the Town Hall Meeting in Calcutta, dated 10 July 1838, 1 August 1838, no. 1, General Department (General) Proceedings, WBSA (henceforth 'Calcutta Town Hall Petition'); 'Coolee Trade Petition', *Calcutta Review* 44 (July 1838), p. 304.

14. 'Meeting for Preventing the Exportation of Coolies', p. 311.

15. Ibid.

16. Ibid.

17. Ibid., p. 315.

18. Ibid., p. 313.

19. Ibid., p. 311.

20. Ibid.

21. Ibid., p. 316.

22. Ibid.

23. Ibid., p. 312.

24. Report in the *Calcutta Courier*, 11 July 1838 (n.p.).

25. 'Meeting for Preventing the Exportation of Coolies', p. 312.

26. Report in *The Englishman*, 11 July 1838, p. 1316.

27. 'Calcutta Town Hall Petition'.

28. For print, readership and reform in India, see Francesca Orsini, *The Hindi Public Sphere 1920–1940: Language and Literature in the Age of Nationalism*

(Oxford: Oxford University Press, 2002); Anindita Ghosh, *Power in Print: Popular Publishing and the Politics of Language and Culture in a Colonial Society, 1778–1905* (New York, NY: Oxford University Press, 2006); Ulrike Stark, *An Empire of Books: The Naval Kishore Press and the Diffusion of the Printed Word in Colonial India* (New Delhi: Permanent Black, 2007).

29. Brajendranath Bandyopadhyay, *Sambadpatre Sekaler Katha* (Representation of Past Times in Newspapers) (Calcutta: Bangiya Sahitya Parishad, 1996); Ghose, *Selections from English Periodicals*.

30. Bandyopadhyay, *Sambadpatre Sekaler Katha*; Muntasir Mamun, *Unish Shatake Bangladesher Sambad-Samayikpatra, 1847–1905* (Nineteenth-Century Newspapers and Periodicals of Bangladesh) (Dhaka: Bangla Akademi, 1985).

31. For popular petitioning and mobilisation in the anti-slavery movement, see Seymour Drescher, 'Whose Abolition? Popular Pressure and the Ending of the British Slave Trade', *Past and Present* 143 (1994): 136–166; Seymour Drescher and Christine Bolt, *Capitalism and Antislavery: British Mobilization in Comparative Perspective* (New York and Oxford: Oxford University Press, 1987). For discussions of indenture in British periodicals, see Jonathan Connolly, 'Indentured Labour Migration and the Meaning of Emancipation: Free Trade, Race, and Labour in British Public Debate, 1838–1860', *Past and Present* 238, no. 1 (2018): 85–119.

32. See *Bengal Hurkaru*, 6 July 1838, p. 19; *Bengal Hurkaru*, 1 August 1838, p. 109; *Bengal Hurkaru*, 18 August 1838, pp. 169–170; *Friend of India*, 23 May 1839, pp. 322–323; *Friend of India*, 20 October 1842, pp. 657–658.

33. See reports in *Bengal Hurkaru*, 10 August 1838, p. 140; *Bengal Hurkaru*, 11 August 1838, p. 144; *Bengal Hurkaru*, 13 August 1838, p. 150.

34. *Friend of India*, 16 August 1838, p. 453.

35. *Friend of India*, 29 September 1842, p. 610.

36. *Calcutta Courier*, 30 July 1838, n.p.

37. *Calcutta Courier*, 14 July 1838, n.p.

38. *Calcutta Courier*, 9 July 1838, n.p.

39. *Bengal Hurkaru*, 13 July 1838, p. 43.

40. *Calcutta Courier*, 10 August 1838, n.p.

41. *Friend of India*, 9 August 1838, p. 438.

42. Letter to the editor of *Bengal Hurkaru*, 7 July 1838, p. 22; *Bengal Hurkaru*, 10 August 1838, p. 140; letter to the editor of *Calcutta Courier*, 21 July 1838, n.p.

43. *Friend of India*, 7 June 1838, p. 291.

44. *Asiatic Journal and Monthly Miscellany* 28 (January 1839), p. 11.

45. 'The Liberated Coolies', letter from C. K. Robison to the editor, *Bengal Hurkaru*, 17 September 1838, in Judicial (Criminal) Proceedings, 6 November 1838, no. 1, WBSA.

46. See Letter to the Editor from C. K. Robison, *Bengal Hurkaru*, 17 September 1838; letter from Chief Magistrate D. McFarlan to F. A. Halliday (Secretary to the Government of Bengal, Judicial Department), dated 27 September 1838; letter from J. W. Birch (Superintendent of Calcutta Police) to Chief Magistrate D. McFarlan, dated 26 September 1838, in Judicial (Criminal) Proceedings, 6 November 1838, nos. 1–3, WBSA.

47. Janette Martin, 'Popular Political Oratory and Itinerant Lecturing in Yorkshire and the North East in the Age of Chartism, 1837–60', unpublished doctoral dissertation, University of York, 2010, especially ch. 4.

48. Hugh Tinker, *A New System of Slavery: The Export of Indian Labour Overseas 1830–1920* (London: Oxford University Press, 1974), p. 61.

49. Letter to the Chief Secretary to the Governor of Mauritius, dated 1 December 1834, 1 December 1834, no. 29; letter to the Chief Secretary to the Governor of Mauritius, dated 29 December 1834, 29 December 1834, no. 24; letter from D. McFarlan to H. T. Prinsep, dated 27 November 1834, 27 November 1834, no. 26, General Department (General) Proceedings, WBSA.

50. Letter from D. McFarlan to H. T. Prinsep, Secretary to the Government of Bengal, dated 12 February 1835, 21 February 1835, no. 12; letter from D. McFarlan to G.A. Bushby, Secretary to the Government, General Department, dated 23 July 1835, 29 July 1835, no. 54, General Department (General) Proceedings, WBSA.

51. *Leeds Mercury*, 21 July 1836, p. 7.

52. Letter to the Chief Secretary to the Governor of Mauritius, dated 1 December 1834, 1 December 1834, nos. 26–27, General Department (General) Proceedings, WBSA. *Chittack* is a measure of weight and *dhooties* or *dhotis* are unstitched lower-body garments worn by men.

53. Letter from Gillanders Arbuthnot & Company to John Gladstone, dated 6 June 1836, Enclosure No. 1 to Gladstone's letters to Lord Glenelg dated 28 February 1838, in *Copies of All Orders in Council, or Colonial Ordinances, for the Better Regulations and Enforcement of the Relative Duties of Masters and Employers, and Articled Servants, Tradesmen and Labourers, in*

the Colonies of British Guiana and Mauritius and of Correspondence Relating Thereof (ordered by the House of Commons to be printed, 2 March 1838) (henceforth *Masters and Employers*).

54. Letter from John Gladstone to Lord Glenelg, dated 29 April 1837, GG/348, Glynne-Gladstone MSS, Gladstone's Library, Hawarden, Wales (henceforth 'GG-MSS').

55. Letter from Lord Glenelg to John Gladstone, dated 16 May 1837, GG/348, GG-MSS.

56. See Indian Labourer's Permit for Bholah, dated 8 December 1837, in appendix to *Letter from Secretary to Government of India, to Committee on Exportation of Hill Coolies: Report of Committee and Evidence* (East India House, ordered by the House of Commons to be printed, 12 February 1841), p. 107; and 'Agreement between William Edmund Browne, Acting on Behalf of the One Part, and the Undersigned Natives of India on the Other Part', Exhibit No. 6, in 'Report of the Calcutta Committee', app., p. 123.

57. Henry Yule, *Hobson-Jobson: A Glossary of Colloquial Anglo-Indian Words and Phrases, and of Kindred Terms, Etymological, Historical, Geographical and Discursive* (new edition edited by William Crooke) (London: J. Murray, 1903 [1886]), p. 486. Literally, *khidmutgar* means the provider of any kind of service (*khidmat*). Indian Labourer's Permit for Peroo, dated November 1837, appendix no. 3 to *Letter from Secretary to Government of India, to Committee on Exportation of Hill Coolies: Report of Committee and Evidence* (East India House, ordered by the House of Commons to be printed, 12 February 1841), p. 106.

58. Indian Labourer's Permit for Peroo, p. 106.

59. See copies of Bengali contracts in General Department (General) Proceedings, WBSA.

60. Exhibit 6, 'Copies of Old and New Contracts', in Appendix to *Letter from Secretary to Government of India, to Committee on Exportation of Hill Coolies: Report of Committee and Evidence* (East India House, ordered by the House of Commons to be printed, 12 February 1841), p. 108.

61. 'Meeting for Preventing the Exportation of Coolies', p. 314.

62. For a detailed discussion of the BFASS's role in the anti-indenture movement, see Madhavi Kale, *Fragments of Empire: Capital, Slavery, and Indian Indentured Labor Migration in the British Caribbean* (Philadelphia: University of Pennsylvania Press, 1998), especially chs. 4–5.

63. *Kendal Mercury*, 21 July 1838.

64. *Taunton Courier and Western Advertiser*, 21 March 1838, p. 3.

65. Ibid.

66. Quoted in 'The Cooly Trade', *Friend of India*, 31 March 1842, p. 194.

67. Quoted in John Geoghegan, *Note on Emigration from India* (Calcutta: Superintendent of Government Printing, 1873), p. 9.

68. *Leicester Chronicle*, 24 July 1841.

69. 'Calcutta Town Hall Petition'.

70. Ibid.

71. Ibid.

72. Ibid.

73. Ibid.

74. *Bengal Hurkaru*, 21 December 1838, p. 628.

75. *Friend of India*, 7 June 1838, pp. 291–292.

76. *The Englishman*, 10 July 1838, p. 1307.

77. *The Englishman*, 30 March 1842, n.p.

78. *Friend of India*, 20 October 1842, p. 658.

79. *Bengal Hurkaru*, 20 July 1838.

80. Ibid.

81. *Friend of India*, 9 August 1838, p. 437.

82. *Friend of India*, 14 January 1838, p. 308.

83. Letter to the editor, *Bengal Hurkaru*, 11 August 1838, p. 144.

84. For discussion of the free–unfree dichotomy and the imagination of ideal indentured migrants as 'free', see Purba Hossain, '"Docile, Quiet, Orderly": Indian Indenture Trade and the Ideal Labourer', in *Across Colonial Lines: Commodities, Networks, and Empire Building*, ed. Devyani Gupta and Purba Hossain, pp. 179–198 (London: Bloomsbury Academic, 2023).

85. See Mrinalini Sinha, 'Anatomy of a Politics of the People', in *Political Imaginaries in Twentieth-Century India*, ed. Mrinalini Sinha and Manu Goswami, pp. 31–50 (London: Bloomsbury Academic, 2022); Karen A. Ray, 'Kunti, Lakshmibhai and the "Ladies": Women's Labour and the Abolition of Indentured Emigration from India', *Labour, Capital and Society* 29, nos. 1–2 (1996): 126–152.

86. Douglas Hay and Paul Craven (ed.), *Masters, Servants, and Magistrates in Britain and the Empire, 1562–1955* (Chapel Hill, NC: University of North Carolina Press, 2005), especially the introduction; Suresh Naidu and Noam Yuchtman, 'Coercive Contract Enforcement: Law and the Labor Market in Nineteenth Century Industrial Britain', *American Economic Review* 103, no. 1 (2013): 107–144.

87. Hay and Craven, *Masters, Servants, and Magistrates*, p. 1.
88. Ibid., pp. 2–3.
89. Alessandro Stanziani, 'Local Bondage in Global Economies: Servants, Wage Earners, and Indentured Migrants in Nineteenth-Century France, Great Britain, and the Mascarene Islands', *Modern Asian Studies* 47, no. 4 (2013): 1218–1251.
90. Hay and Craven, *Masters, Servants, and Magistrates*, pp. 1–2.
91. Ibid., p. 33.
92. See Nitin Sinha, 'Domestic Servants and Master–Servant Regulations in Colonial Calcutta, 1750s–1810s', *Past and Present* 255, no. 1 (2022): 141–188, for the impact of metropolitan master and servant laws on domestic servant regulations in colonial India, which Sinha positions within the framework of 'imperial borrowing'.
93. Hay and Craven, *Masters, Servants, and Magistrates*, p. 8.

3

Investigating Indenture

The Calcutta investigative committee established in 1838 was, in many ways, the culmination of questions raised in the Town Hall meeting. Established as part of an empire-wide decision to set up investigative committees in port cities, the Calcutta committee aimed to investigate whether the indenture trade was exploitative and whether labourers were deceived into migrating overseas. As this chapter goes on to show, the Calcutta committee and its report became an important point of reference in indenture regulations, emerging as one of the most detailed official accounts of the early indenture trade. While the Town Hall meeting showcased voices from elite Calcuttans, the investigative committee became one of the first spaces where the voice of the indentured migrant was heard. With committee members local to Calcutta, and with interviews of migrants and those involved directly in the indenture trade, this investigative committee made Calcutta a key decision-making part of the British Empire.

While reports from Bombay, Madras, Mauritius and Sydney – the other sites of investigative committees – were either considered inconclusive, inadequate or never reached the parliament, the Calcutta committee thrived and succeeded in influencing emigration regulations. John Geoghegan's report of 1873 stated of these committees:

> The Bombay Committee had reported that no such abuses prevailed on that side of India. In fact, emigration from Bombay could hardly then

have been said to exist. The Madras Committee had not contributed anything of value. The records of the Mauritius Committee, if it ever sat, are not forthcoming, and no communication whatever seems to have been received from Sydney.[1]

The two inquiries in British Guiana that had been solicited from England and India were, in fact, never even conducted. By contrast, Geoghegan offered high praise to the Calcutta committee, saying that both parties in parliament found 'an ample armoury of weapons' in the committee report since 'combatants on both sides fought equally in the dark till they got the report of the Calcutta Committee'.[2] Similarly, a letter from the members of a committee based in Mauritius asserted that '[t]he Cooly Trade in all its ramifications [had] been so fully and ably exposed by the Committee appointed in Calcutta'.[3] The decision to establish investigative committees in plantation colonies and port cities was in itself a result of anti-indenture petitions pointing to problems inherent in the indenture system, including letters from Calcutta pressing for investigation. Metropolitan interest in and responsiveness to allegations of mistreatment, exploitation and deception prompted the decision to parcel out the responsibility of investigation and governance to local bodies.

Inquiry and Indenture

Periodic inquiries were a key feature of the indenture trade from its very inception. In 1836, even before the Indian indenture system was sanctioned by parliament, the Government of Mauritius was asked to provide an account of the condition of Indian labourers in Mauritius. They attested to the experiment being a success, with 'labourers and employers seeming in general mutually satisfied with each other'.[4] Reports were also solicited from two members of the Civil Service who had recently visited Mauritius: Parry Woodcock and T. C. Scott. Woodcock and Scott agreed with the Government of Mauritius but pointed to the need for increased regulation.[5] An inquiry was also held by the Law Commission of India in 1836, which swiftly concluded that no changes in legislation were necessary in the indenture system.[6] Such sporadic inquiries aimed at keeping a close eye on the indenture trade reached their apotheosis in the Calcutta committee of 1838.

In August 1838, a six-member committee was appointed in Calcutta to investigate the indenture trade. The committee was under orders to enquire into 'the nature and extent of the abuses alleged to exist in this [Bengal] presidency', with a view to correcting the problems and advising the government on how to remedy and prevent the recurrence of similar abuses.[7] The committee was composed entirely of people local to Calcutta or those with strong ties to the Bengal Presidency.[8] The chairman, Theodore Dickens, was a Supreme Court advocate and a popular speaker at public meetings, as well as the owner of sugar plantations in India. J. P. Grant was a civil servant and judge in the Bengal Presidency with first-hand knowledge of Mauritian emigration. Major E. Archer was a participant and observer in the indenture trade from Calcutta and a member of the military; William Dowson was a merchant in the Calcutta-based firm Henley, Dowson & Bestel (which was involved in emigrating indentured migrants overseas); and Reverend James Charles was a popular reformer.[9] The sixth member, Rosomoy Dutt, (1779–1854) was the first Bengali judge of the Small Causes Court and later commissioner in the Court of Requests. A founder of the Hindoo College (later Presidency College), secretary of the Sanskrit College and secretary to the Council of Education, Dutt was also one of the earliest Indians to be appointed to public commissions of inquiry in British India.[10]

The committee worked by taking detailed testimonies and eyewitness accounts while also basing its investigation on records and correspondences from the Superintendent of Police and from the magistrates of Calcutta and the districts. Those interviewed by the committee included a wide range of people: ships' captains such as Alexander Mackenzie, Edwards, James Smart and John Dyer; ship owners and merchants such as James Rapson, Alexander Colvin, William Frederick Fergusson, John Mackay and William Frank Dowson; labour procurers such as John Hughes and W. E. Browne; colonial officials such as F. W. Birch (superintendent of Calcutta police), J. J. McCann (deputy superintendent of police), J. H. Patton (magistrate of 24 Pergunnahs), D. McFarlan (magistrate of 24 Pergunnahs), Arthur Onslow (civil servant in the Madras Presidency), George Witchlow (officer of the Preventive Service) and William Cracroft (traveller in New South Wales); migrants such as Bibee Zuhoorun, Sheik Manick, Boodoo Khan, Karoo, Suboo and Ramdeen; and citizen-witnesses such as David Hare, Longueville Clarke, Roger Dias, Dwarkanath Tagore, John Floyd, Reverend Thomas Boaz and Thomas William Smyth.[11]

Having accumulated evidence, held interviews and called witnesses
throughout 1838, the committee finally submitted its report in 1839. It
concluded:

> We conceive it to be distinctly proved beyond dispute, that the Coolies
> and other natives exported to Mauritius and elsewhere were (generally
> speaking) induced to come to Calcutta by misrepresentation and deceit,
> practised upon them by native crimps, styled duffadars and arkotties
> [labour recruiters].... We are convinced, in fine, that no laws or
> regulations likely to be passed, short of making the whole land and sea
> transport of Coolies government services, superintended by government
> officers and medical men, will suffice to prevent great misery and
> distress[12]

The report was only signed by three of the original members of the committee,
since Dowson and Grant submitted separate reports contradicting the main
report, and Archer left the committee midway.[13] Nonetheless, this was
accepted as the definitive report by the colonial state. The committee found
most charges of abuse made against the indenture trade to be true. Its report
stated that the emigrants were incapable of understanding the nature of the
contracts and often suppressed their voices for fear of penal consequences.[14]
Calling the trade deceitful and exploitative, it reported that resuming the
indenture trade after its brief suspension in 1839 'would weaken the moral
influence of the British government throughout the world, and deaden
or utterly destroy the effect of all future remonstrances and negotiations
respecting the slave trade'.[15] For the Calcutta committee, the blame fell
squarely on the shoulders of 'native' labour recruiters employed by 'European
and Anglo-Indian undertakers and shippers, who were mostly cognizant of
these frauds'.[16]

With an eye to combatting such abuses, the report recommended regulations
such as entering into contracts with foreign governments with an interest in
the indenture trade and limiting the emigration scheme to only certain Indian
ports. The report considered the economic impact of indentured emigration
as well, arguing that it put undue competitive pressure on the African free
labourers, provided insufficient wages and generally evaded the payment of
full wages.[17] These recommendations of the Calcutta committee would later
be incorporated into future acts, including the revised emigration regulations
instituted in 1842. Issues like mistreatment of labourers on passage, deception

in their recruitment and the problems arising from indentured migrants continuing on the same plantations that previously employed enslaved labour were addressed in the 1842 regulations by increasing surveillance over the mode of recruitment. The 1842 act created the offices of the Protector of Emigrants and the Protector of Immigrants in each participating port and introduced penalties for those who flouted emigration rules. The committee report became a point of reference for parliamentarians, as it helped the state understand and deliberate on the labour and migration policies of the empire.

The Calcutta Committee and the Tradition of Colonial Investigation

Investigative committees in the British Empire had long served the purpose of creating and archiving knowledge systems. Such extra-legal committees offered the public an opportunity to participate in the regulation of colonial labour regimes and served as government acknowledgment of questions around their legitimacy. Scholarship on nineteenth-century investigative commissions has traditionally considered them as policymaking extensions of the government, with Oz Frankel arguing that royal commissions in Britain mirrored parliamentary inquiry processes in an effort to appropriate its legitimacy.[18] According to Frankel, commissions were installed to manage public debates while also making the state visible to the public.[19] This was also true of the indenture committees, which were set up in response to local attitudes towards indenture and were often headed by prominent citizens rather than colonial officials. In fact, instructions for the establishment of the early investigative committees explicitly stated that in order to make their reports satisfactory for 'those who agitate the question at Calcutta', the committees could not be convened by authorities local to the plantation colonies or Company servants visiting the colonies by chance.[20] Instead, the committees should be led by officials appointed by the government explicitly for that purpose and unconnected with the plantation colonies in order to avoid bias.

Adam Ashforth argues that commissions of inquiry were set up for one of four reasons: the need to go beyond politics, limited state resources, distrust between government bodies and pressure from within the bureaucracy.[21] For indenture committees, there was a fifth, more practical reason: the sheer distance and communication difficulties of a multi-sited empire such as the British Empire. As the indenture debates functioned with inputs from disparate parts of the empire, it was impossible to centralise the entire operations. Thus, besides working as a tool to manage public debates, the indenture committees also became one of the earliest colonial committees to gather information on the indenture trade and its transgressions across the empire on such a vast scale. At a time when unfree labour systems were under scrutiny and being criticised in the parliament, having an investigative committee look into their problems gave legitimacy to public concerns on indenture and even legitimised the position of the state as the body in charge of regulating indenture.

At the same time, indenture committees were part of the same process of knowledge production that led to ethnographies, surveys and censuses in colonial India – collecting and fixing present knowledge on the subject while also representing government acknowledgement of criticisms of the indenture trade. Committees not only helped the colonial state gather information and contribute to policymaking, but also played an active role in defining communities in terms of race, gender and other social markers. As Chapter 5 will show, the indenture committees played a key role in racialisation, whereby ideas of race and labour coalesced to formulate the image of the ideal indentured labourer. Thus, the report and interviews of the Calcutta committee not only shaped laws but indeed shaped social mores, influencing the formulation of racial, social and cultural groupings in the indenture trade. Without engaging in an anachronistic exercise that relates inquiry commissions to the ethnographic state that emerged later in the century, it is possible to see in the Calcutta committee the beginnings of techniques of colonial knowledge production.

It was the image of the inquiry as the producer and arbiter of the 'truth' about the indenture system that enabled indenture to continue for almost a century. The report of the Calcutta committee continued to live in official memory as the authoritative account of the early indenture trade. Geoghegan's report of 1873, which emerged as a definitive record of the official history of Indian indenture in its own right, often referred back to the findings of the Calcutta investigative committee.[22] Thus, as much as the setting up of these investigative committees represented government acknowledgement of criticisms of the indenture system, the acceptance and incorporation of their reports in emigration laws were deemed to be adequate safeguarding against those criticisms. The report served simultaneously as a mode of inquiry, a technique of colonial knowledge production, an acknowledgement of voices from Calcutta and a vehicle for the regulation of indenture.

Reading Voices of the Indentured

Besides documentary sources such as official reports, contracts, records of emigration and ships' records, oral testimonies were the main evidence base that the Calcutta investigative committee drew upon. Between August 1838 and January 1839, the Calcutta committee interviewed 36 people about the indenture trade. This practice of gathering oral evidence remained a ubiquitous part of the indenture trade. Over the years, officials continued to periodically examine and interview indentured labourers either when they disembarked in destination colonies like Mauritius or upon their return to Calcutta at the end of their indenture period.

The Calcutta committee did not use a set questionnaire, rather opting for detailed questions catered to the individual experiences of those interviewed. Ships' captains were asked about the size of ships carrying indentured migrants, whether there were any deaths or diseases during travel, whether the migrants were examined by the police and whether they received their stipulated allowances of food and water. Many eyewitnesses were questioned about the process of embarkment from Calcutta and the experience of passage, including the food habits of Hindu and Muslim labourers, the caste background of migrants and the medical provisions on each ship.[23] Questions to the Superintendent of Calcutta Police, F. W. Birch, were focused on his opinion of the slave trade, the indenture trade and the nitty-gritties of the acts and laws regulating the indenture trade. Birch was asked, for instance, about the process by which migrants were documented, whether ships were checked to ensure that contracts were upheld, the examination of migrants before boarding and the languages used for this examination. Birch confirmed that he used 'no translator to assist [him]' since the migrants 'all understood Hindoostanee'.[24] Labour procurers were questioned about labour recruiters, the practice of money advancement to migrants and profits gained by merchant and recruiters from the indenture trade. Migrants were, in turn, mostly asked about their experience of recruitment, signing of the contract, passage and their experience of plantation life. No two persons were asked the same set of questions. However, as the instructions sent to those selected to run the committee included copies of the Town Hall petition to suspend the trade and the Calcutta merchants' counter-petition of 1838, it is reasonable to assume that the questions were at least partially determined by the concerns shown in these two petitions.[25]

Contrast this against, say, the Mauritius committee established at the same time, whose report allegedly never reached the parliament in time. As part of the decision to appoint investigative committees in each participating colony and port city, in October 1838 the Governor of Mauritius appointed a committee to inspect estates employing Indian indentured labourers. It aimed to investigate allegations of abuse and obtain accurate information on the treatment of Indian labourers by visiting 31 Mauritian estates and getting both plantation owners and labourers to answer a set questionnaire. The Mauritius committee was conducted by Special Justice C. M. Campbell, W. Bury, J. Hugon, and J. Villiers Forbes – all of whom had previously been employed by the East India Company. They were to be assisted by magistrates of each district.

Whereas the interview questions of the Calcutta committee were specific to the individual experiences of each interviewee, the Mauritius committee's questions were provided centrally by the Colonial Secretary of Mauritius, which the members of the committee were supposed to personally communicate to the labourers.[26] Queries for Indian labourers included questions about their knowledge of the contract, payment, food provisions, hours of labour, medical supplies and their communication with their families in India, while those for plantation owners focused on the number of employees and returnees, the number of deaths, sickness and absences, and provisions for medical attendance on their estates.[27] The change of vantage point shaped the questions asked. While as a port of embarkation, the committee in Calcutta was concerned with issues of recruitment, exploitation and the voyage, the Mauritius committee focused more on the labourers' condition on plantations and the economic effects of indentured immigration on the colony.

A quick glance at the questionnaire used by the Mauritius committee shows that this was a question of statistics rather than the indenture experience. In contrast to open questions about recruitment, passage and plantation life, the questions by the Mauritius committee were either yes-or-no questions ('Have you any Indians obtained here by transfer?') or required one-word answers ('What is the number of Deaths that have occured [sic] since their arrival?').[28] For the Mauritius committee, the labourers were twice removed from the interview. They were interviewed through interpreters and questioned in the presence of their employers. Further, the questions for labourers were in the third person, while those directed at the planters used the second-person 'you'. As a plantation colony, Mauritius had a disproportionate number of people with mercantile interests in continued migration. As settlers and controllers of the plantation economy in a small colony, planters were close to the power structure and had a strong say in emigration regulations. Moreover, the administrative machinery in plantation colonies had considerable stake in the move against prohibition, since, unlike larger colonies such as British India, they had an undue economic dependence on the plantation economy and its smooth functioning. In contrast to the Calcutta committee, the Mauritius committee concluded that the employment situation in the Mauritian estates was satisfactory and did not need many changes except for regulations around food and working hours.

The Calcutta committee thus offered more space for indentured migrants to voice their opinion, but the labourers were still removed from official discussions of the trade in three distinct ways. First, the spaces for indenture debates were open only to a largely elite group of Calcuttans with access to economic and social capital and the ability to use English as the medium of communication. Indentured labourers were more *allowed* than *welcome* in this space, and the extent to which they could participate and influence the discourse on emigration policies was determined by their elite counterparts. This system expected passivity on the part of the labourers and encouraged a situation where regulations and decision-making were the purview of colonial officials, with limited participation from the labourers. This approach in turn determined which of the reported abuses were addressed. As Rachel Sturman points out, because of restrictions on the voice of the labourer, the regulatory regime ended up not addressing the major grievances of the labourer: 'the withholding, underpayment, and nonpayment of wages; extensions of their labor time; and in some places, restrictions on their free movement off the estates'.[29] Instead, lawmakers focused on the upholding of contracts and resemblance to the slave trade.

The inclusion of labourers' voices, even if as witnesses to the trade, was regulated and limited according to the needs of the discourse. This was partly achieved by having elite Calcuttans speak on their behalf, often at the cost of not having indentured migrants testify to their own experience. For instance, instead of having migrant labourers in local factories or indigo plantations attest to their willingness to migrate, prominent merchant Dwarkanath Tagore's testimony was used by the committee to argue that indentured migrants were unlikely to emigrate if they knew the exact terms and conditions of their voyage and how far they were going. The testimonies of citizen-witnesses David

Hare and Longueville Clarke were similarly used to attest to instances where indentured labourers were visibly unwilling to migrate overseas.

Second, the testimonies of indentured labourers were guided by questions that intended to restrict their voices to specific themes. It is difficult to ascertain if members had the power to compel witnesses to speak, but most seemed eager to offer witness statements willingly. However, the committee was clearly focused on determining whether provisions of the indenture trade were exploitative and reminiscent of slavery. Thus, instead of asking returned migrants open questions about their grievances, committee members asked questions that were very specifically concerned with instances of mistreatment, deception in recruitment and the upholding of contracts. This was because proof of breach of contract strengthened the contention that indentureship was a continuation of slavery. It demonstrated that exploitation or mistreatment during recruitment, during passage and on plantations took place not only because the system was inherently exploitative, but also because regulations could so easily be breached that the mere presence of contracts did not protect labourers from servitude. In this, the Calcutta investigative committee acted as an extension of the colonial state – using the oral testimonies to report on the accusations levied against the trade and reflecting the state's endeavour to determine whether indenture represented an exercise in 'free' or 'unfree' labour. Evidence on the trade was thus guided by questions that the colonial state needed answered, as opposed to concerns that the migrant labourer might have wanted to pose. In the process, testimonies came to be shaped by the way in which questions were framed, by fears of coercion and by the remits of investigation determined by the interviewers.

Finally, the labourer's testimony was considered less reliable than that of elite Calcuttans. Ann Laura Stoler's 'hierarchies of credibility' permeated the records of the Calcutta committee, where 'native evidence' was considered low on the scale of reliability and testimonies were given different weightage on the basis of race, social position and occupation.[30] The committee report stated, for instance, that it had arrived at its conclusions 'after all due allowance [was] made for the habit of exaggeration prevalent among Bengalees and Hindoostanees'.[31] Testimonies from Indians were thus considered fundamentally unreliable. Dowson had submitted a separate report that rejected the findings of the main committee and argued that the problems of the indenture system were remediable through well-implemented regulations and did not warrant its complete prohibition. His report weighed 'native evidence' as even less reliable, arguing:

My colleagues ... are weighing the value and credibility of evidence in a very different manner from that which is laid down as the proper method and principle by all writers on the subject[. They] well know no value can be put ... [on the section of the report that] rests on native evidence.[32]

In *Silencing the Past*, Michel-Rolph Trouillot showed that there are four layers of silencing in the writing of history: silencing during the making or recording of sources, silencing during the creation of archives, silencing by the narrators through their selection of sources and narratives, and silencing by the collective of historians and the public through their selection of particular narratives to become part of the historical corpus.[33] By their very nature, archives privilege certain voices while marginalising others – resulting in a repository where voices are absent as subjects, authors or both. Most historical sources during the early days of the indenture trade included the indentured migrant as a subject, but only very rarely as authors. The voices of women, whether as petitioners or as emigrants, were even more difficult to find in the early period of indenture. In line with Gayatri Chakravorty Spivak's 'Can the Subaltern Speak?' the female indentured migrant suffered 'double displacement' from a position where she could voice her opinion.[34] Thus, it is only through a process of reading against the grain that the labourers' scant testimonies can be used to construct their experiences. Their contributions, voices, interpretations and comments on the indenture trade and their experience of it have to be extracted from records not written with the intent of showcasing their voices.

In spite of such restrictions, however, these interviews represent one of the earliest instances where the voice of the labourer, and his encounter with state machinery, is recorded. They remain, to this date, one of the only official spaces of discussion where early indentured labourers found an opportunity to share their experiences of recruitment, passage and plantation. In stark contrast to the stock-taking approach of the Mauritius committee – where migrants' experiences were bunched together as singular answers from each estate – the detailed interviews of the Calcutta committee individualised the migrant experience and offered knowledge of their quotidian lives. Instead of becoming a statistic in the colonial archive, returned migrants and foremen ('cooly sirdar') such as Bibee Zuhoorun, Karoo, Suboo, Sheik Manick, Boodoo Khan and Ramdeen were able to speak at length about their individual experiences.

Findings of the Committee: Exploitation,
Mistreatment and Deception

The verdict that the indenture trade was similar to slavery in many respects, and hence should be severely curtailed or completely abolished, drew upon a body of evidence that included individual instances of mistreatment, exploitation and deception. While the Town Hall meeting could only offer opinions, accusations and personal accounts, the Calcutta committee was in a position to offer oral and documentary sources that supported this view. By focusing their questions on mistreatment, exploitation, deception and the upholding of contractual obligations, the Calcutta committee made it crystal clear that the main – if not the *only* – important question at the time was whether the indenture trade resembled the slave trade. These quotidian abuses have been discussed here in three phases: during recruitment, during confinement and passage, and in plantations. Taken together, these added cogency and legitimacy to arguments against continued indenture trade. Essentially, the Calcutta committee was able to turn accusations into evidence – evidence that the colonial state and its subjects could agree upon and use in future discussions.

As a port city focused on emigration, discussions in Calcutta were inordinately balanced towards experiences of recruitment and passage. Most interviewed by the Calcutta committee testified to the practice of deception and misdirection in recruiting for the indenture trade. Birch stated that 'kidnapping prevailed in a very great degree in the lower provinces of Bengal'.[35] According to Abdoolah Khan, an Indian doctor aboard ships, labourers on board were unaware that they would be separated from their families for five years, since middlemen often promised that they would only be gone for two months.[36] Similarly, colonial official George Witchlow stated that most migrants did not know that they were going to Mauritius or even where Mauritius was. He mentioned especially the case of a woman kidnapped on her pilgrimage to the Jagannath Temple in Orissa (now Odisha), who was sent in disguise in men's clothing to Calcutta to be emigrated as an indentured labourer.[37] Merchant and committee member Dowson testified to an experiment to shed light on recruitment practices. He had asked an associate, Mr Carapiet, to engage labourers from Chhotanagpur, but only after explaining to them 'the nature of the employment, and that [the labourer] was to leave his country for a period of five years'.[38] According to Dowson, this proved a fruitless mission, since Carapiet did not succeed in procuring a single labourer, even though other middlemen were engaging labourers in the immediate vicinity. Dowson used this to demonstrate that labourers were very often not informed about their destination.[39]

A court-pleader by profession, Roger Dias's testimony was based on his many conversations with labourers who had appeared in front of the police or the 24 Pergunnahs court before embarkation.[40] Fluent in Bengali and Hindustani by his own admission, Dias testified that labourers he spoke to denied the presence of any contract or agreement.[41] Many complained that recruiters had informed them that 'the magistrate would force them to go if they withheld consent, and that all non-compliance would be punished'.[42] This was reminiscent of Dickens's statement at the Town Hall meeting, where he pointed to labour recruiters using 'circulars addressed to judges, collectors and magistrates, which are countersigned and registered by the police' to lead local officers, police agents and emigrant labourers to believe that the middlemen were working under government sanction.[43] An official from the district of Purulia complained in 1838 that 'a few persons are occasionally taken away by men, who I have reason to believe, represent themselves to be servants of the Government'.[44] This made many labourers think that signing up was compulsory rather than voluntary.

Middlemen recruiters also exploited migrants by usurping the wage advance they received when they agreed to the indenture contract. John Hughes testified that besides receiving commission from each agency house for procuring labourers, he received a portion of the advance made to the migrant, 'the whole six months' advance at 30 rupees'.[45] This was corroborated by the Superintendent of Calcutta Police, who informed that at least half of the wage advance was deducted by the *duffadar*s, and formerly 'the whole, or nearly all, was deducted from them'.[46] The Deputy Superintendent concurred, stating that before the government implemented the system of examining migrants, the *duffadar*s kept all of the wages and 'the Coolies had usually no balance at all left of the advance made to them'.[47] They were also often 'plundered of the articles furnished', such as clothing and objects received for joining the indenture trade.[48] Of course, under the new system of examination, even if the migrants received some of their wage advance, they had to pay the Deputy Superintendent a rupee each for inspecting the *duffadar*s' accounts.[49]

There were multiple complaints of middlemen recruiters misstating facts about the voyage and the nature of work. According to Dias, many labourers expected their jobs to be short-term services near Calcutta, allowing them to return to their homes 'as I believe servants are in the habit of doing biennially and triennially'.[50] They were also under the impression that they would be able to make the usual remittances to their families.[51] This meant that they were not aware of the possibility of losing their caste by crossing the *kala pani* – the black water of the seas. As was customary in the nineteenth century, those who crossed the seas could be ousted from their caste and only be reintegrated after offering penance. Although technically only meant to affect Hindu travellers, the social position of Muslims and their relationship with their family could also be impacted. As Dowson testified, the main complaint of labourers was that they had been misinformed about the length of journey, and that by consenting to unknowingly crossing the seas, they could lose their social position.[52] Bibee Zuhoorun, the only female labourer who testified for the committee, stated that she had lost her caste by travelling across the seas: '[E]ven my mother will not drink water from my hand or eat with me.'[53]

Labourers themselves testified to deceptive recruitment practices: Karoo was enticed to Calcutta with the promise of a road-repairing job but was taken to the emigrants' depot instead, where Mauritius was offered as an alternative where he could receive good wages, food and clothing.[54] Zuhoorun (also referred to as Djoram and Juhoorun) had been deceived into thinking Mauritius was only a five-day journey by boat, as opposed to the six-weeks journey it really was. She only found out on the ship that she was travelling outside India.[55] Abdoolah Khan saw *duffadar*s tell migrants that they were to be engaged only for two months and could expect to return to Calcutta in four or five months.[56] Deception was not always explicit. Recruiters made use of legal loopholes and misinformation to ensure that labourers went willingly. Moreover, as Reverend Boaz argued, labourers who came from the hinterland often had no conception of a sea voyage.[57] Captain James Smart testified that migrants were surprised to encounter saltwater on their journey: '[T]hey will lower their lotas [water vessels] on one side to get water, and finding it salt[y], they will go to the other and will lower down again, thinking to get it fresh....'[58] Migrants were also much less likely to understand the contract since they did not speak the common tongue of 'Hindustanee'.[59] In fact, the very idea of work contracts was new to migrants, who were till date used to temporary employment in factories, road works and indigo plantations.

Kidnapping and illegal confinement had become a visible problem of the indenture trade, as many inhabitants of Calcutta testified to their experience with confined labourers. Merchant-entrepreneur Dwarkanath Tagore testified to the committee that the *syce* (horse keeper or groomer) of his partner, William Prinsep, had complained of his brother being confined by recruiters to send him to Mauritius.[60] He also spoke of another friend's servant whom some recruiters had tried to forcibly emigrate to Mauritius. This is reminiscent, of course, of Hare's encounter with indentured migrants confined in a central Calcutta house. Based on his experience with labourers in his factories and indigo plantations in eastern India, Tagore argued that labourers were unlikely to agree to emigrate overseas for a long period of time if they knew the exact terms and conditions.[61] Not only were labourers unable to provide for their families at such distances, but it was also absurd for them to agree to five-year overseas contracts when, in Indian factories, labourers consented to a maximum of eight months away from their families.[62] Such testimonies, however, were not without resistance from government officials. The Superintendent of Police stated that the labourers alleged to have been confined in the central Calcutta house were in fact 'perfectly willing to proceed'.[63]

Treatment of labourers in passage was another cause for concern. Abdoolah Khan painted a picture of despair on board the *Christopher Rawson*: 'They were all crying on board the ship. The captain ordered all their hair to be cut, both of men and women … and he used to lock them below the hatches at four o' clock….'[64] Water provisions on the ship were atrocious: 'It was stinking and thick, something like beer foaming up.'[65] Food provisions could be so lacking that many migrants used what little money they had to purchase water and biscuits from the *lascars*. Labourers were often provided with just rice and tamarinds, with lentils offered twice a week or once every fourth day to save water.[66] Migrants could also be whipped or caned for charges of theft on board their ships.[67] Abdoolah Khan stated that although a doctor on the ship, he himself had been beaten by the ship's captain.[68] Captain Edwards, however, offered a completely different account of the same voyage. When interrogated about the cutting of hair, he stated that it was for reasons of cleanliness. Even though many migrants objected, often on religious grounds, the captain stated: 'I insisted, and it was done; I used no force.'[69] The captain denied that the migrants lacked food provisions, stating that 'they had as much as they liked'. If migrants bought biscuits from the *serangs* and *lascars*, '[t]hey only bought them as a luxury'.[70] He also denied giving the order to hit Abdoolah Khan.[71]

The *Bengal Hurkaru* frequently reported on labourers being mistreated during passage, writing once of a 'coolie ship' where 70 labourers were 'confined in cells' '5 feet by 8 with no light and little air'.[72] Reverend Boaz's account of labourers being confined below deck on their journey overseas became well known in British public circles when he wrote a letter on this issue, extracts from which were read at a public meeting in Exeter Hall, London, and subsequently appeared in journals in Calcutta.[73] In passage, labourers occasionally jumped off ships to escape conditions on board, especially under the assumption that they could swim back to shore.[74] Such testimonies not only highlighted the miseries of passage but also drew attention to similarities with slave suicide during the middle passage. As the Calcutta committee report cautioned, 'if West Indian voyages be permitted, the waste of human life and misery that will fall on the Coolies exported under the name of free labourers will approach to those inflicted on the negro in the middle passage by the slave trade'.[75]

At the same time, this was not a unanimous view. Many indenture officials and recruiters found the evidence contentious. Arthur Onslow, Reverend Anthony Garstin, Doctor Wise, Alexander Mackenzie and Captain R. Rayne – 'all unexceptionable witnesses in point of good faith, character and veracity' – testified to the labourers' 'healthy appearance and their apparent contentment'.[76] Reverend Garstin argued that labourers were 'treated remarkably well, with great humanity, and even tenderness' during passage.[77] Captain Birch testified that there was no incentive for captains and shippers to flout regulations since it would procure unwilling labourers: 'It is [in] the interest of the captain that the provisions which are found by the shippers should be ample, as otherwise the Coolies might come down upon him.'[78] In spite of testifying to the presence of fraudulence in recruitment, Dowson maintained that labourers were content on the Mauritian estates, saying that in his four years of experience, he had 'never seen or heard of a single case of cruelty, injustice or oppression being practised towards a Coolie ... they are treated throughout the island with great tenderness and humanity by their employers'.[79] The Chief Commissary of Police in Calcutta also stated in a letter to Birch that no labourer was sent away without their consent and, in fact, he was always within his rights to refuse.[80] Moreover, while migrants interviewed by the Calcutta committee testified to facing mistreatment, deception and corporal punishment, many returned migrants interviewed at the ports testified to being content with their employment situation, some even eager to renew their contracts.[81]

Finally, there was the question of how labourers were treated on plantations. Labourers testified that middlemen often misrepresented to them the jobs they were expected to perform.[82] Overwork was a common complaint: Sheik Manick testified that the 11 men who died of various illnesses during his stint in Mauritius were actually overworked to death.[83] Manick also reported that his planter Monsieur Riviere always asked him to '[w]ork the Coolies as hard as possible'. When he expressed concern about overworking leading to deaths, Riviere replied that he could always 'get others to supply their places if they die'.[84] Zuhoorun testified that she saw several men die in the plantations: some died after being put in the stocks, three men hung themselves and two men died in the hospital. Although she was not sure why some hung themselves, the rumour amongst the labourers was that 'they could not bear the hardships of the life they led'.[85] Corporal punishment was common on the plantations, where labourers were beaten with canes or leather whips if they stopped working or took a rest.[86] This was often meted out by the Indian overseers. There were other penal clauses, such as punishing unauthorised absence with imprisonment, making labourers break stones and imposing the notorious 'double cut' in wages if labourers missed work due to sickness.[87]

Many testified to long hours of work, working from four in the morning to five or seven in the afternoon, with only an hour's break.[88] In other cases, labourers continued to work till their evening meal, which could be as late as eleven o'clock at night.[89] In exchange, they received two meals a day, consisting of rice, lentils, ghee and dried fish. Labourers were also not allowed to leave their plantations without written permission.[90] Wage cuts for sickness were common, and Sheik Manick and Boodoo Khan testified to receiving no wages at all.[91] Karoo and Suboo both testified to being sent home from Mauritius with only two months' wages because they fell sick (Suboo due to the beatings received from overseers); and in both cases, their wages were forcibly taken away by overseers.[92] The only person who showed an active interest in returning to Mauritius was Ramdeen, who was employed as a *sirdar*. Unlike others, he testified to being treated very comfortably and paid on time and denied that labourers were beaten: '[S]ometimes the Coolies were knocked about, but never beaten....'[93]

Testimonies on mistreatment, deception and lack of adherence to contractual obligations were important pieces of evidence in the indenture debates. It showed, first, that fraudulence and false recruitment practices were a systemic problem, and government-mandated regulations were not enough to counteract them since they could easily be circumvented. A lot of the questions thus revolved around whether migrants received wages and food provisions according to contract and whether their working hours reflected the stipulations in their contracts. There was an implication that deception and misinformation were tantamount to breach of a verbal contract and did not go with the spirit of signing a contract. Second, it indicated that if labourers from eastern India were aware that they had to cross the seas and reside abroad for a minimum of five years, very few would have readily agreed to engage in indenture. Pointing to fraudulence in recruitment was an effective way of arguing that indentured migrants were not in control of their own movement and employment. Rather, they were victims of a system that was not so different from the recently abolished slave trade.

These testimonies were included in the marginalia of the report to substantiate the findings of the committee. Drawing upon them, the committee report argued that there was a deliberate use of kidnapping and false imprisonment in the indenture trade, and strongly condemned the use of 'misrepresentation and deceit' by labour recruiters.[94] Many labourers had, according to the committee, been persuaded to come to Calcutta to work as peons, gardeners or porters under the aegis of the East India Company and did not understand the contracts they signed. When Boodoo Khan agreed to emigrate to Mauritius, he was under the impression that he was to travel by land and arrive in Mauritius in five days. He was also convinced that this was in service of the East India Company, stating to his brother: 'I came for service, and I must go; this is the Company's service, and why should I refuse it?'[95] Despite the regulations of 1837, labourers were often under the impression that they would be liable to penal consequences if they did not comply. In fact, the report implied that fraudulence was central to the recruitment process. It considered the practice of advancing six months' wages to the labourers 'a source of fraudulent and dishonest gain to all the subordinate agents engaged in the export', certain that if such advances were forbidden, 'the prop and mainstay of the Coolie trade ... would be at once removed'.[96] Continuing their insistence on the inefficacy of regulations, the committee report concluded: '[N]o system, we are firmly convinced, would ever suffice completely to counteract the tricks and falsehoods that would be resorted to in India by the Duffadars, Arkotties and other persons engaged in similar avocations....'[97]

Hidden Voices: The Women's Question

By its very nature, the Calcutta committee was selective – selective in its choice of witnesses, of questions to ask each witness and of testimonies that were used to substantiate its final report. With the post-slavery focus on recruitment, exploitation and upholding of contracts, certain experiences tended to be overlooked, key among which was the condition of female migrants. The indenture experience was heavily gendered. While both men and women tilled fields and worked to cultivate and process sugar, some women were employed in the households of plantation owners. Zuhoorun testified to 'making salt, climbing tamarind trees to pick them, sweeping the house, and cutting grass for cattle' in Mauritius.[98] Women also received lower wages and were sometimes expected to wash and cook for the men.[99] Moreover, as women's labour was seen as a form of domestic labour rather than plantation labour – especially in places like Mauritius – planters and recruiters preferred male migrants, thus skewing the gender balance on plantations. John Gladstone found it difficult to engage women in indenture, since '[i]t is the practice of the Hill Coolies to leave their families at home when they come down to Bengal to seek employment'.[100]

Sexual harassment and expectations of sexual favour were a common occurrence on plantations. A particularly harrowing experience was recounted by Zuhoorun, who was asked by the plantation owner Doctor Boileau to be his mistress. She refused his advances, saying: 'I am a Mussulmanee [Muslim woman]. I of course refused. I have degraded myself by going on board ship; I would not further degrade myself.'[101] Her attempts to complain to the police were met with a three-month stint at a house of correction and then a return to Boileau's house, where she was beaten and harassed further. She testified: 'I was beaten, slapped and kicked, and on one occasion my master ran a needle into my breast; it drew blood. I ran to the police; they said, "Why do not you work as you are desired to do?"'[102] Eventually, she decided to return to India before the end of her five-year contract, even if it meant not receiving any wages for her 2.5 years of service. She exclaimed: 'I would not return to Mauritius on any account; it is a country of slaves; I would not go there again; I would rather beg my bread here.'[103]

In spite of her evidence, however, issues of sexual harassment and assault were not explored in the committee report. In fact, the only time the report talked about women was when they discussed the problem of labourers leaving behind their families, stating: '[I]t appears to be contrary to the general Asiatic character, and opposed to the feelings and prejudices of even the lowest classes to emigrate with their women or families....'[104] The report attributed this gendered skew in migration to 'the jealousy and prejudices of Asiatics with regard to the female sex, [and] the want of due accommodation for women in maritime emigration'.[105]

This was a significant omission, not least because discussions of sexual violence and mistreatment of women were common in anti-slavery debates, as well as in later debates over Indian indenture. Henrice Altink has shown that the horrors of slavery were often exposed by abolitionists and anti-slavery activists through the treatment of slave women. This served as an effective way of arousing public sentiments because 'this treatment was diametrically opposed to the gender order of the metropolitan society'.[106] Similarly, the question of female chastity was front and centre in discussions around the abolition of the indenture trade. The early twentieth century saw protests seeking the abolition of overseas indenture led by nationalist leaders such as M. K. Gandhi and Gopal Krishna Gokhale. In these debates, Indian nationalists and anti-indenture activists turned female labourers into symbols of collective protest.[107] Within the gendered framework of the indenture trade, the exploitation of female migrants became an important instrument for exposing the evils of indenture and instigating an emotional response from the public. References to sexual abuse on ships, depots and plantations served to portray an image of decadence and lawlessness. The image of the helpless female labourer was used by Indian nationalists to demonstrate how women were doubly exploited under the colonial and indenture systems, on the one hand, and male oppression, on the other. This aided the portrayal of the indenture trade as dangerous, exploitative and immoral.[108]

Although evidently a strong point of criticism against the indenture trade, the women's question was excluded from the Calcutta committee report, and the issue of sexual assault and violence at the hands of planters was ignored in early legislation. In the early days of indenture, women were yet to be seen as the main victims of the indenture system, or indeed the main participants in the indenture trade. The ideal indentured labourer was then imagined unequivocally as male.

A Regime of Evaluation

Calcutta enjoyed a formidable position within the imperial schema. The Calcutta investigative committee allowed inhabitants of Calcutta to investigate indenture and offer suggestions to the metropolitan government. Its report was not only the most detailed record of the early indenture trade in Calcutta but also a significant body of evidence that came to influence metropolitan regulations. It created a baseline for understanding the indenture trade by formulating questions that targeted the main accusations against it. As allegations of abuse piled up against indenture, and especially as the issue gained ground among the British and Indian public, interviews of returned migrants by indenture officials, police, magistrates and port-officials emerged as a common practice.[109]

The responsiveness of the metropole to debates in the city, and the contribution of these debates to metropolitan lawmaking and trans-imperial notions of servitude, makes the centrality of Calcutta within global indenture networks abundantly clear. As part of the interviews conducted by the committee, shippers and officials were asked for suggestions to improve the trade. James Smart, a master pilot for the East India Company, suggested that there should be native speakers on board ships, provisions for close survey of the ships before it left Indian ports, and a consistent system of mustering the labourers and cleaning and fumigating decks. John Dyer, another master pilot, made suggestions about provisions of water, medicine, appropriate ventilation and proper clothing on deck.[110] These comments were incorporated into the committee's suggestions to the metropolitan government for future lawmaking, demonstrating a collaborative empire in operation.

With the Calcutta committee began a regime of evaluation, where the very presence of periodic evaluations was seen as a safeguard against regression into slavery. Increasingly, colonial officials at ports were instructed to interview returned migrants: a letter from April 1841 instructed the Chief Magistrate of Calcutta to interview migrants on ships returning from Mauritius, urging that 'the examination should be as searching as you can make it'.[111] Later, the Governor General restricted this practice to migrants who had returned before the end of their five years of contractual service.[112] As their findings were distributed to the Governor General, the Superintendent of Police, the Chief Magistrate, district magistrates and other relevant officials, these 'examinations' revealed varied experiences of indenture.[113] All 23 labourers returning from Mauritius on board the *Warrior* in 1842 testified to receiving good treatment, with one of the labourers, Kuntheeram Sirdar from Hazareebaugh, stating that he never witnessed any corporal punishment on plantations.[114] Labourers returning from Mauritius on the *Adina* also reported that they had no complaints about their treatment.[115] Family ties loomed large in these examinations. Many returned migrants, like Khatto, were eager to return to their families in Mauritius and were only visiting Calcutta to see their parents.[116] Some migrants like Buddun carried letters from plantation owners that certified their connection to the estates and even offered to pay for their return travel to Mauritius.[117] Those like Mohun and Khatto were using their visit to Calcutta to persuade some of their family members to join them in Mauritius, as well as to recruit indentured labourers for their respective plantation estates.[118] In many cases, results of these examinations were sought out by Calcutta-based merchant houses. In 1841, while the indenture trade was still suspended, merchant companies like Saunders, May, Sarkies & Company asked the Secretary to the Government of India to furnish copies of the examinations of returned migrants employed in Mauritius.[119]

Even as many returned with no complaints, problems of fraudulent recruitment continued to plague the indenture trade. In January 1840, five people were convicted in Burdwan (Bengal) for 'trepanning [swindling] of Coolies with a view to their being shipped off to the Mauritius'.[120] Sheir Allee Khan was fined 3 rupees for recruiting 8 labourers for Mauritius by convincing the labourers that they were to be employed in an indigo factory in Bengal.[121] Gollam Allee, Nugroo Khan and Hossen Khan were fined 30 rupees for misleading 22 labourers, while Mungloo Khan was fined 30 rupees for convincing 4 labourers that they were to be employed in a local indigo factory rather than a Mauritius plantation.[122] An 1843 letter cautioned district magistrates against *duffadars* who were carrying official-looking orders to induce labourers to migrate through 'fraud[,] extortion or oppression'.[123] It stated that 'such perwannahs are requested by these men to the ignorant people as official documents giving them some degree of authority in their proceedings'.[124] As late as 1859, labourers were found to be misled into joining the indenture trade. Jane Swinton, who accompanied her husband, Captain E. Swinton, on the *Salsette*, wrote: '[O]ut of the 324 Coolies who came on board, I do not believe five, at most, either know where they are going, or what is to be their occupation.'[125]

The committee – through its report and interviews – became an aggregation of the Calcutta debates. With the failure of all other committees to send a detailed report to the parliament in time, the Calcutta committee emerged as an authoritative account, offering rare snapshots into early migrant experience and helping metropolitan officials visualise what imperial labour had come to look like after Abolition. As periodic examinations became a part of the indenture regime, it also cemented metropolitan Britain as the arbiter of the indenture trade – responsible for its continuance and for ensuring a free labour regime. As Radhika Mongia argues in her reading of investigative committees, 'Indenture thus continued not *in spite* of the numerous inquiries, but *because* of them.'[126]

At the same time, the committee had complete control over how the report was written and using whose testimonies. Thus, it was producing selective knowledge about the early indenture trade from a small sample of witnesses, which then became canon. Migrants became a means to an end, and Calcutta emerged not as a space where the indenture debates merely mirrored the debates in Britain but as a separate, autonomous space of debate that was focused on recruitment and emigration. More needs to be done to understand colonial commissions of inquiry as techniques of colonial knowledge production, and indeed to understand their place in global history – perhaps using newer methods such as corpus linguistics to read colonial commissions on a grand scale.[127]

Notes

1. John Geoghegan, *Note on Emigration from India* (Calcutta: Superintendent of Government Printing, 1873), p. 6.
2. Ibid., p. 10.
3. Letter from the Committee of Inquiry on Indian Labourers, Flacq, Mauritius, to G. F. Dick, Colonial Secretary, Port Louis, dated 16 March 1839, in 'Indian Labourers: Indian Enquiry of Flacq, Mauritius', *Papers Regarding the Employment of Indian Indentured Labourers Overseas*, vol. 10: *Report on the Condition of the Labourers on 22 Estates in the Flacq District, Mauritius (Includes Answers to Questionnaires, by Both Employers and Labourers)*, dated February 1839–March 1839, Board's Collections, 1840–1841, vol. 1847, no. 77650, IOR/F/4/1847/77650.
4. Quoted in Geoghegan, *Note on Emigration from India*, p. 2.
5. Ibid., p. 3.
6. Letter from Secretary to the Colonial Office to the Law Commissioners, India, dated 25 May 1836, quoted in letter from Edward Lawford, Solicitor to the East India Company, to David Hill, 12 June 1838, in *Papers Respecting the East-India Labourers Bill* (London: printed by order of the General Court, by J. L. Cox & Sons, 1838).
7. Letter from H. T. Prinsep, Secretary to the Government of India, to Secretary to the Government of Bengal, dated 11 July 1838, Fort William, 1 August 1838, no. 4; letter from H. T. Prinsep, Secretary to the Government

of Bengal, to T. Dickens, Rev. James Charles, W. Dowson, Major Archer, Rosomoy Dutt and J. P. Grant, dated 1 August 1838, 1 August 1838, no. 6, General Department (General) Proceedings, WBSA.

8. *Letter from Secretary to Government of India, to Committee on Exportation of Hill Coolies: Report of Committee and Evidence* (East India House, ordered by the House of Commons to be printed, 12 February 1841), Parliamentary Papers (House of Commons) 16, no. 45 (henceforth 'Report of the Calcutta Committee').

9. *Calcutta Monthly Journal*, August 1838, p. 93; *Calcutta Monthly Journal and General Register*, 1836, n.p.; *Calcutta Christian Observer* 1, 1832, p. 128.

10. *Friend of India*, 14 September 1837, p. 289; Anjali Bose (ed.), *Samsad Bangla Charitabhidhan* (A Dictionary of Bengali Biographies) (Calcutta: Sahitya Samsad, 1998), pp. 461–462; George Smith, 'The First Twenty Years of the Calcutta Review', *Calcutta Review* 59 (1874), pp. 230–231. Historian Romesh Chandra Dutt and poet Toru Dutt were Rosomoy Dutt's great grandchildren.

11. 'Proceedings of the [Calcutta Investigative] Committee, from 22 August 1838 to 14 January 1839', in *Letter from Secretary to Government of India, to Committee on Exportation of Hill Coolies: Report of Committee and Evidence* (East India House, ordered by the House of Commons to be printed, 12 February 1841), Parliamentary Papers (House of Commons) 16, no. 45 (henceforth, 'Proceedings of the Calcutta Committee').

12. 'Report of the Calcutta Committee', pp. 5, 9.

13. Geoghegan reported in 1873: 'Major Archer … went to Europe at an early stage of the proceedings, and I have not been able to obtain his views, if, indeed, he ever put them on record.' Geoghegan, *Note on Emigration from India*, p. 6.

14. 'Report of the Calcutta Committee', p. 5.

15. Ibid., p. 9.

16. Ibid., p. 5.

17. Ibid.

18. Oz Frankel, *States of Inquiry: Social Investigations and Print Culture in Nineteenth-Century Britain and the United States* (Baltimore, MD: The Johns Hopkins University Press, 2006). See also Oz Frankel, 'Scenes of Commission: Royal Commissions of Inquiry and the Culture of Social Investigation in Early Victorian Britain', *European Legacy* 4, no. 6 (1999): 20–41.

19. Frankel, *States of Inquiry*.

20. Letter from G. F. Dick, Colonial Secretary, to the Chief Secretary to Government of Bengal, dated 12 September 1838, in Extract from the Proceedings of the Honourable the President of the Council of India in Council in the General Department, dated 11 July 1838, in *Mauritius: Copies of Correspondence Addressed to the Secretary of State for the Colonial Department, Relative to the Introduction of Indian Labourers into the Mauritius* (ordered by the House of Commons to be printed, 28 May 1840).

21. Adam Ashforth, 'Reckoning Schemes of Legitimation: On Commissions of Inquiry as Power/Knowledge Forms', *Journal of Historical Sociology* 3, no. 1 (1990): 1–22. For how British abolitionists and humanitarians used official inquiries as an important tool, see Zoë Laidlaw, 'Investigating Empire: Humanitarians, Reform and the Commission of Eastern Inquiry', *Journal of Imperial and Commonwealth History* 40, no. 5 (December 2012): 749–768.

22. Geoghegan, *Note on Emigration from India*.

23. 'Proceedings of the Calcutta Committee'.

24. Testimony of Captain F. W. Birch, 30 August 1838, in 'Proceedings of the Calcutta Committee'.

25. Letter from H. T. Prinsep, Secretary to the Government, to T. Dickens, Rev. James Charles, W. Dowson, Major Archer, Rosomoy Dutt and J. P. Grant, dated 1 August 1838, 1 August 1838, no. 6, General Department (General) Proceedings, WBSA.

26. Letter from G. F. Dick, Colonial Secretary of Mauritius, to Special Justice Campbell (Chairman of the Mauritius Investigative Committee), dated 15 October 1838, Colonial Secretary's Office, in 'Correspondence Respecting the Employment of Indian Labourers in the Mauritius', in *Mauritius: Copy of Despatches from Sir William Nicolay, on the Subject of Free Labour in the Mauritius* (ordered by the House of Commons to be printed, 7 February 1840), p. 15.

27. 'Indian Labourers: Indian Inquiry of Savanne, Mauritius', in *Papers Regarding the Employment of Indian Indentured Labourers Overseas*, vol. 6: *Report on the Condition of the Labourers on 24 of the Principal Plantations in the Savanne District, Mauritius*, dated July 1839, Board's Collections, 1840–1841, vol. 1847, no. 77646, Legislative Department, IOR/F/4/1847/77646.

28. Representative questions from the letter from H. M. Self and W. C. Pearce, Stipendiary Magistrates of Moka, to G. Dick, Colonial Secretary, Port Louis, dated 29 July 1839, in *Papers Regarding the Employment of Indian Indentured Labourers Overseas*, vol. 7: *Report on the Condition of the*

Labourers on 24 Estates in the Plaines Wilhelms District, Mauritius, dated June–July 1839, Board's Collections, 1840–1841, vol. 1847, no. 77647, IOR/F/4/1847/77647.

29. Rachel Sturman, 'Indian Indentured Labor and the History of International Rights Regimes', *American Historical Review* 119, no. 5 (2014): 1439–1465, p. 1456.

30. Ann Laura Stoler, '"In Cold Blood": Hierarchies of Credibility and the Politics of Colonial Narratives', *Representations* 37 (January 1992): 151–189.

31. 'Report of the Calcutta Committee', p. 6.

32. William Frank Dowson, 'Minute on the Report of the Committee Appointed to Enquire into the Abuses Alleged to Exist Relative to the Export of Coolies', dated 16 October 1840, in *Letter from Secretary to Government of India, to Committee on Exportation of Hill Coolies: Report of Committee and Evidence* (East India House, ordered by the House of Commons to be printed, 12 February 1841), p. 13.

33. Michel-Rolph Trouillot, *Silencing the Past: Power and the Production of History* (Boston, MA: Beacon Press, 1995). See also Achille Mbembe, 'The Power of the Archive and Its Limits', in *Refiguring the Archive*, ed. Carolyn Hamilton, Verne Harris, Jane Taylor, Michele Pickover, Graeme Reid and Razia Saleh, pp. 19–27 (Dordrecht: Springer, 2002).

34. Gayatri Chakravorty Spivak, 'Can the Subaltern Speak?' in *Marxism and the Interpretation of Culture*, ed. Cary Nelson and Lawrence Grossberg, pp. 271–314 (Urbana and Chicago, IL: University of Illinois Press, 1988).

35. Testimony of Captain F. W. Birch, 20 August 1838, in 'Proceedings of the Calcutta Committee'.

36. Testimony of Abdoolah Khan, 10 September 1838, in 'Proceedings of the Calcutta Committee'.

37. Testimony of George Witchlow, 11 December 1838, in 'Proceedings of the Calcutta Committee'.

38. Testimony of W. F. Dowson, 27 November 1838, in 'Proceedings of the Calcutta Committee'.

39. Ibid.

40. 24 Pergunnahs is an administrative unit in southern Bengal.

41. Testimony of Roger Dias, 29 October 1838, in 'Proceedings of the Calcutta Committee'.

42. Ibid.

43. 'Meeting for Preventing the Exportation of Coolies', *Calcutta Review* 44 (July 1838), p. 314.

44. Quoted in *Friend of India*, 16 August 1838, p. 453.

45. Testimony of John Hughes, 10 September 1838, in 'Proceedings of the Calcutta Committee'.

46. Testimony of Captain F. W. Birch, 27 August 1838, in 'Proceedings of the Calcutta Committee'.

47. Testimony of J. J. McCann, 6 September 1838, in 'Proceedings of the Calcutta Committee'.

48. Ibid.

49. Ibid.

50. Testimony of Roger Dias, 29 October 1838, in 'Proceedings of the Calcutta Committee'.

51. Ibid.

52. Testimony of W. F. Dowson, 27 November 1838, in 'Proceedings of the Calcutta Committee'.

53. Testimony of Bibee Zuhoorun, 20 September 1838, in 'Proceedings of the Calcutta Committee'. For details, see Chapter 5.

54. Testimony of Karoo, 16 November 1838, in 'Proceedings of the Calcutta Committee'.

55. 'Examination of Juhoorun', Exhibit no. 10, Appendix to 'Report of the Calcutta Committee'.

56. Testimony of Abdoolah Khan, 10 September 1838, in 'Proceedings of the Calcutta Committee'.

57. Testimony of Rev. Thomas Boaz, 14 January 1839, in 'Proceedings of the Calcutta Committee'.

58. Testimony of James Smart, 15 October 1838, in 'Proceedings of the Calcutta Committee'.

59. Testimony of Rev. Thomas Boaz, 14 January 1839, in 'Proceedings of the Calcutta Committee'.

60. Testimony of Dwarkanath Tagore, 9 November 1838, in 'Proceedings of the Calcutta Committee'.

61. Ibid.

62. 'Meeting for Preventing the Exportation of Coolies', p. 316; testimony of Dwarkanath Tagore, 9 November 1838, in 'Proceedings of the Calcutta Committee'.

63. Testimony of Captain Birch, 11 October 1838, in 'Proceedings of the Calcutta Committee'.

64. Testimony of Abdoolah Khan, 13 September 1838, in 'Proceedings of the Calcutta Committee'.

65. Testimony of Abdoolah Khan, 10 September 1838, in 'Proceedings of the Calcutta Committee'.

66. Testimony of Abdoolah Khan, 13 September 1838, in 'Proceedings of the Calcutta Committee'.

67. Testimony of Captain A. G. Mackenzie, 13 September 1838, in 'Proceedings of the Calcutta Committee'.

68. Testimony of Abdoolah Khan, 10 September 1838, in 'Proceedings of the Calcutta Committee'.

69. Testimony of Captain Edwards, 17 September 1838, in 'Proceedings of the Calcutta Committee'.

70. Ibid.

71. Ibid.

72. *Bengal Hurkaru*, 6 July 1838, p. 19.

73. Testimony of Thomas Boaz, 14 January 1839, in 'Proceedings of the Calcutta Committee'.

74. Testimony of Captain James Rapson, 22 August 1838, and testimony of F. W. Birch, 30 August 1838, in 'Proceedings of the Calcutta Committee'. See also letter from George Dick, Colonial Secretary, to the Chief Secretary of Bengal Government, Colonial Secretary's Office, Port Louis, dated 18 August 1838; letter from Aubin Real, B. Finck, Andxes Assudo, J. Toris, Antoine and Niace, Fort William, 3 October 1838, no. 7A and 7B, General Department Proceedings, WBSA.

75. 'Report of the Calcutta Committee', p. 9.

76. Ibid., p. 6.

77. Testimony of Rev. Garstin, 29 October 1838, in 'Proceedings of the Calcutta Committee'.

78. Testimony of F. W. Birch, 23 August 1838, in 'Proceedings of the Calcutta Committee'.

79. Testimony of W. F. Dowson, 13 December 1838, in 'Proceedings of the Calcutta Committee'.

80. Letter from John Finniss, Chief Commissary of Police, to Captain Birch, Superintendent of Police, Port Louis, dated 23 May 1838, Appendix no. 16, 26 January 1838, no. 783, in 'Report of the Calcutta Committee'.

81. See letter from Chief Magistrate of Calcutta with statements of five coolies returned from the Mauritius, dated 26 May 1841, no. 47 and 48, Home Department, Public Branch Consultations, NAI; statement from 23 returned Indian labourers in attachment/enclosure to letter from M. Patton, Chief Magistrate, to G. A. Bushby, Secretary to the Government of

Bengal, dated 23 March 1842, no. 18. Home Department, Public Branch Consultations, 6 April 1842, no. 18–19, NAI.

82. Testimony of Abdoolah Khan, 10 and 13 September 1838, in 'Proceedings of the Calcutta Committee'.

83. Testimony of Sheik Manick, 1 October 1838, in 'Proceedings of the Calcutta Committee'. He complained that this was especially true of French planters.

84. Testimony of Sheik Manick, 1 October 1838, in 'Proceedings of the Calcutta Committee'.

85. Testimony of Bibee Zuhoorun, 29 September 1838, in 'Proceedings of the Calcutta Committee'.

86. Testimony of Abdoolah Khan, 10 September 1838, in 'Proceedings of the Calcutta Committee'.

87. Testimony of Abdoolah Khan, 13 September 1838, in 'Proceedings of the Calcutta Committee'. See also Crispin Bates and Marina Carter, 'Sirdars as Intermediaries in Nineteenth-Century Indian Ocean Indentured Labour Migration', *Modern Asian Studies* 51, no. 2 (2017): 462–484, p. 467.

88. Testimony of Abdoolah Khan, 10 September 1838, in 'Proceedings of the Calcutta Committee'; examination of Boodoo Khan, Exhibit No. 11, Appendix to 'Report of the Calcutta Committee'.

89. Testimony of Sheik Manick, 1 October 1838, in 'Proceedings of the Calcutta Committee'.

90. Testimony of Bibee Zuhoorun, 20 September 1838, in 'Proceedings of the Calcutta Committee'.

91. Testimony of Sheik Manick, 1 October 1838, and testimony of Boodoo Khan, 1 October 1838, in 'Proceedings of the Calcutta Committee'.

92. Testimony of Karoo, 16 November 1838, and testimony of Suboo, 16 November 1838, in 'Proceedings of the Calcutta Committee'.

93. Testimony of Ramdeen, 27 November 1838, in 'Proceedings of the Calcutta Committee'.

94. 'Report of the Calcutta Committee', p. 5.

95. Testimony of Boodoo Khan, 1 October 1838, in 'Proceedings of the Calcutta Committee'.

96. 'Report of the Calcutta Committee', p. 5.

97. Ibid., p. 9.

98. Testimony of Bibee Zuhoorun, 20 September 1838, in 'Proceedings of the Calcutta Committee'.

99. Letter from John Gladstone to Lord Glenelg, dated 26 May 1838, GG/358, GG-MSS.

100. Ibid.

101. Testimony of Bibee Zuhoorun, 20 September 1838, in 'Proceedings of the Calcutta Committee'.

102. Ibid.

103. Ibid.

104. 'Report of the Calcutta Committee', p. 9.

105. Ibid.

106. Henrice Altink, *Representations of Slave Women in Discourses on Slavery and Abolition, 1780–1838* (New York, NY: Routledge, 2007), p. 2.

107. See Mrinalini Sinha, 'Anatomy of a Politics of the People' in *Political Imaginaries in Twentieth-Century India*, ed. Mrinalini Sinha and Manu Goswami, pp. 31–50 (London: Bloomsbury Academic, 2022); Karen A. Ray, 'Kunti, Lakshmibhai and the "Ladies": Women's Labour and the Abolition of Indentured Emigration from India', *Labour, Capital and Society* 29, nos. 1–2 (1996): 126–152. A similar rhetoric of victimhood was visible in colonial Malaya; see Arunima Datta, '"Immorality", Nationalism and the Colonial State in British Malaya: Indian "Coolie" Women's Intimate Lives as Ideological Battleground', *Women's History Review* 25, no. 4 (2016): 584–601.

108. For a parallel history of pamphlets, novels, plays and travel narratives written in the late nineteenth century to highlight the mistreatment of indentured women in Assam's tea plantations, see *Justice Murdered in India: The Papers of the Webb Case Recording the Sacrifice of a Daughter of India to the Lust of an Anglo-Indian* (Calcutta: Sadharon Brahmo Samaj Press, 1884), reprinted in Kanailal Chattopadhyay and Sris Kumar Kunda (eds.), *Dwarkanath Ganguli: Slavery in British Dominion* (Calcutta: Jijnasa, 1959); Dakshinacharan Chattopadhyay, *The Mirror of a Tea Planter, or Cha-Kar Darpan* (Calcutta: Jodunath Mandal, 1875); [Ramkumar Vidyaratna], *Udasin Satyasrabar Assam Bhraman* (The Indifferent Truth-Seeker's Travels in Assam) (Calcutta, 1879); [Ramkumar Vidyaratna], *Kuli Kahini: Sketches from Cooly Life* (published by G. C. Home) (Calcutta: Victoria Press, 1888); Jogendranath Chattopadhyay, *Cha-Coolie-r Atmakahini* (Memoirs of a Tea Labourer) (Calcutta: Bengal Medical Library, 1308 BS [1901–1902]).

109. See, for instance, letter from Chief Magistrate of Calcutta with statements of five coolies returned from the Mauritius, dated 26 May 1841, no. 48,

Home Department, Public Branch Consultations, NAI; letter from D. McFarlan, Chief Magistrate of Calcutta, to G. A. Bushby, Secretary to the Government of India, dated 20 April 1841, in *Examination of [Six] Coolies Returned from Mauritius per Gilbert Munro* (Calcutta: Bengal Military Orphan Press, 1841), IOR/V/27/820/23.

110. Testimony of James Smart, Master HC Marine, 17 October 1838, and testimony of John Dyer, 25 October 1838, in 'Proceedings of the Calcutta Committee'.

111. Letter to Chief Magistrate of Calcutta D. McFarlan, dated 19 April 1841, Home Department, Public Branch Consultations, 12 May 1841, no. 40, NAI.

112. Letter to D. McFarlan, Chief Magistrate of Calcutta, dated 1 May 1841, Home Department, Public Branch Consultations, 26 May 1841, no. 46, NAI.

113. Letters with the Chief Magistrate of Calcutta, Home Department, Public Branch Consultations, 17 March 1841, no. 47, NAI.

114. Enclosure to letter from M. Patton, Chief Magistrate, to G. A. Bushby, Secretary to the Government of Bengal, dated 23 March 1842, no. 18, Home Department, Public Branch Consultations, 6 April 1842, nos. 18–19, NAI.

115. Letter from the Chief Magistrate of Calcutta reporting the arrival of 10 Indian labourers from the Mauritius on board the *Adina*, Home Department, Public Branch Consultations, 19 May 1841, no. 25, NAI.

116. Letter from D. McFarlan, Chief Magistrate of Calcutta, to G. A. Bushby, Secretary to the Government of India, General Department, dated 4 May 1841, Home Department, Public Branch Consultations, 26 May 1841, no. 47, NAI.

117. No. 1, statement of Buddun, in attachment to letter from the Chief Magistrate of Calcutta, Home Department, Public Branch Consultations, 26 May 1841, No. 48, NAI.

118. Letter from D. McFarlan, Chief Magistrate of Calcutta, to G. A. Bushby, Secretary to the Government of India, General Department, dated 4 May 1841, Home Department, Public Branch Consultations, 26 May 1841, no. 47, NAI.

119. Letter from Saunders, May, Sarkies & Co, to G. A. Bushby, dated 2 March 1841, Calcutta, General Department, Fort William, 3 March 1841, no. 67, WBSA; list of distribution, Military Orphan Society Press, Home Department, Public Branch Consultations, 17 March 1841, no. 47, NAI.

120. Extract from the proceedings of the Hon'ble President of the Council of India in Council in the Judicial Department under date 23 December 1839, Home Department, Public Branch Consultations, 1 January 1840, no. 8, NAI.

121. Letter from H. C. Metcalfe, Magistrate, to T. Wyatt, Sessions Judge of East Burdwan, Zillah Burdwan Fauzdarry Adawlut, dated 16 September 1839, Home Department, Public Branch Consultations, 1 January 1840, no. 9, NAI.

122. Ibid.

123. Letter from W. Dampier, Superintendent of Police in the LP [Lower Provinces] to Magistrates and Joint Magistrates in the LP, dated 3 November 1843, Judicial (Criminal) Proceedings, 20 November 1843, no. 20, WBSA.

124. Ibid. A *perwannah*, or *parwana*, is an official or royal order, a letter of authority or a license.

125. James Carlile (ed.), *Journal of a Voyage with Coolie Emigrants, from Calcutta to Trinidad, by Captain and Mrs. Swinton, Late of the Ship 'Salsette'* (London: Alfred W. Bennett, 1859), p. 12.

126. Radhika Mongia, 'Impartial Regimes of Truth: Indentured Indian Labour and the Status of the Inquiry', *Cultural Studies* 18, no. 5 (2004): 749–768, p. 763 (emphasis in original).

127. See Stephen Doherty, Lisa Ford, Kirsten McKenzie, Naomi Parkinson, David Roberts, Paul Halliday, Zoë Laidlaw, Alan Lester and Philip Stern, 'Inquiring into the Corpus of Empire', *Journal of World History* 32, no. 2 (June 2021): 219–240.

4

In Defence of Indenture*

The British Empire was, in many ways, contingent on trade and commerce. British merchants helped expand the empire into newer territories, while planters consolidated imperial hold over these newly acquired territories through settlement and commodity production. They played a particularly important role in procuring, employing and legalising the indenture trade. The continuation of indentureship for about a century, and the resumption of indentured emigration in 1842 after its brief suspension in 1839, was a direct consequence of relentless pressure from merchants and planters. Any understanding of the indenture debates, then, is incomplete without a thorough discussion of merchant and planter arguments in defence of indenture. Although there has been substantive work on the West India lobby and planter arguments in the context of slavery, pro-indenture arguments have remained peripheral to the histories of Indian indenture, and indeed to the histories of the British Empire.[1] Most works on indenture debates focus on anti-indenture protest – a narrative that under-represents the voices of merchants and planters who decried prohibition and used their significant political and commercial influence to shape post-slavery labour regulations.

---

* Some of the discussion on merchant networks and John Gladstone builds upon an earlier work: '"A Matter of Doubt and Uncertainty": John Gladstone and the Post-Slavery Framework of Labour in the British Empire', *Journal of Imperial and Commonwealth History* 50, no. 1 (2022): 52–80. All rights reserved.

By situating merchant arguments in Calcutta within a global network of pro-indenture letters, petitions, publications and reports, this chapter inserts merchant and planter voices into the narrative.

Abolition had created labour crises in plantocracies that ranged from permanent decline of the sugar industry in Jamaica, to decline and slow recovery in British Guiana, to fast and successful recovery in Mauritius. With the increasing strength of anti-slavery and anti-indenture lobbies, planters and merchants not only had to prove the need for an alternative source of labour but also demonstrate that Indian labourers were the most well suited for this post-slavery regime. Anti-indenture legislation cut into merchant profits, made them suffer losses from their considerable investment into overseas plantations and turned the sugar trade into a loss-making business. However, instead of a simplistic argument focused on merchant profits, the pro-indenture argument that arose in the aftermath of Abolition was a nuanced and considered one that brought together questions of commerce, justice, rights and free labour. In contrast to a defence of personal profits, pro-indenture petitions resorted to legal, economic and philanthropic arguments. The economic argument linked the rights of merchants and planters to the prosperity of the empire, while the legal and philanthropic arguments countered two of the strongest claims of anti-indenture petitioners – that the indenture trade was a continuation of slavery and that it exploited labourers.

British Merchants and Planters

British merchants and planters were transnational individuals key to the functioning of the empire. They held trading interests in India and the Caribbean, owned plantations across the empire, headed shipping agencies, constituted organisations aimed at the rights of merchants and participated in parliamentary lobbies. As their economic, political and social standing was tied up with the sugar trade and the indentured labour system, the planters and merchants of the British Empire had a direct interest in continuing indenture trade. This section briefly discusses their connections, transnational networks and lobbying power – all of which helped them forward the pro-indenture agenda.

In an imperial system that was economically dependent on commodity production in overseas colonies, planters acted as linkages between the metropole and plantation colonies. British planters have often been described as transatlantic, liminal and absentees.[2] While their business interests sprawled across the empire, many planters in the nineteenth century operated largely from the confines of the metropole. This absenteeism led to the establishment of a large West India planter community in Britain that possessed landed estates and formed a powerful colonial lobby in London.[3] This lobby operated through island agents, members of the Society of West India Merchants, absentee planters living in Britain and members of parliament with West Indian connections and interests.[4] Lobbying was not just confined to London but included regional and provincial merchant organisations.[5]

As the abolitionist movement gained momentum in the beginning of the nineteenth century, metropolitan attitudes towards planters changed from one of ambivalence to criticism. Planters, who had since the eighteenth century been considered liminal but harmless, were now being presented as subjects who fell outside the pale of acceptable British behaviour.[6] Christer Petley relates this to the cultural and political fall of the planter class – 'a fall that was part of a late eighteenth-century reformulation of British identity, as Britons sought to redefine nation and empire in the context of revolutionary changes at home and overseas'.[7] Planters and merchants adapted to this by organising and lobbying to protect their commercial and political interests. This was partly achieved by the activities of the London Society of West India Planters and Merchants and the London West India Committee, which formed the focal point for planter political activity.[8] The former, for instance, petitioned for a tax regime favourable to planters, easy access to North American markets and military protection in the Caribbean, while the latter maintained a strong stand against Abolition and negotiated compensation for planters for 'the loss of his slave'.[9]

Colonists and planters based in the plantation colonies also promoted their interests through provincial bodies, pressure groups, petitions and memoranda. Even if physically removed from the metropole, planters based in Mauritius, for instance, had a say in the implementation of imperial policies, and their landed interests were well represented. Lobbying was complemented by cheap labour strategies such as hindering the formation of an independent black peasantry and drafting of laws to force the emancipated population to the plantation labour market.[10] This perpetuated labour-intensive production techniques instead of necessitating an overhaul of a system dependent on cheap and tractable labour.[11] Taken together, lobbying and cheap labour strategies made the introduction of indentured labourers imperative for the continuation of sugar production.

By contrast, British merchants played a crucial role in straddling the disparate parts of the empire and expanding its political and economic reaches. Established in 1600, the English East India Company spearheaded the empire's relations with the East and West Indies and brought newer territories under economic and political consolidation. As private agency houses emerged, their commercial activities ran parallel to that of the Company. These agency houses acted as agents for domestic manufacturers and merchants by working on commission, and heavily invested in enterprises in the locality of the overseas station, such as indigo plantations in eastern India.[12] Most of these men were from wealthy farming, professional or mercantile families, and their conspicuous wealth, eligibility for borrowed capital and control over local banking and insurance sectors facilitated their position as heavy fixed capital investors.

When Company servants were barred from private trade in 1788, private sector trading passed to the hands of agency houses, and their hold over trade in India became more rooted with the removal of Company monopoly on Indian trade in 1813.[13] By the 1830s, the private sector opened up further as the Company's monopoly in China trade ended in 1833 and as Europeans were granted the right to own land in India. Calcutta, as we saw in Chapter 1, became the site for several private agency houses involved in shipping, insurance, commodity trade and labour migration – businesses that profited from a continued trade in Indian indentured labourers. Coordinating with merchants based in metropolitan port-cities such as Liverpool, Bristol and London, as well as with West India planters, these agency houses came to represent merchant voices against the prohibition of indenture. For these stakeholders in Calcutta, Indian labour not only represented the solution to the post-Abolition woes of planters but also heralded the beginning of a new trade from India that traders based in the East could profit from.

In many cases, merchant houses in Calcutta were connected to plantation owners, and thus in a position to aid each other's commercial interests. Take, for instance, West India planter John Gladstone. Gladstone was a founding member of the Calcutta-based Gillanders Arbuthnot & Company, and its other founding member, F. M. Gillanders, was his wife's cousin.[14] Gladstone had in fact advanced Gillanders a loan of 5,000 pounds to set up his business in Calcutta.[15] The president of the Board of Customs in Calcutta, J. P. Larkins, was also related to Gladstone by marriage (Larkin's wife was niece to Gladstone's wife), and Gladstone frequently used this connection to keep abreast of political and commercial affairs in Calcutta.[16] As a result, voices in Calcutta resonated with merchant and planter arguments from Mauritius, West Indies and metropolitan Britain, even as it remained distinctive by focusing on issues relevant for a procurer of labour, as opposed to a recipient.

Empire of Paper

In the 'paper empire' of the English Atlantic, letters, periodicals and petitions facilitated the formation, circulation and vocalisation of the pro-indenture argument.[17] In the metropole, British planters and merchants wrote letters to publicly argue in favour of indenture and to convince lawmakers of the importance of continued indenture trade. Gladstone's communication with the Calcutta-based Gillanders Arbuthnot & Company was the initial impetus for a continued trade in Indian indentured labourers, his correspondence with parliamentarians and politicians like Lord Glenelg and John Hobhouse was key to legalising the indenture trade, and his letters with fellow merchants helped popularise indenture as an alternative to enslaved plantation labour.[18] Gladstone also used letters as official means of countering anti-indenture claims. In his letter to the Duke of Wellington in February 1838, Gladstone vehemently opposed public accusations of ill-treatment on his West Indian plantations, arguing that 'the most unjust and unfounded representations are now resorted to by those who are opposed to the West India interests, in order to inflame the public mind on this subject'.[19]

In contrast to the more personal and individual tone of letters, petitions expressed the pro-indenture argument publicly and en masse. Pro-indenture petitions were part of a long-standing English tradition of petitioning that dates back to the seventeenth century. By the eighteenth century, petitions had emerged as a standard means of communication between colonies and the imperial centre, commonly used to appeal for relief from natural disaster, to demand reduction in imperial duties or to defend the slave-labour system.[20] West India planters frequently petitioned the metropolitan government to defend planter interests and to prevent or delay Abolition, using petitions as a quasi-constitutional means of seeking redress from the colonial administration. In fact, the very production and handling of such pro-slavery petitions became an exercise in the official registration of grievances. However, in contrast to public petitions of the seventeenth century that constituted open appeals to the general public, many of these were private petitions, 'a traditional, privileged form of communication from periphery to political centre'.[21] These petitions contested the ways in which the British Atlantic was being recast through changes from slavery to abolition to emancipation and, finally, to indenture. Continuing this tradition, pro-indenture petitions came in from Liverpool, London, Glasgow, Calcutta, Mauritius and the West Indies. In the absence of physical contact with the political nerve centre of the empire, petitions became one of the very few ways in which individuals and groups from disparate parts of the British Empire could present grievances to the parliament.

Within Calcutta, merchant arguments were exemplified in a petition from companies like Henley, Dowson & Bestel in July 1838.[22] Closely following the Town Hall petition of 1838 that advocated an end to the indenture trade, this merchant petition argued that the agricultural prosperity of Mauritius depended on the supply of indentured labourers. Its prohibition would ruin the economic prospects of the colony and of those involved in the sugar trade.[23] Similar petitions also came from the plantation colonies. A petition from planters, merchants, traders and British inhabitants of Mauritius called the suspension of indenture 'unconstitutional as restrictive of the personal liberty of all British subjects to take their persons and their industry from any part of the British Dominions to another'.[24] In British Guiana, planters, merchants and clergymen signed a petition in 1839 enumerating the problems of labour shortage since emancipation in the colony.[25] Such petitions were often co-signed by colonial officials based in the plantation colonies, since a continuous and uninterrupted migration of Indian labourers was necessary to sustain the mainstay of the colonies: its sugar plantations.

Even spaces that were overwhelmingly anti-indenture were punctuated by pro-indenture voices, such as the discussions in the Town Hall meeting of 1838 and the Calcutta investigative committee of 1838–1839. In the Town Hall, A. G. Mackenzie said that the indenture trade was not as 'inhuman' as it had been made out to be. In fact, he worried that such a grave and exaggerated narrative of the trade would be 'an acknowledgement, that [people of Bengal] had permitted a slave trade to grow up and flourish under [their] eyes, until exposed to the world by Lord Brougham'.[26] Even Longueville Clarke, who mostly advocated for the end of indenture, stated that if the indenture trade was proved to not be injurious to the labourer, then 'the labourer had a right to seek employment abroad'.[27] Mr Osborne questioned the comparison drawn between the slave trade and the indenture trade, saying that 'the likeness of the two trades was not so great as had been represented'.[28] He argued that there was no proof of the alleged atrocities, stating that if there had in fact been atrocities, people in Mauritius would have questioned it themselves. He urged: 'Why should the benevolence of the whole world be concentrated around this table?'[29]

Although the Calcutta committee report overwhelmingly argued against continued indenture trade, two original members of the committee, William Dowson and J. P. Grant, rejected its findings and submitted separate minutes to voice their opinions. Both argued that the problems of the indenture system were remediable through well-implemented regulations and did not warrant its complete prohibition. Many who testified for the committee agreed, saying that indentured migrants in Mauritius were content and well treated.[30] Reverend Anthony Garstin testified that labourers were treated with great humanity and tenderness during the voyage and had access to abundant food.[31] In talking to hundreds of labourers across several Mauritian plantations, he had found no complaints of ill-treatment. In fact, he believed labourers did less laborious work than they did in India while receiving higher wages.[32] Dissensions within the committee report – a report that featured prominently in the government's decision to regulate the indenture trade – are exemplary of the pervasiveness of merchant voices in the Calcutta debates.

The Legal Argument, or the Question of Contracts

One of the foremost arguments made in defence of indenture was the legal argument. Merchants and planters emphasised that Indian indenture was based on legally binding contractual obligations and that its prohibition was contrary to the tenets of the British justice system. This was a strong rebuttal of claims that indenture was a continuation of slavery, arguing that the very presence of a contract and legal restrictions precluded the indenture trade from reverting to slavery. The indenture system, in this view, was not inherently exploitative and could be kept in check with government-mandated regulations. Alleged problems of the system, such as kidnapping, flogging, unlawful detention in depots and high rates of death and disease on voyages, were either rejected as exaggerated accusations or considered within the acceptable spectrum of problems in a functioning labour system. The legal argument also appealed to the rule of law and notions of imperial responsibility. It emphasised that once contracts were instituted under well-defined and established laws, the system could not be uprooted. In fact, stopping the indenture trade without enquiry and evidence would be prejudicial and would adversely impact British merchants and planters, whom the British government was duty-bound to protect.

The indenture contract, as we saw, was at the centre of the indenture debates. Merchants and planters used their very presence to argue for the legitimacy of the indenture trade, while those against the indenture trade pointed to fallacies within the contractual arrangement to argue for its prohibition. In the post-Abolition context, planter arguments took advantage of the denunciation of slavery and the caveat that any labour system following emancipation must by definition be free. The delineation of 'unfree' and 'free' labour in the aftermath of Abolition was based on a complete and immediate revocation of the Atlantic slave trade – a juxtaposition that pro-indenture voices made use of to defend indenture.

One of the earliest manifestations of the legal argument was in the Calcutta merchant petition of 1838, which argued that the prohibition of indenture was not only pre-judicative and against 'the principle and practice of British justice', but also 'a sure means of entailing a ruinous degree of detriment on the Mauritian Sugar Trade … [and] a Condemnation, without a hearing, of a most respectable body of merchants'.[33] The analogy drawn between slavery and indentured labour was rejected as 'forced and unjust' since indenture involved a voluntary contract.[34]

The legal argument was furthered by Dowson and Grant, who submitted separate minutes denouncing the report of the Calcutta investigative committee. In his evidence for the committee, Dowson agreed that the indenture system was far from perfect. He lamented that labourers were not informed properly that they would travel by sea or that they would be away for five years, and provided anecdotal evidence of how middlemen recruiters resorted to false claims about the indenture trade to procure labourers.[35] However, despite his reservations about the uncontrolled continuation of the indenture trade, Dowson was against its complete prohibition. For Dowson, even if allegations against the indenture trade were true, it was insufficient grounds for abolishing the system.[36] In fact, Dowson insinuated that the committee's report was partial, exaggerated and false, acting rather like 'an advocate commenting upon evidence which he desires to make appear favourable to his own side of the question'.[37] He held that there were some specific failures of the indenture trade, but this problem was not systemic. Ultimately, Dowson argued that the indenture system actually presented 'extremely little hardship to the Coolies' and that every exception to that could be corrected through legislative interference.[38] His position is unsurprising given that he had a direct stake in the continuation of the indenture trade – Dowson was a member of the merchant firm Henley, Dowson & Bestel, a signatory to the Calcutta merchant petition.

Grant also argued that abuses in the indenture system could be countered by stricter regulations. Grant saw indenture as an exercise in free labour and, ultimately, advantageous to the labourer, to India, to the colonies and to the empire at large.[39] Through a re-reading of evidence collected by the committee, Grant argued that abolition should only act as a last resort and that complete prohibition was detrimental to labourers since it restricted 'the movements of free coloured native subjects'.[40] For Grant, many of the allegations – such as abduction, deceitful recruitment and cheating labourers out of their advances – were exaggerated.[41]

The pro-indenture stance was stronger in periodicals. News reports and letters to editors often challenged the government decision to discontinue the indenture trade in 1839 and openly questioned or mocked petitioners who were against the indenture trade. In supporting the legal argument, periodicals put forth two main points: that the presence of contracts made it an open and fair system and that examples of ill-treatment and deception were exaggerated or outright false. A letter to the editor of *The Englishman* stated that lax policing and inefficient magistracy were at the core of the problems, rather than any issues inherent in the indenture system – going to the extent of alleging that the Town Hall meeting was 'a mere farce'.[42] A report quoted in the *Friend of India* argued that 'there is no kidnapping, no confinement, no thrashing, no starvation. Coolies go voluntarily, joyfully, with music and dance.'[43] The *Calcutta Courier* stated that 'it is quite a fallacy to assert that the coolies do not understand their contracts'.[44] It characterised reports of ill-treatment as embellished and 'amount[ing] to a positive *swindle* of the public mind, and a gross abuse of that confidence which the public places in the statements of the papers'.[45] In fact, the *Calcutta Courier* argued:

> No single Coolie gets a permit of embarkation without having a personal interview with the Superintendent of Police. The duffadars are kicked out, the doors of the hall of audience closed – and then from the very lips of the Superintendent himself are they told, where they are going, and upon what contract; that they are perfectly free agents, and with full liberty to go or remain.[46]

The *Calcutta Courier* was convinced that reports of kidnapping, deaths on passage and corporal punishment were exaggerated by rival newspapers: 'extended by the rapid imagination [because] it thrills the blood, and fires the brain'.[47]

The constant communication between merchants and planters in the empire resulted in a transnational pro-indenture argument. Petitions and reports from Calcutta thus need to be studied in relation to voices from plantation colonies like Mauritius. Mauritius was one of the earliest plantation colonies to employ indentured labourers in the production of sugar, with Indian labourers migrating there since 1834. It also boasted a large population of Indian emigrants; an emigration report from 1883 stated that of its total resident population of 369,000, 218,000 (59 per cent) were 'of Indian extraction'.[48] Most French proprietors in Mauritius, unlike their West Indian counterparts, resided in Mauritius, and many maintained an active presence in inspecting and supervising the work in their estates.[49] The strategic position of Mauritius, its commercial significance as a major sugar supplier to the British market and the continued investment of British capitalists in the Mauritian sugar estates created a close association between Mauritian and metropolitan capital.[50] Being answerable to British creditors in the capital, the planters and plantation owners faced immense pressure to increase economies of the estate.[51] Unsurprisingly, then, planters in Mauritius also followed a similar line of argument.

When the Mauritius investigative committee was established to report on Indian labourers in plantation estates, it was immediately followed by a planter petition from Flacq district that criticised the aims and mode of the investigation. The Flacq petition emphasised the 'gentleness and humanity' with which Indian labourers were treated on plantations and asserted that although it was important to enquire into plantation conditions, this particular investigation did not present an accurate account of the state of affairs.[52] Notably, it referred to plantation owners as master (*maître*), reflecting a hierarchical relationship reminiscent of the erstwhile slave–master relations. The Flacq petition questioned the very methodology of enquiry – that of travelling to each plantation estate in each district to ask questions of planters and labourers about their experience of the indenture trade. The petition explained that questioning the indentured Indians en masse would create inaccuracies in the inquiry since some of the labourers were undisciplined and could persuade others to lie. As evidence, it stated that labourers had on several occasions left the plantation to complain on the most frivolous pretexts. But when separated from the group and questioned individually, they declared that they were well treated and had no complaint, but had been influenced (often threatened) to complain by some of their fellow labourers.[53] Consequently, the petitioners recommended that interviews with labourers be translated to a language that the plantation owner understood, so that the latter could justify himself against falsehood and even seek counter-investigation if required.[54] There was a distinct concern that Indian labourers could take advantage of the investigation to spread slander about planters. Ultimately, the petition made clear that the inquiry ought to focus on correct implementation of each article of contract – the upholding of legal tenets – rather than on the experience of indentured Indians. This refocusing of the authorities' attention from the labourers' experience during recruitment, passage and plantation to the upholding of legal contracts was an important feature of the pro-indenture argument.

A separate petition from Mauritius argued that indentured Indians had to go through several checks and procedures before reaching the plantation colony.[55] They signed written bilingual contracts to engage in service, had the contract explained to them by appointed officials of the state, deposited their contracts with police magistrates at the destination colony (such as Mauritius) and were finally inspected by a government medical officer before being transferred to their respective plantation estates.[56] For the petitioners, these regulatory steps sufficiently shielded the indentured labourer from mistreatment or deception.

Planters in Mauritius had an undeniable influence on colonial strategy. Members of the Mauritius investigative committee soon complained to Colonial Secretary G. F. Dick that planters who signed the petition had made it impossible to conduct the investigation 'in the mode proposed ... viz. that of examining each Indian separately and recording each deposition'.[57] In fact, the planters were so persuasive as to make the Colonial Secretary cease the enquiries of the committee.[58] In January 1840, six planters from Mauritius submitted a plan for the establishment of an emigration committee to oversee the introduction of labourers, monitor their conditions in the colony and uphold regulations to prevent their exploitation at the hands of planters and overseers.[59] This shifted the responsibility of ensuring the well-being of the indentured migrants from the colonial government to the employers. Instead of the metropolitan government, this system would make individual planters responsible for the hospitable treatment of labourers and liable to pay penalties for deviating from existing laws. A similar plan was proposed by the Mauritius Free Labor Association, which wanted planters to be at the forefront of recruitment and appoint officials of their own to uphold emigration regulations.[60] The proactive role of planters in suggesting schemes for continued emigration was testament to their pervasive presence and influence in the colony. More importantly, accepting stricter regulations was a strategic compromise to avoid complete prohibition.

Ultimately, this appeal to the rule of law and contractual obligation was the premise on which the legal argument was based. At its core, the legal argument emanating from Calcutta and the plantation colonies emphasised that complete prohibition of the indenture trade was not only opposed to the principles of the British legal system but also an exaggerated response to allegations of ill-treatment. This moved the focus of the indenture debates from the binary of prohibition and continuation to the compromise that problems within the trade should be corrected and regulated. In official eyes, the consent of the indentured labourer was important, but if this consent was obtained in the form of a contract, there remained no objections to the indenture trade. As a letter between parliamentarians and planters from 1841 stated,

> the consent of coolies is indispensably necessary to the validity of the transfer of their services. Yet if that consent was fully and fairly given, we do not see anything illegal in the transaction ... coolies cannot complain of a breach of contract if with a full knowledge of the facts they agree to serve.[61]

The Economic Argument, or the Position of Planters

Such a refocusing of the indenture debates to suit the needs of the post-Abolition environment was also evident in the economic argument. Instead of focusing on how the prohibition of indenture would mean commercial ruin for individual planters and merchants, the economic argument highlighted the plight of the plantation colonies as a whole. Plantation colonies were considered special due to their undue dependence on commodity production. The economic argument thus emphasised the centrality of indenture migration to plantation economies and the centrality of plantations, in turn, to the British economy. Carefully constructed to focus more on the collective than the individual, it posited that the imperial economy and the personal and collective prosperity of merchants and planters were dependent on continued indenture trade and continuous commodity production.

The need-for-labour argument had been used since the turn of the century to argue that if alternative labour forces were not recruited immediately after Abolition, it would lead to the financial ruin of all British plantation colonies. This argument was initially made to counter anti-slavery voices in the parliament, to argue against Abolition and emancipation and to argue in favour of financial compensation for planters for the loss of enslaved labour. After Abolition, the need-for-labour argument became part of the pro-indenture argument, employed to point to the urgent need for alternative labour forces in plantation colonies. In his letter to Liverpool merchant Andrew Colville, for instance, John Gladstone urged that 'if a supply of labourers for [Jamaica and Demerara], who can be bound to serve the Planters for a reasonable number of years cannot be procured from some quarter or other and in considerable numbers, the ruin of both colonies cannot be averted for many years'.[62] Evidently, the planter's loss was also the colony's loss.

One of the earliest to forward this argument, the Calcutta merchant petition of 1838 rejected the Town Hall petition as unfounded on evidence, hostile to merchants and ultimately detrimental to the Mauritian sugar trade and economy.[63] For the merchants of Calcutta, prohibition measures relegated their interests to the background, condemned them financially and questioned their motivations and respectability. The petition sought to draw a direct correlation between the suspension of indentured emigration, the commercial prospects of planters and the 'slur' on the body of merchants, which was taken as a personal affront. It further implied that the suspension would be 'discreditable to the British mercantile character, and opposed to the feelings of true philanthropy'.[64] The petitioners condemned the comparison to slavery, urging: 'Coolie-laborers in the Mauritius, ... are not Slave-laborers, in either the essence or letter of the terms, and [their] just rights are as honestly and vigilantly attended to by Her Majesty's Mauritius Government, as the rights of any native subjects can possibly be by the Government of India.'[65] The petitioners' argument for continued migration operated on three levels: that the cases of maltreatment and deceptive recruiting practices were unproven; that even if they were provable, public opinion was pre-emptively biased against the planters; and that even if the alleged abuses existed, they were remediable and hence not sufficient grounds for suspension of the entire labour system.[66]

More specifically on the economic question, the merchant petition emphasised that those connected with the trade or with Mauritius had made large purchases of land, invested in the trade and diverted capital into Mauritian agriculture – all of which would be detrimentally affected by 'a hasty and arbitrary suspension of the Coolie-labor trade'.[67] Prohibition, it argued, was a disproportionate response to allegations and would necessarily lead to 'a national injury done by destroying its commercial status as a Sugar-producing Island, and that, too, upon the most vague surmises that an evil exists'.[68] Similar arguments emerged in a letter to the editor of the *Calcutta Courier* in July 1838. Accusing journalists of slandering those involved in the indenture trade by accusing them of ill-treatment and forced labour, this letter considered it the duty of a good citizen to correct these assumptions.[69] The letter maintained that suspending the indenture trade would not only deprive the labourers of their freedom by confining them to a state of 'almost serfdom' with little opportunity of employment but also 'annihilate' the colonies.[70]

Similar sentiments were mirrored in the 1839 petition from Mauritian planters, merchants and traders.[71] Although the petition did not mention the names of the undersigned, except that there were 100 signatories, the letter accepting receipt of the petition was addressed to Messrs. Hunter, Arbuthnot & Company, possibly the main merchant house behind the petition. Submitted in May 1839, this protested against the Order in Council of September 1838, which had invalidated any future contracts made outside Mauritius, and those made for a period longer than 12 months. Effectively, this Order in Council stated that Mauritian planters could only employ labourers already on the island, that too for just a year. The petitioners urged that sugar cultivation was the mainstay of the Mauritian economy: 'the staple produce of the colony, and the only article of commerce which is the growth of the soil, so that the fortune of every single individual depends entirely on the success and extent of its culture'.[72] Using hyperbole about the centrality of sugar cultivation in the Mauritian economy, it pointed out that Mauritius produced a considerable amount of sugar with the help of significant investments from British planters. This included 'considerable purchases of land, machinery, cattle, and agricultural implements' and the erection of buildings and infrastructure.[73] Annual average production, it implored, increased from 16,000 tonnes before 1829 to 34,000 tonnes during the 10 years following that, pointing to a direct correlation between agricultural profits and indentured immigration.[74]

Similarly, 773 'Clergy, Planters, Merchants, and other Inhabitants' of British Guiana signed a petition in December 1839 to ask for loans to 'recuperate from a debilitating labor shortage precipitated by emancipation'.[75] The Guiana petition urged that to maintain economic security and prosperity, the British government ought to help West Indian sugar estate proprietors out of the difficulties caused by Abolition. The loan was essential since the colony did not have the resources needed for a sufficiently extensive immigration scheme to enable it to recover from the blows delivered by emancipation. This petition created a direct link between economic and 'moral' ruin by highlighting that prohibiting emigration would affect cropping and idleness on the part of the labourers would increase crime rates.[76] It warned that if no loans were forwarded, the capital used in buildings and machinery would be lost and the labourers would 'speedily degenerate into a state of barbarism'.[77]

The sentiment espoused in these petitions was not confined to the planter class but echoed a popular opinion among government officials in plantation colonies. Governor William Nicolay of Mauritius expressed support for the petitioners when forwarding the planter petition to Lord Glenelg and asked for the speedy removal of the prohibition.[78] Nicolay did not deny the presence of 'nefarious practices' around the employment of labourers but was confident that strong laws and regulations would be able to contain such practices.[79] He emphasised that the proximity of Mauritius to the Indian subcontinent and constant communication between the two countries were particularly conducive for Indian authorities to keep an eye on the true condition of emigrants in the colony.

In May 1841, two Calcutta-based agency houses named Colville, Gilmore & Company and Saunders, May, Sarkies & Company petitioned for the emigration of labourers from Calcutta to Mauritius, even though the indenture trade had been suspended in 1839. What started off as a petition for a small number of labourers seeking passage to Mauritius became one emphasising the indispensability of indentured labourers in the Mauritian economy.[80] Pointing to the losses that Mauritian plantations would suffer if indentured immigration were to discontinue, the letter stated: '[M]uch of the crop that is now upon the ground must otherwise [perish] and serious loss to individuals and injury to the Island be the result, besides increasing the difficulties, which are at present felt in England from the high prices of sugar caused by the short crops from the West India Colonies....'[81] Given the urgency of labourers needed to cut the crops in June and July, they made a case for immediate arrangements for immigration, promising to 'give any security for the good treatment of the people, and the faithful payment of the wages that may be stipulated for'.[82] Due to the large capital investments tied to the crop and its distribution, the petitioners were concerned that metropolitan investors such as the London-based Reid & Company would suffer from the prohibition of indenture. Although their petition was rejected by the Governor General in Council by citing the prohibitory Act XIV of 1839, the statement forwarded by the agency houses reflected a continuation of arguments in defence of indenture.[83]

Ultimately, then, the economic argument was hinged upon three pillars of reasoning. First, since the indenture trade was connected to the sugar trade, colonial economy and plantation economy, its prohibition would not only be disastrous for individual planters but also have a ruinous knock-on effect on these wider networks. Second, prohibition or de-legalisation of indenture was an *a priori* accusation of planters and British authorities in plantation colonies and would disproportionately affect them. A letter to the editor of *The Englishman* argued that prohibition of indenture not only accused colonial officials in plantations of being inefficient but was equivalent to a declaration 'that British laws are deficient, magistrates unmindful, officers powerless, [and] governments incapable or unwilling, to protect the Indian labourers'.[84] Finally, planters and merchants saw the use of enslaved labour, apprentices and Indian indentured labour in their plantations as rights to be protected by the state. Even though five years earlier the conversation was focused on loss and compensation for merchants, it was no longer enough to home in only on merchant woes. Thus, while the focus on merchant profits and economic ruin is unsurprising, it is the way in which the collective was emphasised over the individual that betrays the post-slavery priorities of these pro-indenture petitions.

The Philanthropic or 'Free Labour' Argument

There are parallels between pro-slavery and pro-indenture petitions, as both appealed to planter interests, argued in favour of the sanctity of the plantation economy and referred to the economic effects of changes in sugar production. However, even as the pro-slavery focus on merchant rights, merchant profits and economic health of the British Empire was mirrored in pro-indenture petitions, there had been a fundamental shift in how merchant and planter rights were framed. The early nineteenth century had seen a steady shift in planter petitions – from endorsement of the slave trade to amelioration (gradual reform schemes rather than complete abolition of slavery) to the negotiation of financial compensation for the loss of enslaved labourers. All three, even in the face of anti-slavery protests, imparted a sense that planters were rightfully entitled to the use of enslaved labour in plantations; and if government regulations prohibited that use, planters were entitled to compensation. By the late 1830s, however, this conversation had shifted permanently. The post-Abolition atmosphere had necessitated a change in tactics, where petitions for policy changes required a shift of focus from individual to collective profits and necessitated consideration of the labourers' benefits within the scheme. Thus, the legal and economic arguments came to be conflated with, and often strategically superseded by, the argument that continued indentured emigration benefitted both the planter and the labourer. Within the space of 30 years, the plantation labourer had gone from being enslaved to being emancipated workers to being rights-bearing indentured labourers.

Pro-indenture petitions emphasised that migrant labourers of the British Empire had a right to sell their labour to the highest bidder and choose their employment. By this logic, the prohibition of indenture impinged on the labourers' right of movement and kept them from accepting employment with better payment and working conditions. This argument was strategically deployed as a direct rebuttal of the anti-indenture rhetoric brewing in the colonies and the metropole. In a letter from Mauritius, planters advocated the indenture scheme as beneficial to labourers as well as to British India since it rid India of her 'superabundant population' and provided India with a future supply of workers who had gone abroad and acquired new skills and knowledge in cultivation:

> [T]heir emigration here is unquestionably advantageous to themselves, by their procuring higher wages, in a climate more healthy than their own, and by their removal from a country where, under the Hindu and Mahommedan law, some degree of qualified slavery is still supposed to exist, to an island from whence its last vestige had for ever disappeared.[85]

Focused on how continued indentured emigration was creating a skilled agricultural workforce and guaranteeing employment, higher wages and freer working conditions for labourers, this statement perfectly encapsulated the philanthropic argument. It turned the slavery argument on its head by arguing that unlike British India, where slavery was still not legally abolished, the plantation colonies represented free spaces where the migrant labourers were free from slave-like conditions. The irony of this statement from erstwhile slave owners demonstrates how the planters presumed to speak on behalf of the labourers while distancing themselves from plantation slavery in their own estates. The passage of the parliamentary act to abolish slavery had led to a dangerous stance that had absolved the planter of all responsibility for atrocities committed under the enslaved labour regime.

With the legal abolition of slavery in the British Empire in 1833, and especially in the context of debates on servitude that immediately preceded it, the juxtaposition of 'freedom' and 'unfreedom' had become central to nineteenth-century discourses on labour. As Madhavi Kale points out, indentured labour was successful in 'enabling that crucial dichotomization of slavery and freedom, even as substantially less than "free" labor and social conditions not only persisted but indeed proliferated under the aegis of empire and its (coercive) civilizing mission'.[86] In the aftermath of the anti-slavery movement, it was important for any unfree labour system, or any systematic movement of labourers, to comply with the legal, economic and ethical principles of post-slavery society. This was complemented by the argument that indenture migration not only provided a viable and lucrative employment option but actually saved migrants from the unfortunate socio-economic conditions in their respective villages. Such arguments grew largely out of counterarguments to the prohibition of indentured labour. For instance, the argument that prohibition of indenture bound labourers within the confines of their immediate surroundings was a direct response to the anti-indenture argument that accused the indenture trade of curbing the labourer's freedom. Freedom of labourers – whether the freedom of transcending geographical and sociocultural boundaries or their freedom against exploitation – was a theme common to both those defending and criticising indenture. Alongside legal and economic arguments, improving the conditions of migrant workers formed a central pillar on which planter and merchant arguments rested. This line of argument was evident in petitions from both Calcutta and Mauritius.

The Calcutta merchant petition (1838) stated that far from being a continuation of slavery, the indenture trade represented a 'free labour market' characterised by voluntary emigration.[87] For the petitioners, Mauritian estates not only provided superior wages and better conditions of work than India but also boasted of a wider market for labour.[88] In fact, they argued that the conditions of employment and migration were better than those enjoyed by other labourers across the world:

> a most liberal rate of money payment, an abundant supply of wholesome food, a degree of daily labour far within the physical powers of any race of men, kind personal treatment, and a free passage back to their own country when their time of service has expired.[89]

Emigration was also supposed to bring affluence to the labourers' homes and morally uplift them by 'expand[ing] their minds beyond the narrow circle of their various local prejudices'.[90] The petitioners argued that on general grounds of good policy, indenture was 'not only defensible but worthy of commendation'.[91] In some cases, economic and other arguments were strategically relegated to the background by arguing that, ultimately, it was 'a question involving the rights of British subjects ... to carry their manual labour to the most productive market'.[92] The act of prohibition was feared to set a most dangerous precedent of curbing constitutional liberty. This turned the anti-indenture argument on its head by implying that rather than ensuring the freedom of labourers from exploitation, the abolitionary measure in fact *curbed* their rights of employment and movement.

To prove its confidence in the positive effects of indenture, the Calcutta merchant petition stated that if the allegations of trafficking were substantiated, the merchant community would support any revised regulations because contrary to popular belief, false recruitment negatively affected the commercial interests of merchants. Employing labourers by unscrupulous means, it maintained, would render the labourers 'unwilling' and cause them to spread reports that would make it even more difficult to procure labourers.[93] Crucially, this eliminated the premise for a key point of criticism from the anti-indenture lobby – that planters would allow the indenture trade to continue in spite of allegations of mistreatment and deception. Such assertions not only assuaged them of the guilt of false recruitment and mistreatment but also asserted that deceptive practices were commercially unviable.

The philanthropic argument also appeared in the proceedings of the Calcutta investigative committee. In his minute, Dowson defended indentured emigration as a voluntary act.[94] In fact, he considered that the argument for prohibition was 'a principle destructive of the liberty of the subject ... a species of tyranny not for a moment to be endured, as it would destroy the political free agency of the subject'.[95] Dowson was convinced that prohibiting the indenture trade will prevent labourers from seeking the most profitable market and limit them to 'a country where their labour barely suffices ... to subsist them in the most wretched manner, and where they are subject to almost annual visitations of famine and disease'.[96] He pointed out that some degree of misrepresentation and deception existed in all recruitment, whether of military men, sailors or workers. Thus, it was not fair to consider it an exclusive and abhorrent feature of the indenture trade.[97]

J. P. Grant's report mirrored that of Dowson. Speaking of the unjust effect it had on the labourers' agency, Grant stated that even though the prohibitory act of May 1839 had been passed to counteract abuses in the indenture system, it ended up prohibiting *all* spontaneous emigration:

> [T]his law prohibits all the labouring population of this immense portion of the empire, including skilled labourers or artisans, as well as unskilled labourers, from going of their own accord, as free intelligent workmen, unfettered by any contract, from hence, where their labour may be unable to feed them, to other portions of the empire where their labour may be invaluable.[98]

Grant's main objection to the prohibitory regulations was the effect it might have on labour migrations other than indenture. Calling the 1839 prohibition unwarranted, impolitic and unjust, Grant feared that it would set a legal precedent for all forms of migratory labour and would curtail future labourers from exercising their rights. For Grant, this was a question of

> whether the whole of the labouring population of the vast portion of Her Majesty's territories entrusted to the government of the East India Company ought, or ought not, to be as free as the rest of Her Majesty's subjects in respect to the disposal of their labour, and their right of going about.[99]

Grant not only equated prohibition to severe curtailment of rights but also celebrated continued indenture trade as a triumph of humanitarian values, where the Indian labourer could enjoy the same legal rights as a British citizen to travel and sell his labour. This, then, was a question of equal treatment.

Pro-indenture periodicals celebrated indenture migration as a philanthropic endeavour. A letter published in the *Calcutta Courier* summed this up:

[I]f the cooley is pleased with his conditions and the employer is content with his servant, and that each is shielded by the law from the power of being injured by the other, why should the eager desire of the labourer's friend seek to deprive him of benefitting by his voluntary exile.[100]

The *Courier de Pondicherry*, whose reports were re-published in Calcutta's periodicals, applauded indenture as 'the finishing stroke of the grand and philanthropic measure ... for the emancipation of the slaves'.[101] It argued that labourers migrated voluntarily and enjoyed 'a degree of happiness which they have never tasted before', away from the 'state of degradation and slavery' that they experienced in India.[102] Similarly, according to the *Calcutta Courier*, indentured labourers willingly renewed their contracts because they were 'fat and contented' and free from 'that servility which characterizes them' in India.[103] Writing in 1843, the *Calcutta Star* cited the wealth brought home by returning labourers as evidence of their well-being.[104] Drawing a direct correlation between migration and personal improvement, it argued that 'coolies returned from Demerara [are] morally improved'.[105]

What stood out in pro-indenture periodicals was the reversal of the similarity-to-slavery argument, urging that far from being 'a new system of slavery', the indenture trade was actually a deterrent to slavery. The *Calcutta Courier* argued that suspending the indenture trade from Bengal would warrant increased emigration from French Pondicherry, possibly even of British citizens, where there would be less surveillance and regulations to ensure the labourers' welfare. It asked: 'How much better would it be to strike at the root of the evil here [in India]; ... by exploding the Duffadar system, and leaving the Coolie a free agent.'[106] Playing to the anti-slavery sentiments of the public, this suggested that since slavery was not yet abolished in the French Empire, it would be irresponsible of the British government to let emigration happen from French Indian ports instead of British Indian territories. In a later report, the *Calcutta Star* accused that if the indenture trade from Bengal were to stop because of pressure from the anti-indenture lobby, Britain would have to depend on the import of sugar from territories outside its empire, such as Brazil and Cuba, 'where slavery [was] still present'.[107] Thus, the indenture trade was hailed not only as the solution to the post-Abolition labour shortage but also as the means of achieving global abolition. Championing the indenture trade as the means to abolish rather than to perpetuate slavery was a clever strategic inversion that utilised post-emancipation sentiments to strengthen merchant role in policymaking.

In 1837–1838, the British Empire saw an empire-wide shift from bonded 'unfree' labour systems to nominally 'free' labour regimes.[108] The emergent concept of free labour that developed through negotiations across the empire could be moulded to suit the needs of planters and merchants. The notion of 'free labour' or 'free migration' – terms used interchangeably in merchant and planter petitions – conceptually mirrored the free trade argument in terms of being profit-driven and in advocating opportunities for labourers to sell their labour to the most profitable market. Periodicals referred, for instance, to the 'fair and open hire of labourers' and 'good market[s] for coolee labor'.[109] However, unlike free trade arguments, it advocated government intervention. At least on paper, the rights of labourers – whether 'free' or 'unfree' – emerged as a central point of concern for metropolitan lawmakers. The strategic conflation of economic and philanthropic arguments drew more attention to the labourers' freedom of movement and employment in accordance with the priorities of post-slavery empire. The Court of Directors in London declared that in conversations about lifting the ban on emigration after 1839, the 'primary consideration [was] ... to promote the advantage of certain classes of the people of India, by allowing them free command of their labour'.[110] The philanthropic tinge to the pro-indenture voices and their focus on the open and free migration of indentured Indians ensured their increased reception in post-slavery emigration decisions of the empire.

Lobbying for Indenture

The pro-indenture argument has been missing in works on Indian indenture, barring some mention in Kale's *Fragments of Empire*, which sees pro-indenture petitions as 'the idiom in which sugar entrepreneurs negotiated concessions ... from free trade reformers and imperialists'.[111] As planter petitions found their way to lobbyists, policymakers and legislators, labour shortage came to be accepted as an imminent threat to the colonial sugar industry. Thus, the baseline information for post-emancipation society, which informed metropolitan decisions around the establishment of alternative labour systems such as indentureship, was created and shaped by planter visions. While the shortage-of-labour argument remained an important part of pro-indenture petitions, it was not the only, or even the most forceful, argument made in defence of indenture. Instead of a straightforward argument that equated post-Abolition labour shortage with loss of profits for merchants and planters, the nuanced and complex arguments discussed here brought together issues of wider interest. Taken together, the legal, economic and philanthropic arguments became the cornerstone of the pro-indenture lobby. They appealed to the need to uphold the British justice system, offered a wilful conflation of the commercial interests of the merchant, the planter and the empire, and presented the indenture trade as the means to uplift the Indian labouring class both financially and morally.

As Abolition created the dichotomy of acceptable and unacceptable labour systems, it also created the space for planters to respond to accusations of mistreatment and flouting of labour laws – heralding a new era of debates on migrant labour. By shifting focus away from mercantile profit onto the need to uphold the rule of law, protect the British economy and offer choices to migrant labourers, pro-indenture petitions appealed to the legal and moral requirements of this post-slavery empire. Distinct from pro-slavery arguments that urged for the upholding of merchants' rights to profits, pro-indenture petitions implied that continued indenture trade would positively affect all subjects of the empire – planters and labourers alike.

The indenture debates constituted a constant tussle between petitioners who favoured prohibition and merchants and planters whose commercial well-being depended on continued sugar trade and an assured influx of labourers into the plantation colonies of the British Empire. The positive reception of pro-indenture petitions in the metropolitan government, and the continuation of indenture migration for nearly a century in the face of constant scrutiny and calls for abolition, attests to the impact of merchant and planter voices in defence of indenture. As Chapter 6 will show, merchant apprehensions about emigration from French-owned ports were shared by anti-indenture petitioners from Calcutta, even as they were used to criticise indenture rather than advocate for its continuation. In a unique way, then, Calcutta saw the brewing of both pro- and anti-indenture voices – voices that shaped trade, regulations, migration networks and lives globally.

Notes

1. Although initially neglected among historians of slavery and Abolition, the pro-slavery movement has been widely discussed in recent historiography. See Srividhya Swaminathan, 'Developing the West Indian Proslavery Position after the Somerset Decision', *Slavery and Abolition* 24, no. 3 (2003):

40–60; David Lambert, 'The Counter-Revolutionary Atlantic: White West Indian Petitions and Proslavery Networks', *Social and Cultural Geography* 6, no. 3 (2005): 405–420; Christer Petley, '"Devoted Islands" and "That Madman Wilberforce": British Proslavery Patriotism during the Age of Abolition', *Journal of Imperial and Commonwealth History* 39, no. 3 (2011): 393–415; Michael Taylor, 'British Proslavery Arguments and the Bible, 1823–1833', *Slavery and Abolition* 37, no. 1 (2016): 139–158; Paula Dumas, *Proslavery Britain: Fighting for Slavery in an Era of Abolition* (New York, NY: Palgrave Macmillan, 2016).

2. Andrew Jackson O'Shaughnessy, *An Empire Divided: The American Revolution and the British Caribbean* (Philadelphia, PA: University of Pennsylvania Press, 2000). For details on West India planters, see M. D. North-Coombs, 'From Slavery to Indenture: Forced Labour in the Political Economy of Mauritius, 1834–1867', in *Indentured Labour in the British Empire, 1834–1920*, ed. Kay Saunders, pp. 78–125 (London and Canberra: Croom Helm, 1984); Lowell Joseph Ragatz, *Fall of the Planter Class in the British Caribbean, 1763–1833: A Study in Social and Economic History* (New York, NY: Century Co., 1928); Nicholas Draper, 'The Rise of a New Planter Class? Some Countercurrents from British Guiana and Trinidad, 1807–33', *Atlantic Studies* 9, no. 1 (2012): 65–83; Christer Petley, 'Gluttony, Excess, and the Fall of the Planter Class in the British Caribbean', *Atlantic Studies* 9, no. 1 (2012): 85–106; Christer Petley, 'Rethinking the Fall of the Planter Class', *Atlantic Studies* 9, no. 1 (2012): 1–17; David Beck Ryden, 'Sugar, Spirits, and Fodder: The London West India Interest and the Glut of 1807–15', *Atlantic Studies* 9, no. 1 (2012): 41–64. For a parallel history of indigo and tea planters in India, see Elizabeth Kolsky, *Colonial Justice in British India: White Violence and the Rule of Law* (Cambridge, UK: Cambridge University Press, 2010), especially chs. 4–5.

3. O'Shaughnessy, *An Empire Divided*, p. 15.

4. Ibid.

5. Draper, 'New Planter Class', p. 76.

6. Petley, 'Gluttony, Excess, and the Fall', p. 86.

7. Ibid.

8. For details, see Ryden, 'Sugar, Spirits, and Fodder'.

9. Ibid., p. 42; Extract from a Despatch from Lord Bathurst to Major-General Sir B. D'Urban (Governor of British Guiana), dated 25 February 1826, GG/2865, GG-MSS.

10. North-Coombs, 'From Slavery to Indenture', p. 85.

11. Ibid.

12. S. D. Chapman, 'The Agency Houses: British Mercantile Enterprise in the Far East c. 1780–1920', *Textile History* 19, no. 2 (1988): 239–254, p. 241. Key works on agency houses in Calcutta include Maria Misra, *Business, Race, and Politics in British India, c. 1850–1960* (Oxford: Clarendon Press, 1999); Stephanie Jones, *Merchants of the Raj: British Managing Agency Houses in Calcutta Yesterday and Today* (London: Macmillan Press, 1992); S. B. Singh, *European Agency Houses in Bengal: 1783–1833* (Calcutta: Firma KLM, 1966); Tom Tomlinson, 'The Empire of Enterprise: Scottish Business Networks in Asian Trade, 1793–1810', *KIU Journal of Economics and Business Studies* 8 (2001): 67–83; A. M. Misra, '"Business Culture" and Entrepreneurship in British India, 1860–1950', *Modern Asian Studies* 34, no. 2 (2000): 333–348.

13. B. R. Tomlinson, *The Economy of Modern India: From 1860 to the Twenty-First Century* (Cambridge, UK: Cambridge University Press, 2013), pp. 97–98.

14. Jones, *Merchants of the Raj*, pp. 5–6; Sydney George Checkland, *The Gladstones: A Family Biography, 1764–1851* (London and New York: Cambridge University Press, 1971), p. 121.

15. Sydney George Checkland, 'John Gladstone as Trader and Planter', *Economic History Review* 7, no. 2 (1954): 216–229, p. 219.

16. Checkland, *The Gladstones*, p. 122.

17. Ian Steele calls the English Atlantic 'a literate empire, a paper empire'. Ian Steele, *The English Atlantic, 1675–1740: An Exploration of Communication and Community* (New York and Oxford: Oxford University Press, 1986), p. 265.

18. For Gladstone's epistolary networks, see Purba Hossain, '"A Matter of Doubt and Uncertainty": John Gladstone and the Post-Slavery Framework of Labour in the British Empire', *Journal of Imperial and Commonwealth History* 50, no. 1 (2022): 52–80. For a parallel story of personal networks aiding plantation economy, imperial connections and the emigration of indentured labourers into Ceylon (modern-day Sri Lanka), see Stan Neal, 'Imperial Connections and Colonial Improvement: Scotland, Ceylon, and the China Coast, 1837–1841', *Journal of World History* 29, no. 2 (June 2018): 213–238.

19. Letter from John Gladstone, Andrew Colville and Henry Davidson to the Duke of Wellington, dated 28 February 1838, in 'Correspondence on the Taking of Coolies to British Guiana', GG/358, GG-MSS.

20. Lambert, 'The Counter-Revolutionary Atlantic'. For parallels with how African slaveholders used petitions to oppose abolition, see K. O. Akurang-Parry, '"A Smattering of Education" and Petitions as Sources: A Study of African Slaveholders' Responses to Abolition in the Gold Coast Colony, 1874–1875', *History in Africa* 27 (2000): 39–60.

21. Lambert, 'The Counter-Revolutionary Atlantic', p. 408.

22. 'Petition of Messers Henley, Dowson & Bestel and Others, or the Respectful Representation of the Merchants of Calcutta, Who Are Connected with the Trade of the Mauritius, in a Memorial Addressed to the President in Council of India in Council', dated 23 July 1838, Calcutta, General Department (General) Proceedings, 1 August 1838, no. 2, WBSA (henceforth 'Calcutta Merchant Petition'). See also 'Coolie Petition: The Representation of the Merchants of Calcutta, Who Are Connected with the Trade of the Mauritius, to the President of the Council of India in Council', *Calcutta Courier*, 31 July 1838.

23. 'Calcutta Merchant Petition'.

24. Quoted in *Bengal Hurkaru*, 19 July 1839.

25. Letter from Governor Light to Lord Russell, dated 22 December 1839, in *British Guiana: Copies or Extracts of Any Correspondence between the Secretary of State for the Colonies and the Governor of British Guiana, Respecting the Immigration of Labourers into that Colony* (ordered by the House of Commons to be printed, 24 March 1840), p. 39. See also enclosure to this letter, 'Petition Adopted at a Public Meeting of the Inhabitants of British Guiana', dated 21 December 1839 (henceforth, the 'Guiana Planter Petition').

26. 'Meeting for Preventing the Exportation of Coolies', *Calcutta Review* 44 (July 1838), p. 312.

27. Ibid., p. 315.

28. Ibid., p. 312.

29. Ibid.

30. See, for instance, testimony of Captain J. Rapson, 22 August 1838; testimony of Captain R. Rayne, 30 October 1838; testimony of A. P. Onslow, 11 December 1838, in 'Proceedings of the [Calcutta Investigative] Committee, from 22 August 1838 to 14 January 1839', in *Letter from Secretary to Government of India, to Committee on Exportation of Hill Coolies: Report of Committee and Evidence* (East India House, ordered by the House of Commons to be printed, 12 February 1841), Parliamentary Papers

(House of Commons) 16, no. 45 (henceforth, 'Proceedings of the Calcutta Committee').

31. Testimony of Reverend A. Garstin, 29 October 1838, in 'Proceedings of the Calcutta Committee'.

32. Ibid.

33. 'Calcutta Merchant Petition'.

34. Ibid.

35. Testimony of William Frank Dowson, 27 November 1838, in 'Proceedings of the Calcutta Committee'.

36. William Frank Dowson, 'Minute on the Report of the Committee Appointed to Enquire into the Abuses Alleged to Exist Relative to the Export of Coolies', dated 16 October 1840, in *Letter from Secretary to Government of India, to Committee on Exportation of Hill Coolies: Report of Committee and Evidence* (East India House, ordered by the House of Commons to be printed, 12 February 1841), p. 13 (henceforth 'Dowson's Minute').

37. Ibid., pp. 13, 15.

38. Ibid., p. 17.

39. 'Copy of Mr. J. P. Grant's Minute on the Abuses Alleged to Exist in the Export of Coolies', dated 1 March 1841, in *Hill Coolies: Copy of Papers Respecting the Exportation of Hill Coolies* (ordered by the House of Commons to be printed, 21 June 1841), pp. 1–42 (henceforth 'Grant's Minute').

40. Ibid., p. 4.

41. Ibid.

42. Letter to the editor, *The Englishman*, 20 July 1838, pp. 1379, 1380.

43. *Friend of India*, 26 July 1838, p. 405.

44. *Calcutta Courier*, 14 July 1838, n.p.

45. *Calcutta Courier*, 4 July 1838, n.p. (emphasis in original).

46. Ibid.

47. *Calcutta Courier*, 9 July 1838, n.p.

48. George Abraham Grierson, *Report on Colonial Emigration from the Bengal Presidency* (with diary) (Calcutta: n.p., 1883), p. 2.

49. Marina Carter, *Servants, Sirdars and Settlers: Indians in Mauritius, 1834–1874* (New Delhi and New York: Oxford University Press, 1995), p. 214.

50. North-Coombs, 'From Slavery to Indenture', pp. 88–89.

51. Carter, *Servants, Sirdars and Settlers*, p. 214.

52. 'Petition of Planters from Flacq, Mauritius', enclosure to letter from C. M. Campbell, J. Hugon, J. Villiers Forbes and W. Bury to G. F. Dick, Colonial Secretary, dated 18 February 1839, Flacq, in *Papers Regarding the Employment of Indian Indentured Labourers Overseas*, vol. 10: *Report on the Condition of the Labourers on 22 Estates in the Flacq District, Mauritius*. Board's Collections, 1840–41, vol. 1847, no. 77650, IOR/F/4/1847/77650, February–March 1839 (translations mine).

53. Ibid.

54. Ibid.

55. 'Petition of Planters, Merchants, Traders, and Other Inhabitants of Mauritius', enclosure 1 to *Correspondence Respecting the Employment of Indian Labourers in the Mauritius*, no. 62 (printed by the House of Commons, 7 February 1840) (henceforth 'Mauritius Planter Petition').

56. Ibid.

57. Letter from C. M. Campbell, J. Villiers Forbes, J. Hugon and W. Bury to G. F. Dick, Colonial Secretary, dated 18 February 1839, Flacq, in *Papers Regarding the Employment of Indian Indentured Labourers Overseas*, vol. 10: *Report on the Condition of the Labourers on 22 Estates in the Flacq District, Mauritius*, dated February 1839–March 1839. Board's Collections, 1840–41., vol. 1847, no. 77650, IOR/F/4/1847/77650.

58. Letter from G. F. Dick, Colonial Secretary to C. M. Campbell, President of the Committee of Inquiry on Indians (in Mauritius), dated 28 February 1839. 'Indian Labourers: Indian Enquiry of Flacq, Mauritius' in *Papers Regarding the Employment of Indian Indentured Labourers Overseas*, vol. 10: *Report on the Condition of the Labourers on 22 Estates in the Flacq District, Mauritius*, dated February 1839–March 1839, Board's Collections, 1840–41, vol. 1847, no. 77650, IOR/F/4/1847/77650.

59. Letter from James Edward Arbuthnot, C. Brownrigg, M. T. Rowlandson, Henry Barlow, Robert Bullen and Edward Chapman to Lieutenant-General Sir William Nicolay, dated 17 December 1839, Port Louis, Mauritius. Home Department, Public Branch Consultations, 13 May 1840, no. 16, NAI.

60. Letter from Edward Chapman, Halir Griffiths, H. Hunter and Henry Barlow to Lieutenant General Sir Lionel Smith (Governor), dated 14 January 1841, Port Louis, in *Papers Regarding the Emigration of Indian Labourers to the British Colonies*, vol. 2: *Hill Coolies: Report of the Committee, Minutes of Council*, dated 22 April 1841–12 May 1842, Board's Collections, 1840–41, vol. 1909, no. 81645, IOR/F/4/1909/81645.

61. Letter from J. Campbell and Thomas Wild to Lord Russell, dated 9 February 1841, in 'Miscellaneous Correspondence, 1806–1849', GG/2768, GG-MSS.

62. Letter from John Gladstone to Andrew Colville, dated 11 November 1839, in 'Letters from Andrew Colville (from London), 1831–49', GG/100, GG-MSS.

63. 'Calcutta Merchant Petition'.

64. Ibid.

65. Ibid.

66. Ibid.

67. Ibid.

68. Ibid.

69. 'The Cooly Question', letter to the editor, *Calcutta Courier*, 21 July 1838, n.p.

70. Ibid.

71. 'Mauritius Planter Petition'.

72. Ibid.

73. Ibid.

74. Ibid.

75. 'Guiana Planter Petition'.

76. Ibid.

77. Ibid.

78. Despatch from Sir William Nicolay to Lord Glenelg, dated 4 May 1839, *Correspondence Respecting the Employment of Indian Labourers in the Mauritius* (printed by the House of Commons, 7 February 1840). See also Despatch from Sir William Nicolay to Lord Glenelg, dated 21 May 1839, in the same document.

79. Ibid.

80. Letter from Messrs Saunders, May, Sarkies and Co. to I. R. Colvin, Private Secretary to Governor General, dated 3 May 1841, Calcutta, in *Papers Regarding the Emigration of Indian Labourers to the British Colonies*, vol. 2: *Correspondence of Two Calcutta Houses of Agency, viz. Messrs Colville, Gilmore and Co. and Messrs Saunders, May, Sarkies*, dated March 1841–May 1841, Board's Collections, 1840–41, vol. 1909, no. 81646, IOR/F/4/1909/81646.

81. Ibid.

82. Ibid.

83. Letter from G. A. Bushby, Secretary to the Government of India to Messers Saunders, May, Sarkies and Co., dated 5 May 1841, in *Papers*

Regarding the Emigration of Indian labourers to the British Colonies, vol. 2: *Correspondence of Two Calcutta Houses of Agency, viz. Messrs Colville, Gilmore and Co. and Messrs Saunders, May, Sarkies*, dated March 1841–May 1841, Board's Collections, 1840–41, vol. 1909, no. 81646, IOR/F/4/1909/81646.

84. Letter to the editor, *The Englishman*, 14 July 1838, p. 1341.

85. Extract from the Proceedings of the Honourable President of the Council of India in Council in the General Department, dated 11 July 1838, in *Correspondence Respecting the Employment of Indian Labourers in the Mauritius* (printed by the House of Commons, 7 February 1840).

86. Madhavi Kale, *Fragments of Empire: Capital, Slavery, and Indian Indentured Labor Migration in the British Caribbean* (Philadelphia, PA: University of Pennsylvania Press, 1998), p. 175.

87. 'Calcutta Merchant Petition'.

88. Ibid.

89. Ibid.

90. Ibid.

91. Ibid.

92. Ibid.

93. Ibid.

94. 'Dowson's Minute', p. 13.

95. Ibid.

96. Ibid.

97. Ibid.

98. 'Grant's Minute', pp. 3–4.

99. Ibid., p. 1.

100. Letter to the editor, *Calcutta Courier*, 19 July 1838, n.p.

101. 'The Courier de Pondicherry and the Cooly Trade', *Friend of India*, 26 July 1838, p. 405.

102. Ibid.

103. *Calcutta Courier*, 11 December 1840, n.p.

104. *Calcutta Star*, 9 October 1843, p. 1923.

105. Ibid.

106. *Calcutta Courier*, 12 July 1838, n.p. See also letter to the editor, *Calcutta Courier*, 19 July 1838, n.p.

107. *Calcutta Star*, 8 August 1844, p. 1515.

108. See Kate Boehme, Peter Mitchell and Alan Lester, 'Reforming Everywhere and All at Once: Transitioning to Free Labor across the British

Empire, 1837–1838', *Comparative Studies in Society and History* 60, no. 3 (2018): 688–718.

109. Letter to the editor, *The Englishman*, 20 July 1838, pp. 1379–1380.

110. Letter to Lord Ellenborough (Governor General of India) from the Court of Directors of the East India Company, London, dated 22 March 1842, quoted in 'Grant's Minute'.

111. Kale, *Fragments of Empire*, p. 55.

5

Race in the Making of
Indentured Labourers*

When John Gladstone wrote to Gillanders Arbuthnot & Company about procuring Indian labourers, the latter suggested labourers from eastern India as ideal for Gladstone's West Indian plantations. Speaking of their previous experience of sending Indian labourers to Mauritius, Gillanders Arbuthnot & Company wrote:

> [T]he tribe that is found to suit best in the Mauritius is from the hills to the north of Calcutta, and the men of which are all well-limbed and active, without prejudices of any kind, and hardly any ideas beyond those of supplying the wants of nature.... They are also very docile and easily managed, and appear to have no local ties, nor any objection to leave their country.[1]

Gladstone's stipulations for labourers to replace enslaved labour in his plantations were clear – they needed to be active, able-bodied, experienced in hard labour, easily manageable in a plantation context and willing to travel overseas for work. The response to his stipulations, however, betrayed an essentialised understanding of the Indian labouring class. Gillanders

---

* This chapter builds upon ideas developed in an earlier work: '"Docile, Quiet, Orderly": Indian Indenture Trade and the Ideal Labourer', in *Across Colonial Lines: Commodities, Networks, and Empire Building*, ed. Devyani Gupta and Purba Hossain, pp. 179–198 (London: Bloomsbury Publishing, 2023). All rights reserved.

Arbuthnot & Company's choice of men 'from the hills to the north of Calcutta' drew upon a combination of assumptions about docility, lack of ties to the land, physical fitness and climatic compatibility. Essentially, the labourer's purported ignorance, docility and eagerness to travel abroad were not seen as individual circumstances but as racial characters – common to the entire community and determined by race.

Such assumptions were not restricted to merchants and planters but were, in fact, a ubiquitous feature of the Calcutta public sphere. Spokesmen in Calcutta employed a similar language of racialisation when referring to indentured Indians, particularly when arguing for the need for spokesmen to intervene in the indenture trade. Debates at the Calcutta Town Hall, discussions of the Calcutta indenture committee and articles in the press played a crucial role in creating the idea that Indian indentured labourers constituted a singular, undifferentiated group. In previous chapters, we saw how post-slavery constructions of labour were centred around ideas of freedom and, in many cases, around the idea that only male migrants were appropriate plantation labourers. This chapter demonstrates how race and caste fit into this narrative. The ideal indentured labourer was not only imagined as free and male (at least in the early days of indenture) but also as docile, outside the restrictions of caste society, and racially predisposed towards hard labour. Thus, the very trope that considered indentured Indians as primitive, ignorant and undifferentiated in terms of race and religion also celebrated them as ideal labourers. This chapter explores the personal, experiential and quotidian implications of the Calcutta debates and engages closely with how notions of race, caste and primitivism punctuated the indenture debates in Calcutta.

The Interplay of Race, Caste and Indenture

Social divisions in South Asia do not always work along lines of race and are in fact often a nebulous mixture of class, caste, regional variation and other forms of difference. Historians, sociologists and anthropologists have thus deliberated for long over the South Asian equivalents of race. Peter Robb's 1995 edited collection recognised the difficulty of using race as a unit of analysis in the study of South Asia and developed the working definition of race as an 'essentialising of groups of people which held them to display inherent, heritable, persistent or predictive characteristics, and which thus had biological or quasi-biological basis'.[2] Susan Bayly argued that the works of 'scholar-officials' with Indian careers alluded to ethnological, evolutionary and racial hierarchies in South Asia and offered a hierarchical notion of civilisation.[3] She wrote:

> The most significant approach to India as an ethnographic problem in the colonial period was the theme of race, with its accompanying ... notions of evolutionary historic race conquests, its belief that civilisation was the unique achievement of ethnologically 'advanced' races, and its insistence on eternal deep-seated antipathies between so-called higher peoples and those of inferior or debased and degenerate 'blood'.[4]

The concept of race had changed dramatically in the late eighteenth century from being linguistically and environmentally defined to mid-nineteenth-century 'scientific' conceptions of race, where race was defined along evolutionary, predetermined terms.[5] In colonial India, this was further complicated by hierarchical notions of caste, prevailing understandings of taxonomy, ethnography and regionalism, and Victorian understandings of race and scientific racism.

Race is a contested term when used in the context of colonial India, but the complex interplay of racial and caste-based assumptions, the sustained language of hierarchy and difference, the focus on inheritable and biological characteristics, and the range of social interaction and classification at play in the indentured debates can only be encompassed when using the terms 'race' and 'racial division' broadly. The defining features of this complex process of categorisation, in keeping with Robb's definition, were essentialisation, hierarchisation and the idea that behavioural characteristics had a biological basis and could be inherited. In other words, cognitive and behavioural features were seen as directly related to physical and hereditary ones.

This shaped how colonial officials, merchants and spokesmen talked about migrant labourers in three crucial ways. First, the rhetoric that emerged from the indenture debates in Calcutta equated one's position in the social hierarchy with intelligence, employability, primitivism and labouring capacity. Indian 'coolies', it was argued, were the ideal post-slavery labourers because they were ignorant, docile and hard-working people with minimal (read: primitive) needs and could be easily convinced to travel overseas. Second, it created a false equivalence between climate and racial characteristics. Finally, in conjunction with official and planter attitudes towards migrant labourers, the Calcutta debates flattened social and cultural identities of migrant labourers into terms that defined the person only in relation to their utility to the indenture trade. The complex process of defining, essentialising and cementing the social identity of indentured Indians not only shaped the indenture experience but also influenced indenture regulations. This racialisation was key to recognising indentured Indians as the ideal post-slavery plantation labourer and as the antidote to the post-Abolition labour crisis. These constructions, in turn, went on to shape understandings of servitude, mobility and labour rights across the empire.

The choice of Indian labourers for colonial plantations was based on contemporaneous understandings of race and racial behaviour, as Indian and European ideas of social division came together to validate indentured Indians as the successor to the plantation regime. On the one hand, the indenture debates drew upon European ideas of race, such as assumed linkages between race and climate, or connections between race and docility.[6] On the other, it drew from Indian understandings of caste hierarchy, including caste-based restrictions on travel and supposed connections between caste and physical characteristics. Ideas of caste in fact derived not just from traditional understandings of the Indian caste system in terms of inclusion–exclusion and historical precedence around losing one's caste but also from the colonial state's understanding of caste identity as intrinsically related to physical and behavioural characteristics. As a result, indenture debates essentialised the identity of indentured Indians into one compatible with the tropical climate, outside traditional caste society and without any ties to land or country.

In the correspondence between Gladstone and Gillanders Arbuthnot & Company, for instance, attention was paid to choosing labourers who had 'no local ties'.[7] Having 'no religion' and no objection to leaving the country indicated labourers who were not restricted by traditional caste rules, thus adding to their ability to be ideal migrant labourers. For Hindu men and women of the time, crossing the seas (colloquially known as *kala pani*, or the dark waters) equalled losing their position within caste society. As the caste system imposed strict hierarchies of ritual status and firm guidelines over one's social interactions, it was believed that these guidelines could not be adequately followed outside the country. Thus, those crossing the seas were either permanently ousted from their position within caste society or had to perform penance to be allowed back.[8]

This was a key deterrent to overseas migration. As Roger Dias testified to the Calcutta investigative committee, 'natives of the north-western provinces would lose caste by a sea voyage; and … to the natives of the lower provinces a sea voyage would be more dreadful than incarceration for life'.[9] When asked about the caste backgrounds of migrants on board his ship, Captain James Rapson reported that his ships carried indentured migrants of three distinct religious backgrounds: 'Mussulmen who cooked on board, Hindoos who would not eat rice on board, and low caste Hindoos who did not object to eat rice cooked on board....'[10] Rapson was well aware of caste-based concepts of touch and impurity and the implications of eating with people not of the same caste. He kept provisions for 'parched rice, sugar and parched peas' for those who could not eat food cooked by members of other (generally lower) castes; and even when some of these men went over to the other mess that served boiled rice, Rapson would not let them: 'I said I would have no converts until these stores were finished....'[11] Since traditionally caste determined who one could dine with, and whose touch was considered 'polluting', losing one's caste often resulted in complete social ostracisation. Bibee Zuhoorun testified that in Mauritius, she often sought the help of other women on the plantation, whom she referred to as 'two black Caffre girls', to do work that she could not do without losing her caste.[12] After returning from Mauritius, she had lost her position within caste society, stating that 'even my mother will not drink water from my hand or eat with me'.[13] Although Zuhoorun's testimony specifically mentioned 'I have lost my caste', it is possible that instead of a particular caste taboo, the social ostracisation she faced was the result of leaving her homeland for a destination overseas where it was impossible to ensure that she upheld her religious obligations. As a married woman, it could also be tied to aspersions over her character after being away from her home and husband for two and a half years. As her testimony makes its way to us through translation and possible abridgement, it is impossible to determine if, as a Muslim woman, she was talking about the caste taboo on crossing the *kala pani* or a general socio-religious taboo.[14]

Moreover, caste status was seen as intricately linked to the propensity for physical labour, as labourers from upper castes were considered ineligible for plantation labour by recruiters. In an account from 1883, emigration agent H. A. Firth stated: '[O]n no account whatever must you send any more Brahmins. They also give much trouble in the Colony and are strongly objected to.'[15] Mrinalini Sinha argues that Totaram Sanadhya, who later became an important voice for the abolition of indenture, was listed in his emigration pass as a *thakur* of the Kshatriya caste rather than as a Brahmin precisely because recruiters were expressly discouraged from recruiting Brahmins.[16] In another case, an emigration agent from 1901 told his sub-agent: 'I will take the thakurs you have already recruited if they are paka labourers but don't collect any more if you can get lower castes....'[17] Emigration statistics in works like Marina Carter's *Servants, Sirdars, and Settlers*, Surendra Bhana's *Indentured Indian Emigrants to Natal* and Brij Lal's *Girmitiyas* show that although there have always been upper-caste emigrants, their proportion was significantly lower than those from lower castes.[18]

Caste-based epithets like *dhangar* were used constantly to refer to the ideal migrant. The *dhangar* was considered an appropriate and even lucrative labourer due to his perceived position outside caste society and, by implication, his freedom from caste restrictions on food and mobility. For instance, J. R. Mayo commented in a deposition in 1837 that 'in several parts of India there are people to be found who have no caste, especially the Hill Coolies of Bengal, a fine athletic race of people, who eat fresh meat or any other kind of food without scruple. They are free from the prejudices of the Hindoos and Mahometans.'[19] John Mackay stated: '[T]he Dangurs entertain no prejudices of caste [or] religion, and they are willing to turn their hands to any labour whatever....'[20] He went on to praise their simple lives: 'Their clothing is simple and scanty, and they eat only once, rarely twice, in 24 hours.'[21] Although Mackay's contention about food habits is debatable, it added to the argument for seeing *dhangars* as a cost-effective and commercially viable labour pool. A proto-ethnographic categorisation was at play here. As Mayo asserted, 'I should prefer employing the Hill Coolies of Bengal, especially as they are ... free from caste....'[22] Apparently falling outside the caste system, they could be relegated to the realm of the primitive and could easily be persuaded to cross the *kala pani* without affecting their social position. This not only implied for the colonial state a cheaper reserve of labour but also one that was more controllable and mobile.

Docility, Primitivism and Labouring Capacity

Besides caste background, docility and labouring capacity were considered key qualities for labourers who were to inherit the plantation complex across British colonies. This involved equating position in the social hierarchy with intelligence, employability, primitivism and labouring capacity. In fact, racialisation was central to the continuation of Indian indenture for 80 years precisely *because* it was intimately tied to ideas of labouring capability.

Fitness and physical capacity were at the forefront of planter demands, as they insisted upon young, healthy migrants who were free from disease. Correspondence with planters and lawmakers often centred around the physical features of migrants. In a letter to Colonial Secretary Lord Glenelg in 1839, Governor Henry Light reported: 'The Coolies on Mr. Gladstone's Property are a fine healthy Body of Men; they are beginning to marry or cohabit with the Negresses.... The magnificent Features of the Men, their well-shaped, though slender Limbs, promise well for the Mixture of the Negress with the Indian.'[23] This insistence continued well into the latter half of the century: instructions from an indenture report in 1883 required that surgeons should examine indentured emigrants and choose only those who were physically fit, 'free from contagious disease', experienced in agricultural labour and with 'horns on the palmar base of the fingers, showing that the emigrant is accustomed to hard work'.[24] As Yoshina Hurgobin has shown, the colonial state saw the worker's body as a crucial link to the regime of production processes since workers' productivity was predicated on health.[25]

The racialised idea of 'hill coolies' as strong and unintelligent helped planters imagine them as perfect for plantation work (Figure 5.1). In a letter from 1836, British merchants pointed out that 'though not physically nearly as strong as the natives of Africa, [Indian labourers] are able to bear long continued exertion as well as any people in the world'.[26] Gillanders Arbuthnot & Company's insistence on labourers from 'hills to the north of Calcutta' was also grounded on the assumption that they were 'well-limbed and active'. In fact, it was their residence in the hills – in the peripheries of civilisation, as it were – that bestowed upon them qualities appealing to planters.[27] Uday Chandra has shown that primitivism was 'an imperial ideology of rule that infantilized so-called savage or tribal peoples and subjected them to a protectionist yet developmentalist regime'.[28] It arose from encounters with landscapes that clashed with the East India Company state's vision of a civilised and ordered agrarian society, especially at 'frontier zones' such as the Chhotanagpur region.[29] This reading of primitivism facilitated, for instance, the official segregation of 'tribes' as primitive subjects of the colonial state to be identified with hills and forests. A central ideology in the administration of the Company state and in the delineation of its migrants, understandings of primitivism influenced how the migrant labourer was described in the indenture debates. In fact, Kaushik Ghosh has argued that it was colonial obsession with the primitive that led to their fetishisation as a solution to colonial demands for labour across its territories.[30]

Figure 5.1 'Indian huts on a sugar plantation, Plain William near Port Louis', c. 1853

Source: Photograph by Frederick Fiebig; photo 250/(25), British Library, https://imagesonline.bl.uk/asset/144238 (accessed in March 2024).

In the Town Hall meeting and the discussions of the Calcutta committee, Calcuttans drew a causal link between racial characteristics and potential for labour, often expressed through comparison with African labourers.[31] Captain R. Rayne testified that an able-bodied male *dhangar* was equal to an enslaved labourer for field labour, but not for work on board ship or on the wharf since 'they have not the bodily strength of the African for labour, requiring a great exertion of muscle, but they have perhaps more endurance, and can work for a longer time without fatigue'.[32] Rapson argued: 'An Indian Coolie could not do as much labour as an African', while Captain Edwards stated: '[T]here is as much a difference between an Indian Coolie and a negro apprentice as between a ship lascar and an English sailor.'[33] This comparison was not confined to elite Calcuttans but one shared by the migrants. Abdoolah Khan testified that indentured Indians whom he met in Mauritius wished that 'Caffres' were sent in their place since they were 'much stronger' and more suited to the heavy work that planters demanded.[34] Dwarkanath Tagore, in his capacity as proprietor of indigo factories that employed migrant labourers, compared these 'men from the hills' to workers from Bengal. He complained: 'The natives of Bengal are naturally an idle set of people…. Hence they are not good workmen, and the Dhangas or Hill Coolies, being much better workmen, are preferred by indigo planters, and others who employ many labourers.'[35]

Others, however, were of the opinion that physical abilities were not the only desirable attribute in an indentured labourer: 'the mild temper and cautious habits of the Hindoo, with the increased energy which the fine climate produces, renders him a much superior character to the African negro'.[36] Captain Rayne argued that the 'Calcutta Coolies were more docile and worked harder than any other labourers'.[37] The report of the Mauritius investigative committee stated as well that the 'Hill Cooley [sic]' was 'mild and inoffensive'.[38] Docility was in fact a key attribute of the quintessential indentured migrant. His docility not only made him an ideal addition to the plantation complex (as seen in Gillanders Arbuthnot & Company's insistence on 'docile and easily managed' labourers) but also made it essential for spokesmen to speak on his behalf.

This interplay of racial background and labour, particularly the assumption that certain communities were predisposed towards hard labour, has parallels in other labour systems. Jonathan Connolly has shown that race was key to explaining the perceived economic failure of the emancipation system since '"[i]ndolence" [of emancipated slaves] was linked to savagery; [and] resistance to labour discipline attributed to racial incapacity'.[39] Similar racialised rhetoric pervaded the discourse on 'coolie' migration to the Andamans, as evident in the works of Philipp Zehmisch.[40] Known as 'Ranchis', labourers were contracted from the Chhotanagpur region of India to clear forests and erect infrastructure in the Andaman Islands, and they are even today referred to as 'simple', 'hard-working' and 'submissive'.[41] Zehmisch argues that contemporary stereotypes of the Ranchi Adivasis were derived from colonial classifications that constructed 'the primitive as both exotic tribal and everyday manual labourer'.[42] Their suitability for labour was ascribed to collective racial characteristics such as docility, submissiveness and physical strength.[43] The Ranchis thus suffered the same racial stereotype of the 'hill coolie' from the Chhotanagpur region as the indentured Indians. Outside the Indian subcontinent, Stan Neal shows that the colonial desire to experiment with Chinese migrant labour in Assam, Ceylon, Hong Kong and Australia derived from ideas of a 'distinctly Chinese racial character', which was constructed in the Anglo-Chinese contact zone of Singapore.[44] Much like stereotypes about indentured Indians, stereotypes of Chinese deceitfulness, entrepreneurship and commercial-mindedness were based on the assumption of an 'unchanging racial character'.[45]

Besides implications of a docile and disciplinable reserve of labour whose position outside caste society made them ideal candidates for the post-slavery labour regime, Indian labourers were desirable for several other reasons. Their viability as good labourers was tied to their migratory nature, familiarity with the seasonal labour market and their experience in labour organisation and collective bargaining. In an account from 1838, Mackay stated: '[T]hey will travel a distance of five hundred miles in search of employment, and know the value of money, and carefully save the wages they earn in Calcutta and on the plains, and carry them back to their country to spend with their families....'[46] Indian labourers were also considered a cheap alternative. In a letter from 1835, Calcutta merchant George Arbuthnot stated that India was perfect for procuring labourers because the cost of employing Indian labourers was 'not one-half that of a slave'.[47] British merchant John Moss reiterated this sentiment, arguing that 'East Indians are the best conducted and the cheapest labourers in the world, with the fewest wants'.[48]

'More Allied to Monkeys than to Men'

The interplay of racial and caste-based assumptions had created a hierarchy of plantation labourers. Primitive labourers from the hills were considered low on the scale of intelligence but high on that of physical fitness, while upper-caste migrants were considered the inverse. As these hierarchies were consolidated and left lasting impacts on recruitment and the indenture experience, 'ignorance' emerged as another key rubric. During the East India House debate in 1842, prominent abolitionist George Thompson described indentured migrants thus:

> Look at his ignorance; he was ignorant of the character of those by whom he was first engaged; he was ignorant of the geography, and knew not the position nor the relation of the country to which he would be sent; he was ignorant of the elements and considerations which constituted a fair and equitable bargain; he was ignorant still more of the character of those by whom he was to be employed; he knew nothing of their avarice, their subtlety, their love of power, their past treatment of their

coloured slaves, and the means which they possessed … of setting aside
and rendering nugatory the most important clauses in the paper contract
which had been mutually signed in India.[49]

Broadly referring to low intelligence and lack of understanding about
where they were going and how long they would be gone, ignorance was
a coveted trait for recruiters in India. At the same time, it was precisely
this ignorance that put labourers at risk of misinformation and deception.
Asserting the ignorance of the labourers who migrated was thus a key anti-
indenture argument. Speaking at the Town Hall meeting of 1838, Bishop
Daniel Wilson urged that although he would not normally support petitions
that limit freedom of action, that principle did not apply here because the
labourers were too ignorant to know where they were going or what their
indenture contracts were about.[50] Reverend James Charles rested his entire
argument at the meeting on the contention that the labourers were capable
neither of understanding the contract nor of defending their rights in terms
of that contract.[51] According to reports in the *Calcutta Courier*, he found it
necessary to 'restrain the helpless and ignorant Coolies from entering into
engagements which they could not understand, and from binding themselves
down by contract, to the evils and privations which awaited them in the lands
of their labour'.[52]

In a statement that betrayed his belief that indentured migrants were
inferior, Reverend Charles described indentured Indians as 'more allied
to monkeys than to men; their only care consisted in eating and drinking;
these wants being satisfied, they thought of nothing else, and would never
reflect on the probable consequence of what might befall them hereafter'.[53]
This racialised and paternalistic characterisation sat well with the audience
and was applauded and repeated at several intervals. Barrister Longueville
Clarke stated later in the meeting: 'The coolie was represented, as but little
removed from the monkey, so wild, so deplorably ignorant, as to be utterly
helpless; what then would become of him in a foreign and distant land, where
his language was unknown, and his wants and habits were strange?'[54] This
rhetoric was also repeated in periodicals. The *Friend of India* wrote that the
'coolies' were 'the most simple, ignorant and degraded of the population of
Bengal' and that European planters took advantage of their 'ignorance and
simplicity, to inveigle him into a distant servitude'.[55] Other reports referred to
the indentured migrants as simple, ignorant, 'wretched', 'half civilized' and
'too abject to vindicate their own rights'.[56]

There was thus a direct correlation between the migrants' character and their need for spokesmen. Imagining the indentured labourers as ignorant, helpless, unfit and almost child-like provided space for the Calcutta elite to speak for them and make decisions on their behalf. It was also key to proving that regulations were not sufficient in controlling abuses of the trade. Reverend Charles argued that even if the police authorities who examined the labourers prior to embarkation were competent enough to explain the terms of contract, the labourers were incapable of understanding them.[57] He pointed out that it was difficult to find translators in Calcutta who spoke the language of the '*dhangurs*' and near impossible for the superintendent to explain to around 6,000 migrants the terms of the contract to their perfect comprehension.[58] Although Mr Osborne contested this by saying that not all migrants were *dhangars* from the hinterland but came from Bengal and other provinces, whose language the police officers spoke and understood, such voices were few and far between.[59] Most of the contemporaneous discussion revolved around an essentialised idea of the 'coolie' as hill men who were incapable of understanding the terms of their employment.

The second resolution of the Town Hall meeting brought this concern to the fore, stating that 'the hill coolies and other natives of India, who are induced to emigrate, do not understand, and are not capable of understanding the terms of the contract into which they are said to enter'.[60] This point was reiterated in the Calcutta committee report, which stated that indentured migrants were 'really incapable of understanding the nature of the contracts they were said to have entered into, even when an opportunity of explanation had been afforded apparently sufficient for the purpose'.[61]

Assumptions of ignorance also pervaded the interviews conducted by the Calcutta investigative committee, and there was a distinct hierarchy of labourers agreeable to all attendees of the committee without being explicitly spelled out. Deputy Superintendent of Police J. J. McCann pointed out that people engaged in Calcutta as domestic servants and mechanics were 'certainly much more intelligent than those called Coolies'.[62] Captain Alexander Mackenzie stated that from his limited interaction with the labourers, it seemed that they held 'very vague notions of the nature of their engagement' and were at times 'totally ignorant of it'.[63] This seemed to be the consensus of most respondents. Ship's captain John Dyer held that the migrants had 'no conception as to where they were going, or the length of their voyage', while Roger Dias argued that it was impossible for labourers to comprehend the terms of their engagement, since those he saw in court 'were generally illiterate and extremely ignorant'.[64] Magistrate Patton concurred, saying: 'I doubt whether the majority even understood a word of what was said at the police ... neither I, nor any man in my court, could make them understand one word....'[65]

Since labourers were seen as incapable of understanding contracts and thus not in charge of their own agency, it naturally followed that they could only have been duped into joining the trade. Reverend Thomas Boaz asserted that their close family bond made it unlikely that labourers would leave for Mauritius had they understood the nature of the contract. He testified: 'It is contrary to the habits of the people of India to leave their own country; and this is more particularly the case with the Hill Coolies.'[66] Based on his experience with labourers employed in his indigo factories, Dwarkanath Tagore concurred that they were difficult to retain in factory employment at the end of the manufacturing season.[67] He testified that the 'lower class of natives' who formed the bulk of the labour pool could easily be influenced to leave their homes and join the trade, 'but if they perfectly understood that they would be required to go [on] a voyage of a month or six weeks, it would be difficult to get their consent'.[68] They were more likely to comply if they believed that they were to be employed in European households ('for whom they have a great respect') and that they would return soon.[69] This implied that it was easy to recruit labourers through misrepresentation, and indeed they could *only* be recruited through misrepresentation. The emphasis on the ignorance of migrants was directly related to an essentialised view of the primitive and ignorant migrant from the hinterland. This was in line with the colonial state's understanding of primitivism and its push for subjugation and improvement of those it identified as primitive.

Climate and Race

The choice of Indian labourers was also predicated on the false equivalence created between climate and racial characteristics. Nineteenth-century ideas of scientific racism drew a direct link between race, climate and behaviour, often equating the climate of the tropics with docility and aversion to labour. Drawing upon this, West India planters demanded labourers from tropical climates, and especially from communities traditionally considered to be docile and controllable.

Indian labourers were seen as ideal for the warm tropical climate of plantations, which was otherwise considered a hindrance for European and Chinese labourers. As Gladstone stated in a letter to the parliamentarian John Hobhouse, experiments involving plantation labourers drawn from Germany, Madeira and Ireland were unsuccessful due to 'the influence of the climate generally producing reluctance to labour, and increasing the desire for the spirituous liquors'.[70] Gladstone argued elsewhere that 'the extreme heat and relaxing influence of the climate produce ... a disposition of indolence and an aversion to labour' for the African slave population.[71] By contrast, Indian labourers were not only used to working in the tropical climate, but were also familiar with seasonal migrations necessitated by the largely agrarian nature of pre-colonial and early colonial Indian economy. They were thus a perfect fit for the climatic and agricultural needs of the plantation complex.

What's in a Name? The 'Coolie', the 'Hill Coolie' and the 'Dhangar'

In *Along the Archival Grain*, Ann Laura Stoler argues that scholars of colonial societies need to not only read against the grain of archival sources but also question the very grains – the social categories – that these archives produce and perpetuate.[72] One such social category perpetuated in colonial records is that of the 'coolie'. This term homogenised an entire group of heterogeneous people and flattened their diverse social identities into a singular term that defined the person solely in relation to their position in and their usefulness to the indenture trade. The use of umbrella terms like 'coolie', 'hill coolie', and caste epithets such as 'dhangar' was central to the process of racialisation and, indeed, to the anti-indenture argument. Through the conflation of social categories and the imagination of all indentured Indians as part of a singular, undifferentiated social class, the indenture debates in Calcutta aided racialisation and the continuation of the trade itself. Both planters and citizen-spokesmen were guilty of perpetuating the idea that Indian indentured labourers were an undifferentiated group. In studying the term 'coolie' and similar epithets, this section thus engages with the very archival grains that Stoler asks scholars to read along.

As the indenture trade was sanctioned by the parliament and the indenture debates became more common in the early nineteenth century, it became important to denote migrants by a singular term. 'Coolie', which was originally used in British India as an umbrella term for various kinds of physical and manual labourers – whether working on roads, railways or construction sites – came to be co-opted for official purposes to mean Indian indentured migrants specifically.[73] This, however, did not entail a complete replacement of the term, as 'coolie' continued to denote non-indentured labourers. Archival records from the time mentioned 'coolies' employed by the military to perform manual labour. They constructed roads; removed jungles; carried sick *sepoys*; repaired buildings, roads, causeways and bridges; carried ammunition and medicine chests; watered horses; and were employed in the role of *bhistees* (water carriers and suppliers), sweepers, 'elephant coolies' and cooks.[74] Still, terms such as 'coolie', 'hill coolie' and 'dhangar' were used interchangeably in the Town Hall meeting, in interviews of the Calcutta committee, in newspapers and in letters between Calcutta merchants and British planters to denote hill communities from the Bengal Presidency, possibly to differentiate between indentured migrants and other Indian labourers. The absence of preliminary definitions of either term, or even a delineation of their occupational and social characteristics, was tied to unsaid stereotypes of the labouring population that were well known and acknowledged in public discourse. These assumptions can be traced to varying ideas about the local labouring population.

Primarily a caste epithet, *dhangar* refers to an untouchable caste in Bengal and a herding caste in Maharashtra. Within the indenture trade networks, however, this caste epithet was used interchangeably with 'coolie' and 'hill coolie' to denote migrant and indentured labourers. Letters from the Chief Magistrate of Calcutta frequently referred to 'Dhangur labourers', 'Dhangur coolies' and 'coolies of the Danghur caste', who had been engaged to serve in Mauritian sugar plantations from as early as 1835.[75] As Ghosh points out, the term *dhangar* 'embodied a language of primitivism', as aboriginality emerged as a new language for classifying Indians as labourers fit for plantation work.[76]

In the Town Hall meeting and the Calcutta committee, the majoritarian view was that those who migrated were overwhelmingly 'hill coolies' and *dhangars*. Abdoolah Khan, designated as 'native doctor' on board ship, testified that the migrant labour pool was a mixture of *dhangars* and others from Chhotanagpur and the Bengal Presidency.[77] W. E. Browne maintained that the majority of labourers on board his ship were 'hill coolies'.[78] Not only were the categories of 'hill coolie' and 'dhangar' essentialised and undefined, but the interviewers and interviewees seemed to also share an idea of the 'hill coolie'. Certain social, cultural, racial and ethnographic characteristics of the 'hill coolie' were mutually agreeable to both parties without further clarification. Members of the Calcutta public sphere were conversant with ideas of the caste system and the hierarchical and ethnographic assumptions that accompanied it. At the same time, having been educated in the English tradition, they were intimately aware of nineteenth-century colonial ideas of race and racial difference. Thus, the category of the ideal labourer, which included very specific and nuanced ideas of race and caste, was immediately apparent to everyone as they inherited, internalised, employed and adhered to a common framework of difference.

In fact, the racial stereotypes accompanying the term were only clarified when Gillanders Arbuthnot & Company described their choice of labourers for Gladstone's plantations.[79] The letter compared *dhangars* to monkeys and characterised them as illiterate and ignorant communities who could be easily convinced to migrate: '[The] Dhangurs, are always spoken of as more akin to the monkey than the man. They have no religion, no education, and in their present state no wants beyond eating, drinking and sleeping; and to procure ... labour.'[80] Even in more official spaces, the indentured migrant was now confidently identified as the primitive 'hill coolie'.

Statistical reports from the time, however, tell a more varied story. John Geoghegan reported in 1873 that of all emigrants from Calcutta, the majority hailed from 'lower agricultural and labouring castes of Hindus', even as he conceded that 'there [was] some mixture of all castes'.[81] Of the 323,877 migrants who sailed from the Calcutta port between 1842 and 1870, Geoghegan reported that 218,973 were Hindus, 49,860 were Muslims, 54,956 were 'Aborigines' and 88 were Christians.[82] George Abraham Grierson's 1883 investigation reported on the fallacy of assuming that only men of lower castes joined the indenture trade.[83] Even though both Indians and Europeans assured Grierson of this assumption, Grierson countered through his investigation that 'two-thirds of the Hindus recruited belong to castes of higher and medium social position. Only one-third can be considered of decidedly low social position.'[84] His analysis of emigration registers for 1883 demonstrated that of the 1,226 migrants from northern Bihar in that year, 264 were Muslims, 231 hailed from upper castes (such as Brahman, Rajput and Chhatri), 454 from castes 'of medium social position' like Teli, Baniya, Kahar, Kurmi and Gowala, and the rest from lower castes such as Chamar and Dusadh.[85] Caste background continued to be a point of contention and was reported in most ships' lists and emigration reports, although many such reports resorted to using more encompassing terms like 'Hindu' or 'malabar' when unsure of caste-names.

Such essentialisation and categorisation of Indians into groups by their supposed racial characteristics was happening before colonial ethnographic projects had taken off in South Asia. Once ethnographic works began to be published, the terms 'hill coolie' and 'dhangur/dhangar' were attributed varying characteristics. The *Asiatic Journal and Monthly Register* saw one of the only discussions on *dhangars* in the first half of the nineteenth century, stating: 'The Dhangur Kholes, who inhabit Chota Nagpur and its vicinity, are described by all who have spoken of them as a lazy, degraded, and mean-spirited race. They are utterly untinctured with Hinduism, and speak a peculiar dialect.'[86] Later works offered alternative theories about their origins. R. V. Russell argued that *dhangar* in the central provinces referred to shepherding communities.[87] William Crooke, on the other hand, considered *dhangars* 'a Dravidian tribe found in eastern district of the north-western provinces' such as Gorakhpur and Mirzapur, and Oraons as 'the typical Dhangar labourers of Chota Nagpur'.[88]

Many of these observations defined the community by physical features. George Campbell described *dhangar* labourers in Calcutta as distinguishable from 'the flat broad-nosed features of the Santals' by their 'peculiar little "pique" "retrousse" sort of nose'.[89] Other ethnographic works considered them in terms of occupation and labouring potential. *Hobson-Jobson*, a historical dictionary of Anglo-Indian terms, stated that *dhangar* was 'the name by which members of various tribes of Chutia [*sic*] Nagpur, but especially the Oraons, are generally known when they go out to distant provinces to seek employment as labourers'.[90] Edward Dalton considered *kols* and *dhangars* as aboriginal people distinct from the population in the plains, and as 'industrious and energetic'.[91] Matthew Sherring described *dhangars* as 'an industrious and active people', 'able-bodied and well-conducted', 'chiefly employed in felling the jungle'.[92] In an account from the late nineteenth century, prominent colonial ethnographer H. H. Risley related the term to *dhan*, or paddy, arguing: 'The *dhangar* system of payment is so general in Chota Nagpur that the term is virtually synonymous with labourer, and these nomadic labourers describe themselves, and are known throughout Bengal, as "Dhangars" ...'. [93]

In an article on missionaries in Bengal, Sangeeta Dasgupta talks of German missionaries who wrote about 'kols' and 'dhangurs' serving in colonial Calcutta as menial workers.[94] They were employed to sweep streets, clean canals and perform other public works (Figure 5.2). Contemporary

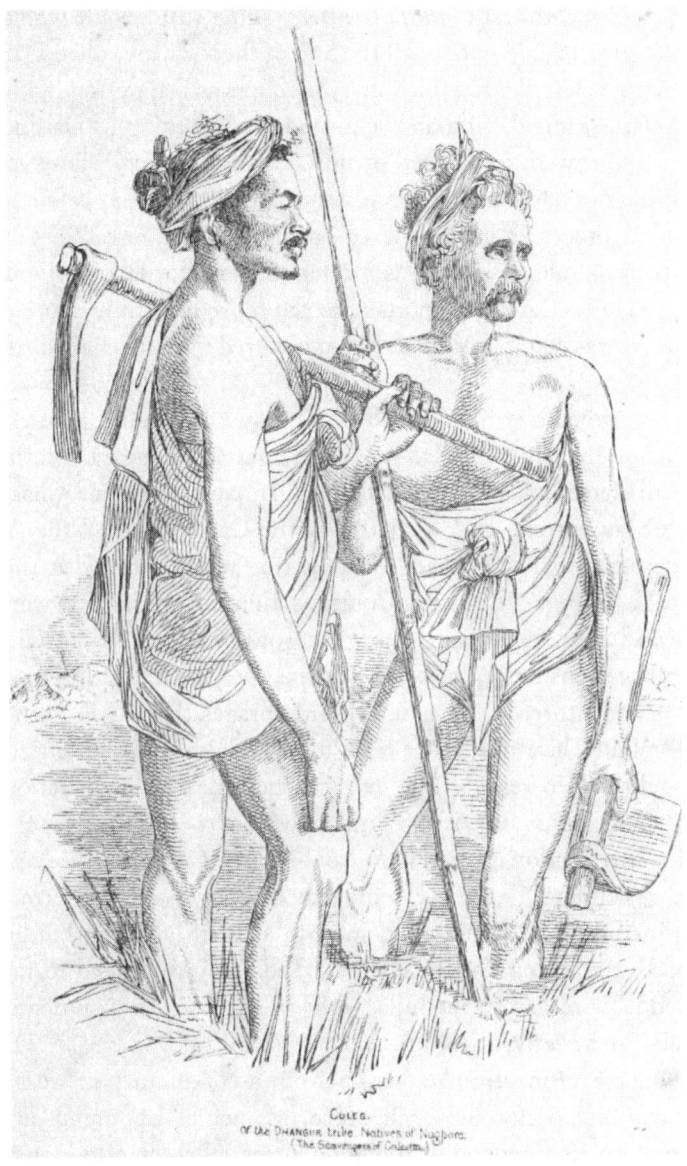

Figure 5.2 'Coles of the Dhangur tribe; natives of Nagpore (the Scavengers of Calcutta)'

Source: 'Coles of the Dhangur Tribe; Natives of Nagpore (the Scavengers of Calcutta)', in *A Series of Miscellaneous Rough Sketches of Oriental Heads* (Calcutta: Colesworthey Grant, 1844), p. 81, Wikimedia Commons, https://commons.wikimedia.org/wiki/File:ORIENTAL_HEADS_ p081_Coles_of_The_Dhangur_tribe._Natives_of_Nagpore,_(The_Scavengers_of_Calcutta).jpg (accessed in April 2024). Original held and digitised by the British Library.

sources concur, with the *Calcutta Courier* writing that 'people who clean the drains in Calcutta, and remove all the filth of the town are called Danghurs'.[95] These men are described in missionary accounts as 'happy and light-hearted' but also dark-skinned, wild and semi-nude.[96] According to Dasgupta, both *kol* and *dhangar* were terms used by upper-caste Bengalis, whose vocabulary the missionaries had borrowed to characterise the men.[97] It is fair to assume that similar processes led to the co-opting of these terms in official and private correspondences, often as a catch-all term for labourers from lower castes. Even as emigration reports reflected movement from across the caste spectrum, it was commonly held that indentured migrants hailed from lower castes.

The very process of naming, classifying and cataloguing the experience of the indentured migrant also led to the consolidation of the term 'coolie'. Today, this term holds various meanings. In parts of India, it has come to mean railway porters. In large parts of the Caribbean and the Americas, it is a derogatory slur. Lomarsh Roopnarine recently called it the 'Indian "C word"', urging: 'The word Coolie is the most explosive word in the Caribbean Indian experience. No other word has come close to having the same ability to insult.... The word disrupts the peasant tradition of Indians in former indentured colonies. The word enrages them.'[98] For scholars like Khal Torabully, however, it is a term to be reclaimed. Torabully coined the term 'coolitude' to refer to the cultural identities and interactions of the Indian labour diaspora.[99] At the time, however, 'coolie' was part of common parlance. The dictionary entry on 'coolies' in *Hobson-Jobson* demonstrates its myriad connotations.[100] According to *Hobson-Jobson*, the term has been in use since the 1550s and could refer to a hired labourer, burden carrier or an indentured migrant. In northern India it was applied to lower-class unskilled labourers from the hills, while in southern India it denoted hired wage labourers (derived from the term *kuli*, meaning wages).[101] For Walter Hamilton, the term originated from Koli, a community in western India 'who have long performed such office [as menial labourers], and whose savagery, filth, and general degradation attracted much attention in former times'.[102] Hugh Tinker argues that although derived from words such as 'Koli', by the end of the eighteenth century, the term 'ceased to have any connection with any group and race [and] was used to describe those at the lowest level of the industrial labour market'.[103] For instance, the term was used to refer to manual labourers who built the new Fort William in Calcutta in 1757–1775.[104]

This undifferentiated and imprecise articulation of the migrant labourer formed a crucial link to ideas of colonial philanthropy and need for spokesmanship. Andrea Major makes clear how racial, imperial and commercial discourses contributed to the portrayal of the 'hill coolie' as the quintessential migrant labourer in the Australian indenture scheme.[105] The British and Foreign Anti-Slavery Society's (BFASS) rationale for excluding Indian migrants from the global market was based on an essentialist understanding of 'inherent racial characteristics of the Indian labourer, his lack of information about the world, and his supposed place within a static, timeless, and unchanging village India'.[106] This applied to discourses in Calcutta as well, where the labourer's ignorance and inability to understand contracts was seen as tied to racial characterisations that negated his ability to exercise autonomous agency. As Major shows, highlighting the labourers' helplessness and perceived lack of agency was the preliminary step to rendering them 'appropriate subjects of colonial philanthropy'.[107]

The indenture debates in Calcutta operated within the rubrics of early colonial ethnography, which drew upon a perceived link between primitivism, ignorance and labouring potential. *Kol* and *dhangar* were used interchangeably in colonial archival documents and came to represent the ideal labourer. *Kol*s also made an appearance in discussions about military recruitment with similar stereotypes tied to their names. Acting political agent Captain Wilkinson wrote in an 1832 letter about recruiting from the Chhotanagpur region.[108] He argued that the Lurka 'coles' of Singbhum would make good soldiers 'if disciplined', but other 'coles' from the Chhotanagpur region were not appropriate since they would not submit to military discipline and would not agree to be employed away from their homes 'to which their attachment is very great'.[109] On the other hand, Wilkinson considered the 'Dhunger or Ouran Coles of Chotah Nagpoor' to be hard-working men, but they were 'want[ing] [in] spirit for soldiers' and had previously been discharged as unfit for military service.[110] Straddling colonial notions of the tribal and the primitive, *kol*s were classified as 'tribes' in Chotanagpur but became 'the labouring caste par excellence in modern Bengal'.[111]

This stereotyping and flattening of diverse identities aided in the continuation of the indenture trade. Purported to consist mainly of hill communities, indentured migrants offered a primitive and readily available labour market – an untapped and abundant source of labour for the empire known for their propensity for hard labour and their familiarity with temporary seasonal migration. This cycle of self-fulfilling stereotype heavily influenced the anti-indenture discourse, where the 'hill coolie' emerged as the ideal plantation labourer precisely because *all* indentured migrants were perceived as 'hill coolies' and *all* 'hill coolies' perceived as primitive.

The Ideal Plantation Labourer

This chapter challenges the periodisation of works on race and ethnography in colonial South Asia. It shows that categorising Indians into groups by their racial characteristics, assuming connection between the physical, the behavioural and the cognitive, and considering intelligence and labouring capacity to be racially determined were already a prominent feature in the early nineteenth century. Thus, the race–caste–primitivism triad that pervaded conversations about indenture predated more entrenched discussions about ethnography in colonial India. Clare Anderson has shown that in the late nineteenth and early twentieth centuries, Indian prisoners and convicts acted as a convenient sample for the colonial state's construction of biological hierarchies of race.[112] In fact, the nineteenth century saw a split among British administrators – some viewed caste as a social category while others saw it as a biological category.[113] The racialisation of indentured migrants took place towards the beginning of this split. It manifested before ethnographic and anthropological reports were published in the late nineteenth century, and before ethnographic classifications aided the delineation of incarcerated communities and 'criminal tribes'.

The image of the ideal plantation labourer was forged in the crucible of global indenture debates – shaped by the demands of planters, parliamentarians and abolitionists, by post-slavery understandings of labour, and by colonial ideals of race. Stereotyping was not limited to the colonisers and agents of the British state. Indian elites also employed racialised language and furthered racial stereotypes as they discussed the indenture question. Ultimately, in the process of defending the rights of indentured migrants, Calcuttans ended up shaping and entrenching the very oppressive structures that guided their lived experience.

In Britain, as Gladstone negotiated with parliamentarians to allow for a legal system of indenture migration, he perpetuated the stereotypes bestowed on him by Gillanders Arbuthnot & Company. In a letter to Sir Hobhouse, Gladstone repeated the assertions from Gillanders Arbuthnot & Company about labourers from the hills, calling them 'docile, quiet, orderly, and able-bodied People, of whom a great Number are constantly employed as Labourers in Calcutta'.[114] Through such conversations, racialised understandings of Indian migrants made their way into official reports and regulations. As a result, planters and recruiters targeted specific regions and castes when procuring indentured labourers. As late as 1896, the emigration agent for Natal, R. W. Mitchell, directed his recruiter to ensure that all recruited emigrants 'belong to the agricultural castes, with hard hands, sound healthy bodies, ample chests, and muscular limbs'.[115]

As the relationship between race, labouring capability and ignorance that was drawn in the indenture debates permeated official and public discourse, it had a distinct impact on policy. In a memorandum from Mackay in 1837, the ideal indentured migrant was identified as the 'Dangur', who 'are willing to turn their hands to any labour whatever'.[116] His primitive nature was exemplified in his willingness to eat 'any kind of animal food' including 'snakes, lizards, rats, mice', his 'simple and scanty' clothing, and his 'equally simple and confined' habitations.[117] Such ideas had a very real impact upon the indenture contract, as food provisions were kept to a bare minimum of rice, lentils, ghee and salt. Rapson testified that his ships originally served the indentured migrants two meals a day, but he reduced it to one meal a day on the insistence of *sirdars*, who argued that 'they [the migrants] had never been used to any thing of the kind'.[118]

Similarly, the idea that 'hill coolies' were excellent physical labourers who did not need much leisure influenced their allotted leisure hours in the indenture contract. In discussions of the Mauritius investigative committee, Charles Anderson's characterisation of indentured labourers as overworked and living in unclean conditions was rejected on grounds that this was common for Indians.[119] The committee suggested that 'had Mr Anderson ever visited India', he would understand that living in less than ideal lodgings and sleeping on the bare floor were customary for Indian labourers.[120] In newspapers, the 'dhangur coolie' from eastern India came to be imagined as the solution to the post-Abolition labour deficit. In fact, the image of the strong but unintelligent 'coolie' was made popular in public discourse through newspapers. The *Friend of India* argued that 'coolies' are 'the most simple, ignorant and degraded of the population of Bengal', 'but one remove[d] from the animals which graze upon their hills'.[121]

Reshaad Durgahee showed how ethnic and professional terms were turned into racial slurs in Mauritius. By the 1880s, *malabar*, the term for the south-western coast of the Indian peninsula, had become an offensive term for Hindus while *lascar*, the word for Indian seamen, was appropriated as a derogatory term to describe Muslims.[122] In Fiji, Indian labourers were seen as domesticated and easy to manage as long as they were engaged under the contract, but those who stayed on after the end of their contract were considered 'animal-like'. Perceived as wild, uncontrollable and threatening, time-expired Indians were deliberately separated from the indigenous Fijian population.[123] These later stereotypes were, in many ways, legitimised by the language and essentialised terms employed in the Calcutta debates in the 1830s and 1840s. The default image of the indentured labourer remained that of a dark, strong man eager for labour – an image that Calcuttans had a direct role in perpetuating.

This chapter, then, is an un-entanglement of the complex processes that led to the formation of the ideal labourer trope within global networks of indenture. As indentured migrants were framed around hierarchies of race, caste, ethnography and post-slavery labour ideals, anyone who did not fall within these categories was simply erased from the imagination of the ideal migrant. Thus, although they took place in closed meetings, the indenture debates in Calcutta came to shape wider official and public notions of the labourer. He was free to sell his labour overseas and free in his decision to migrate, but his ignorance required him to be represented by elite spokesmen. As it cemented the image of the quintessential indentured labourer and, in particular, defined the labourer as primitive and ignorant, the debates in Calcutta also helped substantiate the role of the citizen-spokesman.

Notes

1. Letter from Gillanders Arbuthnot & Company to John Gladstone, dated 6 June 1836, in *Copies of All Orders in Council, or Colonial Ordinances, for the Better Regulations and Enforcement of the Relative Duties of Masters and Employers, and Articled Servants, Tradesmen and Labourers, in the Colonies of British Guiana and Mauritius and of Correspondence Relating Thereof* (ordered by the House of Commons to be printed, 2 March 1838) (henceforth *Masters and Employers*).

2. Peter Robb, 'Introduction: South Asia and the Concept of Race', in *The Concept of Race in South Asia*, ed. Peter Robb, pp. 1–76 (New Delhi: Oxford University Press, 1995), p. 1.

3. Susan Bayly, 'Caste and "Race" in the Colonial Ethnography of India', in *The Concept of Race in South Asia*, ed. Peter Robb, pp. 165–218 (New Delhi: Oxford University Press, 1995), p. 167.

4. Ibid., p. 168.

5. Ibid.

6. For a discussion of nineteenth-century racial theory in the context of colonial India, see Thomas R. Metcalf, *Ideologies of the Raj* (Cambridge, UK: Cambridge University Press, 1994); Mark Brown, 'Ethnology and Colonial Administration in Nineteenth-Century British India: The Question of Native Crime and Criminality', *British Journal for the History of Science* 36, no. 2 (2003): 201–219.

7. Letter from Gillanders Arbuthnot & Company to John Gladstone, dated 6 June 1836, in *Masters and Employers*.

8. For details of the trope of the *kala pani* in the context of indentured and other migrants, see Crispin Bates and Marina Carter, 'Kala Pani Revisited: Indian Labour Migrants and the Sea Crossing', *Journal of Indentureship and Its Legacies* 1, no. 1 (2021): 36–62.

9. Testimony of Roger Dias, 25 October 1838, in 'Proceedings of the [Calcutta Investigative] Committee, from 22 August 1838 to 14 January 1839', in *Letter from Secretary to Government of India, to Committee on Exportation of Hill Coolies: Report of Committee and Evidence* (East India House, ordered by the House of Commons to be printed, 12 February 1841), Parliamentary Papers (House of Commons) 16, no. 45 (henceforth, 'Proceedings of the Calcutta Committee').

10. Testimony of J. Rapson, 22 August 1838, in 'Proceedings of the Calcutta Committee'.

11. Ibid.

12. Testimony of Bibee Zuhoorun, 20 September 1838, in 'Proceedings of the Calcutta Committee'.

13. Ibid.

14. Ibid.

15. Quoted in Thomas Metcalf, *Imperial Connections: India in the Indian Ocean Arena, 1860–1920* (Berkeley, CA: University of California Press, 2007), p. 147.

16. Mrinalini Sinha, 'Totaram Sanadhya's Fiji Mein Mere Ekkis Varsh: A History of Empire and Nation in a Minor Key', in *Ten Books That Shaped the British Empire: Creating an Imperial Commons*, ed. Antoinette Burton and

Isabel Hofmeyr, pp. 168–188 (Durham, NC: Duke University Press, 2014), p. 174.

17. Quoted in Metcalf, *Imperial Connections*, p. 162. *Paka* can be translated as strong, reliable or experienced.

18. Marina Carter, *Servants, Sirdars and Settlers: Indians in Mauritius, 1834–1874* (New Delhi and New York: Oxford University Press, 1995); Surendra Bhana, *Indentured Indian Emigrants to Natal, 1860–1902: A Study Based on Ships' Lists* (Delhi: Promilla & Company, 1991); Brij V. Lal, *Girmitiyas: The Origins of the Fiji Indians* (Lautoka: Fiji Institute of Applied Studies, 2004 [1983]).

19. J. R. Mayo, 'Remarks upon the Employment of Indian Labourers Out of Their Own Country', dated Sydney, 1 May 1837, enclosure 3 in no. 32, appendix to *Report from the Select Committee on Transportation (Communicated by the Commons to the Lords)* (ordered by the House of Commons to be printed, 16 August 1838), p. 175.

20. John Mackay, 'Indian Immigration: On the Introduction of Indian Labourers – Memorandum for the Consideration of His Excellency the Governor of New South Wales and Its Dependencies', enclosure 3 in no. 32, appendix to *Report from the Select Committee on Transportation (Communicated by the Commons to the Lords)* (ordered by the House of Commons to be printed, 16 August 1838), p. 173.

21. Ibid.

22. Mayo, 'Employment of Indian Labourers', p. 175.

23. 'No. 7: Extract of a Despatch from Governor Light to Lord Glenelg, dated 11 January 1839, Governor's Residence, Demerara', Governor Light to Lord Glenelg, 29 January 1839, in *Correspondence Relative to the Condition of the Hill Coolies and of Other Labourers Who Have Been Introduced into British Guiana* (ordered to be printed by the House of Lords, 26 July and 12 August 1839), in *The Sessional Papers Printed by Order of the House of Lords or Presented by Royal Command in the Session 1839*, vol. 7, p. 74.

24. H. A. Firth, 'Instructions for Surgeons When Examining and Selecting Emigrants in the Mufassal before Proceeding to This Agency' (Calcutta, 1881), in Basdeo Mangru (ed.), *Colonial Emigration from the Bengal Presidency* (Hertford: Hansib Publishers, 2014), app. 2, pp. 101–102.

25. Yoshina Hurgobin, 'Making Medical Ideologies: Indentured Labor in Mauritius', in *Histories of Medicine and Healing in the Indian Ocean World,*

Volume Two: The Modern Period, ed. Anna Winterbottom and Facil Tesfaye, pp. 1–26 (New York: Palgrave Macmillan, 2016), p. 4.

26. Letter from Livingston Syers and Co. to Messers Taylor, Potter and Co., dated 4 February 1836, in 'Miscellaneous Correspondence, 1806–1849', GG/2768, GG-MSS.

27. For parallels in the Afghan border region, where the 'violent geographies' of the region were purported to create a lawless and violent frontier population beyond the pale of civilisation, see Martin J. Bayly, *Taming the Imperial Imagination* (Cambridge, UK: Cambridge University Press, 2016); Martin J. Bayly, 'Imperial Ontological (In)Security: 'Buffer States', International Relations and the Case of Anglo-Afghan Relations, 1808–1878', *European Journal of International Relations* 21, no. 4 (2015): 816–840.

28. Uday Chandra, 'Liberalism and Its Other: The Politics of Primitivism in Colonial and Postcolonial Indian Law', *Law and Society Review* 47, no. 1 (2013): 135–168.

29. Ibid., p. 142.

30. Kaushik Ghosh, 'A Market for Aboriginality: Primitivism and Race Classification in the Indentured Labour Market of Colonial India', in *Subaltern Studies X: Writings on South Asian History and Society*, ed. Gautam Bhadra, Gyan Prakash, and Susie Tharu, pp. 8–48 (New Delhi: Oxford University Press, 1999), p. 18.

31. Similar assumptions of biological hierarchies of race and connection between physical attributes and behaviour also shaped the treatment of global convicts and incarcerated communities. See Clare Anderson, *Legible Bodies: Race, Criminality and Colonialism in South Asia* (Oxford and New York: Berg Publishers, 2004); Clare Anderson, 'The Andaman Islands Penal Colony: Race, Class, Criminality, and the British Empire' *International Review of Social History* 63, no. S26 (2018): 25–43. For a parallel history in Southeast Asia, see Syed Hussein Alatas, *The Myth of the Lazy Native: A Study of the Image of the Malays, Filipinos and Javanese from the 16th to the 20th Century and Its Function in the Ideology of Colonial Capitalism* (London: Frank Cass, 1977).

32. Testimony of Captain Rayne, 30 October 1838, in 'Proceedings of the Calcutta Committee'.

33. Testimony of J. Rapson, 22 August 1838; testimony of Captain Edwards, 17 September 1838, in 'Proceedings of the Calcutta Committee'.

34. Testimony of Abdoolah Khan, 13 September 1838, in 'Proceedings of the Calcutta Committee'.

35. Testimony of Dwarkanath Tagore, 9 November 1838, in 'Proceedings of the Calcutta Committee'.

36. Letter from Thomas Wise to Theodore Dickens, dated 19 September 1838, appendix to *Letter from Secretary to Government of India, to Committee on Exportation of Hill Coolies: Report of Committee and Evidence* (East India House, ordered by the House of Commons to be printed, 12 February 1841), Parliamentary Papers (House of Commons) 16, no. 45 (henceforth 'Report of the Calcutta Committee'), p. 174.

37. Testimony of Captain Rayne, 30 October 1838, in 'Proceedings of the Calcutta Committee'.

38. Letter from the Committee of Inquiry on Indian Labourers to Captain G. F. Dick, Colonial Secretary, Port Louis, dated 16 March 1839, in 'Indian Labourers: Indian Enquiry of Flacq, Mauritius', in *Papers Regarding the Employment of Indian Indentured Labourers Overseas*, vol. 10: *Report on the Condition of the Labourers on 22 Estates in the Flacq District, Mauritius (Includes Answers to Questionnaires, by Both Employers and Labourers)*, dated February 1839–March 1839, Board's Collections, 1840–41, vol. 1847, no. 77650, IOR/F/4/1847/77650.

39. Jonathan Connolly, 'Indentured Labour Migration and the Meaning of Emancipation: Free Trade, Race, and Labour in British Public Debate, 1838–1860', *Past and Present* 238, no. 1 (2018): 85–119, p. 109.

40. Philipp Zehmisch, 'The Invisible Architects of Andaman: Manifestations of Aboriginal Migration from Ranchi', in *Manifestations of History: Time, Space, and Community in the Andaman Islands*, ed. Frank Heidemann and Philipp Zehmisch, pp. 122–138 (New Delhi: Primus Books, 2016).

41. Quoted in ibid., p. 123.

42. Ibid., p. 124.

43. Ibid., p. 133.

44. Stan Neal, *Singapore, Chinese Migration and the Making of the British Empire, 1819–67* (Woodbridge: Boydell Press, 2019), p. 2.

45. Ibid.

46. Mackay, 'Indian Immigration: On the Introduction of Indian Labourers', p. 173.

47. Letter from George Arbuthnot to Robert Gladstone, dated 18 July 1835, quoted in Sydney Checkland, *The Gladstones: A Family Biography*

1764–1851 (London and New York: Cambridge University Press, 1971), p. 315.

48. Letter from John Moss to John Gladstone, dated 10 September 1836, in 'Letters from John Moss (of Otterspool), Liverpool Merchant and Demerara Planter', GG/297, GG-MSS.

49. 'Debate at the East India House: East-India Labourers', *Asiatic Journal and Monthly Register for British and Foreign India, China, and Australasia* 38 (1842): 191–215, p. 207. For details of George Thompson's anti-slavery and anti-indenture activities, see Andrea Major, *Reimagining Empire in India: George Thompson, Anti-Slavery Activism, and the Global Networks of British Colonial Reform, 1831–1858* (London: Bloomsbury Publishing, 2025).

50. 'Meeting for Preventing the Exportation of Coolies', *Calcutta Review* 44 (July 1838), p. 313.

51. Ibid., pp. 311–312.

52. Quoted in *Calcutta Courier*, 11 July 1838, n.p.

53. 'Meeting for Preventing the Exportation of Coolies', p. 311.

54. Ibid., p. 315.

55. *Friend of India*, 24 May 1838, pp. 261–62; *Friend of India*, 9 August 1838, pp. 537–538.

56. *Friend of India*, 30 August 1838, pp. 486, 487; *Friend of India*, 24 May 1838, pp. 261–262.

57. 'Meeting for Preventing the Exportation of Coolies', p. 311.

58. Ibid., p. 313.

59. Ibid.

60. Ibid., p. 314.

61. 'Report of the Calcutta Committee', p. 5.

62. Testimony of J. J. McCann, 6 September 1838, in 'Proceedings of the Calcutta Committee'.

63. Testimony of Alexander Mackenzie, 13 September 1838, in 'Proceedings of the Calcutta Committee'.

64. Testimony of John Dyer, 25 October 1838; Testimony of Roger Dias, 25 October 1838, in 'Proceedings of the Calcutta Committee'.

65. Testimony of Magistrate Patton, 15 October 1838, in 'Proceedings of the Calcutta Committee'.

66. Testimony of Reverend Thomas Boaz, 14 January 1839, in 'Proceedings of the Calcutta Committee'.

67. Testimony of Dwarkanath Tagore, 9 November 1838, in 'Proceedings of the Calcutta Committee'.

68. Ibid.

69. Ibid.

70. Letter from John Gladstone to Sir John Cain Hobhouse, President of the Board of Control, London, dated 23 February 1837, 6 December 1837, no. 54, General Department (General) Proceedings, WBSA.

71. John Gladstone, *A Statement of Facts, Connected with the Present State of Slavery in the British Sugar and Coffee Colonies, and in the United States of America, Together with a View of the Present Situation of the Lower Classes in the United Kingdom, Contained in a Letter Addressed to the Right Hon. Sir Robert Peel* (London: Baldwin & Cradock, 1830), in 'A Statement of Facts Connected with the Present State of Slavery ... Together with a View of the Present Situation of the Lower Classes in the United Kingdom, Contained in a Letter Addressed to ... Sir Robert Peel, Bart. by John Gladstone', GG/2868, GG-MSS.

72. Ann Laura Stoler, *Along the Archival Grain: Epistemic Anxieties and Colonial Common Sense* (Princeton, NJ: Princeton University Press, 2009).

73. The use of the term 'coolie' continued throughout the nineteenth and early twentieth centuries, until a law was passed in 1950 to replace the term with *mazdoor* to signify Indian labourers. 'Replacement of the Term Coolie by the Word "Mazdoor" in Official Correspondence', Ministry of Labour: Resolution, New Delhi, 27 May 1950, no. L.W.I.56(6)/50, Ministry of Home Affairs, Government of India, Home Department, Public Branch, NAI.

74. See index of the Home Department, Public Branch, 1835–43, NAI; Index of the Military Department, Military Branch, 1835–43, NAI.

75. See letter from Chief Magistrate to Officiating Secretary to Government, General Department, dated 13 May 1835; letter from D. McFarlan, Chief Magistrate, to G. A. Bushby, Secretary to the Government, General Department, dated 23 July 1835; letter from G. A. Bushby, Secretary to the Government, to G. F. Dick, Chief Secretary to the Government of Mauritius, dated 29 July 1835, Fort William, 29 July 1835, no. 453, General Department (General) Proceedings, WBSA.

76. K. Ghosh, 'A Market for Aboriginality', p. 32.

77. Testimony of Abdoolah Khan, 13 September 1838, in 'Proceedings of the Calcutta Committee'.

78. Testimony of W. E. Browne, 11 October 1838, in 'Proceedings of the Calcutta Committee'.

79. Letters between John Gladstone and Gillanders Arbuthnot & Company, in 'Correspondence on the Taking of Coolies to British Guiana, Including Letters from Andrew Colville, George C. Arbuthnot and Sir George Grey, and Copy Letters to the Duke of Wellington', 1838, GG/358, GG-MSS.

80. Letter from Gillanders Arbuthnot & Company to John Gladstone, dated 6 June 1836, enclosure no. 1 to Gladstone's Letters to Lord Glenelg, dated 28 February 1838, in *Masters and Employers*.

81. John Geoghegan, *Note on Emigration from India* (Calcutta: Superintendent of Government Printing, 1873), p. 68.

82. Ibid.

83. George Abraham Grierson, *Report on Colonial Emigration from the Bengal Presidency* (with diary) (Calcutta: n.p., 1883).

84. Ibid., p. 36.

85. Ibid.

86. *Asiatic Journal and Monthly Register for British and Foreign India, China, and Australasia* vol. 8 (London: Parbury, Allen & Co., 1832), pp. 264–265.

87. R. V. Russell, *Tribes and Castes of the Central Provinces of India* (London: Macmillan & Company Limited, 1916), pp. 18, 41.

88. William Crooke, *The Tribes and Castes of the North-western Provinces and Oudh*, vol. 2 (Calcutta: Office of the Superintendent of Government Printing, 1906), pp. 267–270.

89. George Campbell, *The Ethnology of India* (Calcutta: C.B. Lewis, 1866), p. 29.

90. Henry Yule, *Hobson-Jobson: A Glossary of Colloquial Anglo-Indian Words and Phrases, and of Kindred Terms, Etymological, Historical, Geographical and Discursive* (London: J. Murray, 1903 [1886]), p. 296.

91. Edward Tuite Dalton, *Descriptive Ethnology of Bengal* (Calcutta: Office of the Superintendent of Government Printing, 1872). See also Dalton, 'The Kols of Chota Nagpore', *Journal of the Asiatic Society of Bengal* 35, no. 2 (1866): 153–200.

92. Matthew Atmore Sherring, *Hindu Tribes and Castes* (Calcutta: Thacker, Spink & Company, 1872), p. 403.

93. H. H. Risley, *The Tribes and Castes of Bengal: Ethnographic Glossary*, vol. 1 (Calcutta: Bengal Secretariat Press, 1892), p. 219.

94. Sangeeta Dasgupta, '"Heathen Aboriginals", "Christian Tribes", and "Animistic Races": Missionary Narratives on the Oraons of Chhotanagpur in Colonial India', *Modern Asian Studies* 50, no. 2 (2016): 437–478, pp. 446–447.

95. *Calcutta Courier*, 9 July 1838, n.p.

96. S. Dasgupta, 'Heathen Aboriginals'.

97. Ibid.

98. Lomarsh Roopnarine, 'Review of Coolies of the Empire: Indentured Indians in the Sugar Colonies, 1830–1920 by Ashutosh Kumar', *Labor History* 60, no. 5 (2019): 590–591.

99. Marina Carter and Khal Torabully, *Coolitude: An Anthology of the Indian Labour Diaspora* (London: Anthem Press, 2002).

100. Yule, *Hobson-Jobson*, pp. 249–251.

101. Ibid.

102. Walter Hamilton, *Description of Hindostan and the Adjacent Countries*, vol. 1 (Delhi: Oriental Publishers, 1820), p. 609.

103. Hugh Tinker, *New System of Slavery: The Export of Indian Labour Overseas 1830–1920* (London: Oxford University Press, 1974), pp. 41–42.

104. See Kaustubh Mani Sengupta, 'The New Fort William and the Dockyard: Constructing Company's Calcutta in the Late Eighteenth Century', *Studies in History* 32, no. 2 (2016): 231–256.

105. Andrea Major, '"Hill Coolies": Indian Indentured Labour and the Colonial Imagination, 1836–38', *South Asian Studies* 33, no. 1 (2017): 23–36.

106. Ibid., p. 26.

107. Ibid., p. 27.

108. Letter from Acting Political Agent Captain Wilkinson to G. Swinton, Chief Secretary to Government, dated 8 July 1832, Fort William, Home Department, Public Branch, 16 July 1832, no. 57, NAI.

109. Ibid.

110. Ibid.

111. Uday Chandra, 'Kol, Coolie and Colonial Subject: A Hidden History of Caste and the Making of Modern Bengal', in *The Politics of Caste in West Bengal*, ed. Uday Chandra, Geir Heierstad and Kenneth Bo Nielsen, pp. 19–34 (Oxon and New York: Routledge, 2015), p. 20.

112. C. Anderson, *Legible Bodies*.

113. Ibid., p. 60.

114. Letter from John Gladstone to Sir John Cain Hobhouse, President of the Board of Control, London, dated 23 February 1837, 6 December 1837, no. 54, General Department (General) Proceedings, WBSA.

115. Letter from R. W. Mitchell to Benoy Krishna Gupta, dated 30 September 1896, quoted in Thomas R. Metcalf, '"Hard Hands and Sound

Healthy Bodies": Recruiting "Coolies" for Natal, 1860–1911', *Journal of Imperial and Commonwealth History* 30, no. 3 (2002): 1–26, p. 23.

116. Mackay, 'Indian Immigration', p. 173.

117. Ibid.

118. Testimony of J. Rapson, 22 August 1838, in 'Proceedings of the Calcutta Committee'.

119. Letter from Charles Anderson to the Colonial Secretary G. F. Dick, dated 30 November 1838, in 'Correspondence Respecting the Employment of Indian Labourers in the Mauritius', in *Mauritius: Copies of Despatches from Sir William Nicolay on the Subject of Free Labour in the Mauritius* (ordered by the House of Commons to be printed, 7 February 1840), pp. 37–38.

120. Letter from C. M. Campbell, J. Hugon, J. Villiers Forbes and W. Bury to G. F. Dick, dated 5 December 1838, in 'Correspondence respecting the Employment of Indian Labourers in the Mauritius', in *Mauritius: Copies of Despatches from Sir William Nicolay on the Subject of Free Labour in the Mauritius* (ordered by the House of Commons to be printed, 7 February 1840), p. 40.

121. *Friend of India*, 24 May 1838, p. 261.

122. Reshaad Durgahee, *The Indentured Archipelago: Experiences of Indian Labour in Mauritius and Fiji, 1871–1916* (Cambridge, UK: Cambridge University Press, 2022), p. 69.

123. Ibid., pp. 113–114.

6

Subjects, Citizens, Spokesmen

By creating a new category of unfree labour migrants, the indenture trade had opened up the question of subjecthood and citizenship. Some of the earliest Indian theories of modern polity and society were generated in relation to the rights of mobile peoples, such as seamen, traders, *lascar*s and Indians soldiers.[1] Both British officials and Indian liberals saw land rights as customary, but for mobile peoples, rights had to be created anew by the state.[2] As indentured labourers began to push legal categories by moving abroad, it became necessary to consider their rights on ships, on plantations and in colonies that fell outside the remits of the British Empire (such as in French and Dutch colonies). The very movement of indentured migrants to serve in plantation colonies had raised them to the status of mobile subjects of the empire whose rights had to be upheld by the colonial state and whose well-being was the responsibility of the state. A new, nuanced understanding of subjecthood was at play here.

Although scholars of indenture have mainly focused on the labourer, the indenture trade had, in reality, created roles for both the labourer and the spokesman. In the process of debating the indenture trade and petitioning for the rights of mobile subjects of the British Empire, petitioners from Calcutta had emerged as vocal citizens of the empire. While the trope of the racialised labourer shaped the indenture experience by influencing recruitment practices, indenture contracts and allotments of food on plantations, petitions from spokesmen in Calcutta entrenched the latter further into the Calcutta public sphere as active participants. Ultimately, the indenture debates in Calcutta contributed to a novel understanding of imperial citizenship that was vocal, participatory and aspirational. The citizen-spokesman based in Calcutta became an important participant in the global machinery of indenture as he questioned, criticised and debated the indenture trade and employed a rhetoric of rights, responsibility and imperial benevolence. This chapter explores how subjecthood, citizenship and labour rights were negotiated in the Calcutta debates and how commercial, reformist, humanitarian, political and imperial interests came together in these negotiations.

Labourers as Rights-Bearing Subjects

Rachel Sturman argues that indenture migration represents one of the earliest contexts where international labour rights were discussed and championed, leading to the establishment of several key concepts in transnational human rights and the early conceptualisation of international labour regulations.[3] Although the indenture system was exploitative and coercive, for Sturman, it 'occasioned new ideas … about what constituted a legitimate and humane labor system'.[4] While Sturman's argument for a direct link between the treatment of indentured migrants and the emergence of a distinct rhetoric of 'human rights' in the twentieth century is based on a loose definition of rights, humanitarian concerns undoubtedly underlined the indenture debates. In the post-slavery empire, Indian indenture posited both a legal question and a moral one.

The labourer's position within the British Empire was predicated on the idea that their primitiveness precluded them from speaking for themselves and that their migratory nature transformed them from regional subjects of the British Indian government to subjects of the empire, thus making them more vulnerable and susceptible to exploitation. When Bishop Daniel Wilson asked those attending the Calcutta Town Hall meeting '[w]here were the laws to protect them in an old slave colony and from the tyranny of task-masters who had spent a whole life in driving slaves' or when Longueville Clarke posed the question 'what then would become of him in a foreign and distant land, where his language was unknown, and his wants and habits were strange', the question was clearly one of rights.[5] The term 'rights' was not entirely uncommon in the Calcutta debates, used, for instance, in the Town Hall petition: '[the emigrants] have been the subjects of transfer [from] one master to another at Mauritius and other places … many of them had suffered as men and citizens in their persons their purse and their *civil rights*'.[6] Clarke urged in the Town Hall meeting that if it could be proven that the trade was not exploitative, then 'the labourer had a *right* to seek employment abroad without reference to the interests of those cultivators at home'.[7] Mr Charles urged the attendees of the Town Hall meeting to extend to the indentured migrants the sympathy and advocacy that enslaved labourers received during the abolition debates:

> The Negro has had the benefit of the genius, the talent, the energy, the humanity of the great and good men of our own country. Not so the poor Cooley in the Mauritius. No one there will advocate his rights, few will sympathise with his wants, he will have *no Wilberforce* to plead for him, no Brougham to thunder in his favour ... let us not then send him to distant bondage, where he will find neither friend nor advocate.[8]

Similarly, pro-indenture petitions frequently referred to rights, justice and subjecthood when expressing the need for continued emigration. For signatories of the Calcutta merchant petition of 1838, indenture was a question 'involving the rights of British subjects ... to carry their manual labour to the most productive market', while also securing to the labourers 'ample opportunity to exercise their rights as free subjects'.[9] In a letter to the editor of the *Calcutta Courier*, an anonymous French writer urged that preventing Indian labourers from migrating overseas was at variance with the principles of the metropolitan government and in fact opposed to the constitutional rights of English subjects.[10] Stopping emigration, he argued, would amount to 'violating their person and their liberty, as they are English subjects. It would deprive them of their free will. It would be to substitute slavery for liberty; for if the free man cannot go everywhere he wants, he is no longer free, he becomes a slave....'[11]

The discussion around indenture was thus couched in a language of morality and concern for the migrant. Within the space of three decades, the conversation had shifted from an economic question of commodity trade, profits, labour retention and planter compensation to whether the indenture trade was aiding or hindering the migrant labourer's rights. Pro-indenture petitions emphasised the right of the labourer to seek employment, while anti-indenture arguments pointed to the labourer's right to better living and working conditions and his right to security from deception and abuse. As the act of migration raised indentured Indians to the status of rights-bearing subjects, subjecthood and labour rights became intricately linked. Indeed, it was as a subject of the British Empire that the migrant had rights – the right of being protected against exploitation, the right of return to their country of origin and the right to seek redress. As the *Calcutta Star* urged in 1843: 'coolies returned from Demerara ... have been awakened to a sense of their rights as citizens; ... from mere listless hangers on upon society they have been elevated into men and citizens'.[12]

As the discussions in Calcutta shaped the question of how rights accrued to the labourers, it also prompted imperial labour policies that worked to ensure those rights. In the aftermath of the anti-slavery movement and the abolition debates in Britain, it was imperative for any migrant labour system to comply with the economic and ethical principles of the post-slavery empire. For those who criticised the indenture trade, strict regulations and contracts were the means to achieve this. The second resolution passed in the Town Hall meeting of 1838 stated that the meeting did not intend to 'interfere with the civil rights of any class of her Majesty's subjects' or stifle free migration.[13] However, in this case, the indentured migrant's freedom of movement and employment was overshadowed by the responsibility of the British state to protect its subjects, especially subjects who were seen as incapable of understanding the terms of their indenture.[14] In essence, the Town Hall resolution contended that the argument that labourers should be allowed to choose their mode and place of employment and escape what planters often depicted as miserable economic conditions at home applied only with the caveat that they were not entering unregulated, coercive labour systems. Turning the free labour argument on its head, this implied that the labourer's right of mobility was nullified by his right to be protected from mistreatment. It tied together imperial responsibility with labour rights by proposing a situation where the colonial government should maintain strict regulatory rights over the trade to ensure the labourers' safety from unfree labour regimes. By implication, the rights of labourers and their capacity to enjoy those rights had to be upheld by the colonial state, and any infringement of these rights could warrant government intervention.

As this opened up space for government interference in economic affairs, it attracted criticism from the pro-indenture lobby. For merchants and planters, the *laissez-faire* economy that Britain purported to represent required that labourers be allowed to 'sell' their labour to the highest bidder. Hence, they discouraged any regulation that restricted indentured emigration or potentially limited the migrant's right to seek employment. In fact, planters used indenture contracts to show that labourers already enjoyed a say in determining their future conditions of employment, or at least had prior knowledge of their rights and of the conditions of work in plantations. In his minute for the Calcutta investigative committee, J. P. Grant framed indenture as a question of rights of the empire's subjects 'in respect to the disposal of their labour, and their right of going about'.[15] Thus, for both pro- and anti-indenture petitioners, the rights of the migrant labourer remained at the centre of their arguments.

Geographical Limits of Subjecthood

Besides allusions to the 'ignorance' of migrants around how far they were going and how long they would be gone for, the Calcutta debates were also concerned with protecting indentured migrants in colonies situated beyond the remits of British legal structures. In the Town Hall meeting, Reverend Charles pointed out that it would be difficult – perhaps even impossible – to adequately protect the labourers in plantation colonies because they were located outside the regulatory boundaries of the colonial Indian government.[16] Essentially, regulations made in Britain or British India could not necessarily be implemented in faraway British plantation colonies because of geographical, legal and policing limits. As the reverend argued, labourers were more prone to ill-treatment in Demerara because its large European population was known for constantly defying parliamentary authority.[17]

This concern became more acute with indentured emigration to French plantations. Returned migrants had testified to having a different experience on French-owned plantations. Sheik Manick testified to the Calcutta investigative committee that '[t]hose who were employed by Englishmen said that they got sufficient to eat; but [not] those who were employed in the service of Frenchmen.... Those employed by English gentlemen got their pay monthly, but not those employed by French gentlemen.'[18] When asked if he would recommend others to work in Mauritius, he was frank about the disparity, saying that they would get their pay and clothes if employed by English planters, but not if employed by French planters.[19] Although Mauritius was a beautiful country and he was willing to go back there, Manick maintained that 'the Frenchmen are very bad'.[20] Bibee Zuhoorun's personal ordeals aside, she also testified to collusion between planters and the police that made it difficult for labourers to seek redress. When she was denied wages for the two and a half years that she worked in the plantation of Dr Boileau, the police did not help her.[21] She complained to the committee: 'The police did not interfere in my behalf; what could they do? He [Boileau] was a Frenchman, and the magistrates of police I went before were Frenchmen; they understand one another.'[22]

French planters were not the only cause for concern – many labourers emigrated to and from colonies belonging to the French Empire. W. F. Dowson testified before the Calcutta committee that more labourers were being exported from French Pondicherry than from Calcutta and other Indo-British ports.[23] Since slavery still existed in the French Empire, some expressed doubt that changes in regulation within the British Empire could solve the labourers' problems. Dowson was of the opinion that precautionary and restrictive measures adopted merely in British ports would not only be ineffective in stopping abuses in the system but would also push the indentured traffic from British ports to French ones.[24] He argued that only the suspension of trade with French colonies like Bourbon could stop further exacerbation of the situation. As the Calcutta committee cautioned: 'A prohibition to receive Coolies into British colonies in foreign vessels might no doubt be enforced, but the exportation to foreign colonies could not be checked....'[25] Indenture migration between the two empires, especially emigration from the French Indian ports of Pondicherry and Karikal, continued to be a point of diplomatic debate, building up to the Anglo-French convention on emigration of labouring population in 1860.[26]

The question of discrepancy in regulations between French and English colonies and the legal ambiguity of labourers moving between English and other colonial regimes was a question of belonging. In post-Abolition Britain, the fear of indenture migration reverting into slavery continued to be a strong point of criticism. Comparison with the French Empire put pressure on the British Empire to ensure that its labourers were safe from mistreatment and exploitation. Thus, by appealing to a sense of imperial benevolence and responsibility, these peripatetic labourers came to be imagined as subjects of the British Empire whose rights had to be protected by British law. Unsurprisingly, the concept of imperial benevolence remained ubiquitous in these debates.

The Paternal and Benevolent State

Petitions from Calcutta frequently referred to imperial benevolence and responsibility towards indentured migrants. In the Town Hall meeting,

Longueville Clarke commented that British rule in India played a paternal role, and he worried about the fate of labourers outside it: '[R]emoved from the paternal care of this Government, and many of its excellent servants, what was then to save him from oppression?'[27] Participants in the Town Hall meeting compared indentured Indians to child labourers in England, urging that they were 'unable to help themselves, and require[ed] the protection and interference of government'.[28] The Town Hall petition compared the empire's responsibility of protecting the civil rights of its indentured labourers to its responsibility of removing slavery from British dominions.[29] Viewing the colonial state as responsible for protecting its migrant labour forces from slave-like conditions, the petition asked that 'the evils so long inflicted on the Negro race' not be allowed to be transferred to the inhabitants of British India.[30] Taken alongside the notion of ignorant migrants incapable of helping themselves, such statements pressed the need for government intervention. As the previous chapter outlines, imagining the indentured labourer as ignorant, helpless, unfit and child-like allowed the Calcutta elite to speak on their behalf.

Spokesmanship was thus couched in the language of paternalism, betterment and humanitarianism. The Calcutta elite saw themselves as necessary interventionists who understood what was good for the migrants even if the migrants could not see it themselves. In the British Empire, humanitarianism was linked to the colonial world, especially with organisations like the British India Society (BIS), the Aborigines Protection Society (APS) and the British and Foreign Anti-Slavery Society (BFASS) employing a humanitarian rhetoric.[31] Although many works on imperial humanitarianism focus on the late nineteenth and twentieth centuries, the term had come into everyday use by the early nineteenth century.[32]

Michael Barnett argues that humanitarianism instilled new kinds of commitments on the part of the fortunate as it brought together notions of imperial trusteeship, compassion, welfare, Christian ideals and morality.[33] This humanitarianism was paternalistic and interventionist, existing alongside Christianity, colonialism and commerce 'that deemed the "civilized" peoples superior to the backward populations'.[34] He recognises the role of the anti-slavery movement in spearheading humanitarianism since it caused the British public to 'broaden its moral imagination and to recognize its special responsibilities to the colonized'.[35] Zoë Laidlaw argues that in the era immediately following the French Revolutionary and Napoleonic Wars, British humanitarians called for imperial reform that was at once 'benevolent and self-interested, moral and political'.[36] For Laidlaw, the 1830s marked the high point of British humanitarian influence on empire with discussions of abolition and emancipation, challenges to convict transportation to Australia and inquiries into indigenous–settler relations.[37]

At the same time, imperial humanitarianism functioned with inherent contradictions such as existing alongside settler colonialism. Just when calls to abolish slavery, to reform governance at home and to campaign on behalf of indigenous populations were emerging, and colonial officials were being given instructions to govern humanely, thousands of Britons were involved in invading and occupying indigenous people's lands on an unprecedented scale.[38] Similarly, there was the contradiction in implementing policies legalising indenture while abolishing the slave trade. William Green argues that abolishing the slave trade but allowing the Indian indenture trade to flourish was not an example of British hypocrisy or of derailed imperial trusteeship when confronted by powerful vested interests. It was merely a necessary compromise: 'a vital, if disagreeable, bulwark in a basically humane Atlantic strategy, not the calloused or wilful adoption of a "new system of slavery"'.[39] Kate Boehme, Peter Mitchell and Alan Lester argue that there were hierarchies in the moral obligations of the British Empire, stating: 'The moral obligation that the imperial government owed to enslaved and indentured Indians, apprenticed Mauritian creoles, recaptives, and convicts was evaluated separately, and less critically, than that owed to the enslaved in the Caribbean....'[40]

Imperial humanitarianism, then, was neither static nor absolute. In the Indian context, Peter Marshall refers to the 'moral swing to the East', whereby British imperial interests moved away from the Atlantic and turned towards the East as it tried to make India the centrepiece of the nineteenth-century British Empire.[41] This was because humanitarianism of the late eighteenth-century Cornwallis era was seen as compatible with Britain's national advantage, and was part of an argument that while West Indians continued to deny 'their blacks' the essentials of civil society and protection under law, the East India Company was actively extending such benefits to Indians.[42] It was within this context that the Calcutta debates flourished. Post-slavery ideals of humanitarianism and imperial morality seeped into the Calcutta public sphere through the cross-imperial transmission of ideas in newspapers and letters and shaped how indenture was debated. Many of the participants in the Town Hall meeting and the Calcutta petition referred to 'imperial benevolence' and demonstrated belief in the colonial state to take the right moral decision. The language of these debates is reminiscent of the 'civilising argument', where it was the responsibility of the coloniser to institute good governance for the moral and material progress of the colonised.

The use of non-subversive language and the insistence on colonial responsibility towards labourers was a unique feature of the early indenture debates. Far from questioning rules of imperial governance, these petitions reaffirmed the political position of British rule in India by appealing to the metropolitan government to make regulatory changes. The Calcutta investigative committee reported, for instance:

> We have a full trust that the benevolent and commanding intellects employed in the consideration of the whole subject in England, both within Parliament and out of it, cannot fail to lead the legislature to right conclusions; and we rest humbly confident in the conclusion, that whatever may be the result, Parliament and the people of England ... will not permit injustice to be done to the Indian subjects of the Crown ... from any motives of political advantage, however weighty, or of mercantile gain, however large.[43]

The committee thus asserted their 'full trust' in the benevolence of the lawmakers in Britain and their confidence in the British parliament to prevent any injustice from befalling the indentured migrant. Similarly, the Town Hall petition of 1838 was laudatory of the colonial state and reiterated their trust in the 'humane intentions' of the government:

> Your petitioners trust that your Honor in Council ... will be able so to investigate and decide that the blessings of civil and religious freedom enjoyed by nearly all Her Majesty's subjects may be continued and extended to those residing within Her densely populated possession under your Honor in Council in the East.[44]

The role of the state in protecting labourers' rights was also reiterated in official discussions. In a letter from 1844, Governor General Henry Hardinge wrote that '[c]oolies are not their own masters as regards emigration', and asserted that indenture regulations to protect the labourer's rights were necessary since 'they are hired by the [government] [towards] whom they are to look for protecting them in all their rights'.[45] Clearly, labour rights were bestowed upon the indentured migrant by the colonial government, who held the authority to enforce it. These discussions not only lauded the paternal role of the colonial state but also pointed to the state as the regulator of indenture and, indeed, the purveyor of justice.

Such language – critical of policies, but at the same time panegyric, justificatory and even apologetic for taking up the state's time – was evidence of a public petition that sought imperial benevolence while also cementing the colonial state's position as an imperial power. Rather than questioning the colonial regime for initiating the indenture trade, petitioners from Calcutta criticised specifics tenets of the trade while expressing unwavering confidence in the decisions of the imperial regime and in the benevolence of their regulations. Instead of being a criticism of the state, this was in fact an admittance that the legal structures and decisions of the colonial state were supreme. This politics of non-subversion helped entrench petitioners and spokesmen in Calcutta into their position as allies of the colonial state. This was in keeping with the tone of public debates and petitions at the time, which often highlighted loyalty to the British colonial state. For instance, a letter from Dwarkanath Tagore on the occasion of him receiving a gold medal from the Company's Court of Directors referred to the 'just and liberal rule of the honourable court', 'the invincible power of the protecting state', and its 'pure and benevolent intentions, [and] noble solicitude for the welfare and improvement of the millions'.[46]

This non-subversive reaction to the indenture trade stood in stark contrast to movements advocating for the rights of plantation labourers later in the century. In the late-nineteenth-century movement criticising inland emigration to Assam, the tone was firmer and more subversive. In 1886–1887, prominent Brahmo Samaj activist Dwarkanath Ganguli published a series of articles on the condition of indentured labourers in Assam's tea plantations. In his criticism of Assam indenture, Ganguli emphasised that it was the duty of the colonial Indian government to ensure the welfare of its migrant labourers. He considered the government to be 'morally bound' to ensure that migrants were 'not compelled to lead the life of bond-slaves in tea-gardens'.[47] His voice, however, was more critical than panegyric – angry at the fact that the 'pitiable conditions' of the migrant labourers could easily be removed by the government 'if it were so disposed'.[48] Ganguli expressed particular frustration at how several tenets of the emigration acts that governed indentured emigration to Assam's tea plantations were invalidated or interpreted to favour the planters. He lamented that 'impartial administration of justice can hardly be expected from those who do not scruple to interpret the law of the land in the interests of the planting community and at complete variance with the benevolent intentions of the Legislature'.[49] Similarly, the early-twentieth-century movement for the abolition of overseas indenture saw Indian nationalists publicising harrowing stories of indentured migrants being detained, mistreated and deceived and pushing strongly for its immediate abolition. Evidently, there had been a shift in public attitude towards the colonial government through the course of the century.

Imperial Citizenship and the Art of Petitioning

Whilst indentured migrants were being raised to rights-bearing subjects of the British Empire, the act of petitioning was bringing spokesmen from Calcutta closer to the political nerve centre of the empire. Public petitions, as we saw, had emerged as a key way of expressing grievances with indenture regulations. Planters from destination colonies and merchants from Calcutta frequently petitioned the metropolitan government to express their concerns with the trade, while vocal inhabitants of Calcutta petitioned to curtail or abolish indenture. The metropole, which was physically removed from the indenture trade, formed a complex and crucial linkage between planters, merchants, colonial officials and the parliament. Petitioning was a way of harnessing this space and developing a trans-oceanic public sphere. The next few pages unravel the aspirational citizenship that emerged in the Calcutta debates through petitioning and, indeed, tethered the urban public sphere together on the issue of indenture. Unlike ideas of citizenship that centre around nation and nationality, this was a dutiful, active and aspirational citizenship that made spokesmen from Calcutta visible to the metropolitan centre.

Although colonial citizenship has rarely been seen in this light, the link between petitioning and citizenship is well established in histories of early modern Britain.[50] In England, the stabilisation and consolidation of procedure by the seventeenth century and the belief in the security of written records necessitated petitioning as a formal means of communication with the Crown.[51] By the seventeenth century, the right to petition had become a salient right held by individuals and collectives.[52] Mass petitions, whether to the Crown, the parliament or local magistrates, also became the means by which a politically discursive public sphere emerged in England. Petitions facilitated the flow of information and political messages from the periphery to the political centre.[53] Thus, the emergence of petitions had attributed an unprecedented authority to public opinion in politics, and this was not just confined to metropolitan Britain.

In the South Asian context, the use of petitions has been substantively studied in very few works, notable amongst which is the 2019 special issue of *Modern Asian Studies*, titled 'Petitioning and Political Cultures in South Asia'.[54] Exploring the use of petitions from the Mughal period to the late colonial period, this special issue argues that the written petition has long been an important vehicle of political dissent and popular mobilisation, while also embodying expressions of community and individual rights.[55] Taken together, the articles in the issue show that petitioning in South Asia has played three major roles. It has been a mechanism of centralising and bureaucratising of state power as well as a mode of standardising and routinising political relations. It has been a vehicle for creative forms of protest, dissent and popular public engagement. Finally, petitioning has played a powerful symbolic role, as written petitions retained traces of a patrimonial form of rule with a face-to-face relationship between the ruler and the petitioner.[56]

In his work on colonial Bombay, Prashant Kidambi shows that petitioning activities had become 'exercises in the public performance of the "political"', whereby petitions were discussed in assemblies that claimed to represent public opinion.[57] As Bhavani Raman contends, petitioning created 'a world of officially acceptable dissent under colonial rule'.[58] Robert Travers relates petitioning practices during Company rule to written petitions (*arzis*) in Mughal South Asia, arguing that Company-era petitioning established Calcutta as the political capital of Bengal and the East India Company as the sovereign source of authority and justice.[59] In many cases, petitioning also became an important stimulus for new administrative regulations.[60] Later in the century, petition writing was linked to the emergence of early Indian nationalism, so much so that the colonial state made it a practice to scrutinise petitions for expressions of rebellion or sedition.[61] This happened in the context of a 'petitioning explosion' across the British Empire, with the parliament receiving petitions from India, Canada, the Australian colonies and New Zealand.[62] Richard Huzzey and Henry Miller have enumerated more than a million petitions sent to the House of Commons between 1780 and 1918, demonstrating how colonial subjects demanded attention from Westminster.[63] As petitioning was celebrated as a universal right of all British subjects, studies of colonial petitioning have added considerably to our understanding of subjecthood. For spokesmen in Calcutta, however, petitioning allowed them to bridge the subject–citizen divide.

The act of petitioning implied that someone based in Calcutta could comment on a migratory labour system sanctioned by the metropole while also making the connection between the ruler and the ruled more direct. The legitimacy of the petition was shaped by its ability to travel through proper channels. As David Lambert argues in the case of petitions relating to slavery, 'the highly deferential style of writing demonstrates that petitioners sought to influence, and not challenge … metropolitan authority'.[64] The expression of opinion, the petitioning of metropolitan government and the underlying belief in imperial legal structures made the petitioners participants in imperial processes. Through petitions, the spokesmen in Calcutta were transformed from passive subjects of the British Empire to vocal citizens who debated the rights of the empire's labourers, voiced their opinions on matters of public interest, exercised their right to protest and express grievances and contributed to changing emigration regulations. This rendered the spokesman of Calcutta part of a civil society broader than just the city. In the absence of well-formed ideas of nationhood in early- and mid-nineteenth-century India, these facilitated the understanding of citizenship as not being limited to the city or the nation but extended to the empire.

What, then, makes an imperial citizen? Daniel Gorman argues that citizenship is 'a primary means through which societies assert, construct and consecrate their sense of identity'.[65] It is defined by a sense of civic belonging, comprising both social and legal–political identities.[66] However, there is no singular definition of citizenship in South Asia. It has been conceptualised differently during Company rule, under Crown rule, during the independence movement and in the post-independence era. Nineteenth-century British India itself bore witness to changing notions of nationhood, subjecthood and citizenship. Sukanya Banerjee points out that the ideal of the 'universal citizen-subject' assumed singularity through overlapping trajectories in the late nineteenth century.[67] This universal citizenship came with the caveat of being necessarily dual: 'Indians, after all, were "imperial" citizens, citizens only because of their position as localized "Indian" subjects of the Crown.'[68]

The notion of citizenship was further complicated by decolonisation. Joya Chatterjee sees citizenship of post-partition refugees through the lens of occupation of space, the rights of property and mobility and the right to return.[69] Minority citizenship in South Asia was thus produced by complex and violent interactions between government and a range of non-state actors, and it was the distinctive acts of agency of the stranded minority population that helped cement ideas of citizenship for the displaced and the refugees. By inserting refugees as active agents in the consolidation of citizenship rights, Chatterjee juxtaposes South Asian citizenship against models derived from the West.[70] For Aihwa Ong, certain transnational groups even deployed a flexible citizenship, exercising their rights flexibly and opportunistically.[71] As Frederick Cooper shows for French Africa, negotiations for citizenship of the empire could lead to demands for social, economic and political equality, to the abolition of distinctions between colonial subject and citizen, and to the juxtaposition of autonomy and belonging.[72]

Despite varying definitions of citizenship, at its core, the term represents a sense of belonging to a nation, state or empire. Most works on citizenship in colonial South Asia focus on its consolidation in the late nineteenth and early twentieth centuries, especially with the emergence of anti-colonial nationalism and nationhood.[73] Taylor Sherman, William Gould and Sarah Ansari argue that the interval between the 1930s and the 1960s was a formative period in South Asian history in terms of citizenship, while Banerjee shows that the category of the citizen was not formally codified in British law until well into the twentieth century.[74] By contrast, this book focuses on a time before the Queen's Proclamation of 1858, itself a watershed moment in the conceptualisation of subjecthood and citizenship. Notions of citizenship and subjecthood in relation to the early indenture trade functioned within a unique interplay of ideas of civilisation, spokesmanship and protectionism at a stage before the legal codification of the category. Unlike citizenship ideals that emerged from the dichotomy of belonging to the Indian nation and the British Empire, the citizenship that spokesmen in Calcutta appealed to was embedded in a sociopolitical scene before the emergence of a clearly defined nationalism.

Citizenship has primarily been framed as a question of rights, including right to residence, right to property and right to vote. T. H. Marshall saw citizenship as constitutive of civil, political and social rights, and Chatterjee relates it to rights of property, mobility and return.[75] However, while citizenship and subjecthood can be bestowed, they can also be achieved through performance. Gunnel Cederlöf argues that subjecthood is an act:

'When people and communities assert themselves and make claims to various rights or privileges within a polity, they perform subjecthood; that is through this act, they come into being as subjects or citizens at a particular time and place.'[76] Performance was an important framing principle for the indenture debates in Calcutta. It was not by the declaration of rights but by the performance of duties – such as asserting the rights of their fellow men and writing petitions to the metropolitan government – that the Calcutta spokesmen elevated themselves to citizens of the empire and aligned themselves to the wider imperial sphere. Constant appeals for changes in metropolitan regulations emerged from a vision of global indenture networks that could only be regulated through a centrally consolidated legal framework that was responsive to inputs from its subjects and citizens.

In some ways, this aspirational citizenship required a non-citizen subject to juxtapose themselves against. The imagined community of the citizen-spokesman in Calcutta thus also included migrants – even if not as citizens, at least as British subjects.[77] The only thing connecting spokesmen from Calcutta to metropolitan lawmakers was that they were tied by the same idea of responsibility towards its migrant-subjects. Their invocation of notions of civic duty altered the perception and scope of political space. It suggested that the metropolitan parliamentarian had the same duty as a spokesman from Calcutta to make sure that migrant labourers of the empire were protected from mistreatment. The figure of the imperial citizen was thus manifest in the self-appointed spokesman appealing for legal changes to the indenture schema – a citizenship that could only be reached by the active performance of duties expected of a citizen.

Huzzey and Miller have recently argued that even as all subjects of the British Empire technically enjoyed the right to petition, there were practical inequalities of opportunity separating citizens in the imperial metropole from colonial subjects.[78] The active, aspirational and participatory citizenship of Calcutta's spokesmen attempted to blur this citizen–subject divide. By criticising indenture regulations, arguing for the rights of indentured labourers as migrant subjects of the empire and appealing to the imperial benevolence of the colonial state, spokesmen in Calcutta entrenched themselves firmly into the imperial public sphere. As members of the public sphere in Calcutta – Indian and European alike – took part in claims-making exercises to assert their own legal belonging to the empire, they forced a rethinking of the chronologies of imperial citizenship.

The Spokesmen of Calcutta

Merchants and planters were invested in defending the indenture trade due to a straightforward reason – continued labour emigration was the only way for them to maintain profits from the sugar trade in the aftermath of Abolition. Arguments against the trade, however, were more complex. Many spokesmen who participated in the Town Hall meeting or in the Calcutta investigative committee had no explicit vested interest in the indenture trade. Why, then, were they invested in the indenture question, and particularly in openly opposing colonial decisions, when they had no connection to indentured labourers? Why did merchants like Dwarkanath Tagore and Rustomjee Cowasjee, who held commercial interest in labour emigration, actively criticise indenture and petition for its abolition? This final section focuses on the coming together of commercial, reformist, humanitarian and imperial interests in negotiations around the indenture question to demonstrate that these interests did not operate in isolation but in a space where the urban elite straddled various roles at once.

Crispin Bates and Marina Carter argue that many of those who resisted indenture migration – including Chairman of the Calcutta investigative committee Theodore Dickens and prominent anti-indenture voice Dwarkanath Tagore – were railway and colliery managers, landholders and indigo planters. By virtue of their involvement in labour-intensive enterprises, they had a vested interest in challenging the export of Indian labour.[79] In other words, for them, it was not a question of whether the indenture trade was continued, but a question of *where* labour was employed. This argument is in keeping with Clarke's speech in the Town Hall in 1838, where he argued that local interests were tied to the indenture question: 'If the trade would be prevented, it might injure the sugar colonies, to the benefit of the sugar planters here [in India]. It might also give the planters here the benefit of that labour which would otherwise be abstracted.'[80] Planters in Bengal, according to Clarke, had a lot to gain from the abolition of indenture, in terms of both reduced competition from West Indian sugar and a larger labour pool to choose from in the absence of overseas emigration. While this argument might hold true for some, the situation was more complex than commercial interests could explain. Many Calcuttans who argued against the indenture trade were reformists with no commercial stake in either its continuation or abolition, while merchants like Tagore and Cowasjee straddled *zamindari*, commercial and reformist interests. Instead of judging just by their professions, the motivation behind their anti-indenture stance can be attributed to a combination of reformist interests, concern that indentured emigration could cause a shortage of domestic labour, the intellectual pressure of abolitionism and the example of social reform movements at home.

In the public debate on indenture, post-slavery humanitarianism came together with South Asian reformism, the influence of the Bengal Renaissance and Indian traditional philanthropic habits.[81] Within Bengal, the early- and mid-nineteenth century was a time of social reform movements where Indians negotiated with the colonial government for social betterment and welfare. During the so-called Bengal Renaissance, Bengal's reformers rallied against *sati* (widow immolation) and perpetual widowhood and in favour of issues such as widow remarriage, freedom of the press, increased printing presses and easier access to legal frameworks of the state. The indenture debates were part of this wider reformist trend, drawing also from Indian traditions of philanthropy, where *zamindar*s and rich members of society were historically responsible for philanthropic activities such as building wells, donating to the destitute and funding educational institutions.[82] It was also shaped, as we saw, by aspirations of belonging to a transnational public sphere.

At the same time, philanthropy and reformism did not necessarily mean that Tagore and Cowasjee were acting out of the goodness of their hearts. Philanthropy was a political move – a way of fulfilling the moral obligations of the post-slavery empire, performing the role of a good citizen and cultivating fame within Calcutta society. In many ways, participation in the indenture debates was a means to be heard and to becoming close to the ruling structure. It was a way to cultivate social and political capital. This reformism allowed elite spokesmen from Calcutta to argue for the rights of labourers whom they did not identify with socially or culturally and did not often afford rights to themselves, when employing them in households, agricultural works, plantations and public works. In fact, the philanthropy of Calcutta's spokesmen was mocked in a letter to the editor of the *Calcutta Courier*, which called them philanthropists in name only ('philanthropes en paroles') and recommended that they be philanthropic not with their pens but with their money.[83] Thus, a graded and nuanced reformism was at work here. As Sturman points out, the indenture system exemplified how labour welfare worked in 'fundamentally non-democratic contexts', where understandings of labour rights, discussions on labour welfare as a humanitarian concern and criticisms of bonded labour were fully compatible with imperial subjecthood.[84]

The next few pages explore the careers of Tagore and Cowasjee to locate their anti-indenture stance in the context of their other public activities. They were perfect examples of 'merchant-reformers'. Tagore was a landholder and entrepreneur with interest in indigo and sugar production. He owned shipping companies and held shares in various trading and banking organisations. Cowasjee was a merchant and shipping magnate with commercial interest in shipping between India and Mauritius. In view of the potential for profit from recruiting, accommodating and shipping indentured labourers from Calcutta to plantation colonies, both Tagore and Cowasjee's resistance to the trade seems counterintuitive. As a landholder and the owner of indigo plantations, Tagore particularly fits Bates and Carter's criteria for merchants who resisted indentured emigration as a form of labour strategy.[85] Yet their careers suggest that their reformist and merchant interests did not necessarily clash. Instead of a singularly commercial or reformist role in society, they were merchants and reformers at once.

Dwarkanath Tagore (1794–1847) was one of the most well-known participants in the Calcutta indenture debates (Figure 6.1). An entrepreneur, industrialist and philanthropist in his own right, Tagore was also the father of prominent Brahmo Samajist Debendranath Tagore, grandfather to Nobel Prize-winning poet and writer Rabindranath Tagore and great-grandfather to artists of the Bengal School of Art, Gaganendranath and Abanindranath Tagore.[86] He was the first Indian to become the director of a bank (the Union Bank) in 1828, and in 1834, he established the first Anglo-Indian trading agency with equal partnership, Carr, Tagore & Company, which was involved in emigrating labourers and servants from India.[87] Besides the ships he employed for trading, he also held shares in some Company ships.[88] He held *zamindari* land in eastern Bengal and was a shareholder in the Commercial Bank, the Laudable Society and the Oriental Life Assurance Society.[89]

As Carr, Tagore & Company gained traction, Tagore expanded into industrial ventures in eastern India – setting up an indigo factory at Silaidaha, establishing sugar factories in Baruipur, Ghazipur and Pabna, managing coalfields in Raniganj and reviving work at the government silk factory in Kumarkhali.[90] His Raniganj coalfields made him one of the earliest suppliers of energy for steamships in Bengal. In his sugar factories, he used Chinese and Mauritian sugarcanes and introduced new technologies of sugar production, such as the steam engine.[91] He testified to the Calcutta investigative committee that he was 'the first person who commenced cultivating sugar-cane by the

Figure 6.1 Dwarkanath Tagore

Source: 'Dwarakanath Thakur', in *Ramtanu Lahiri, Brahman and Reformer: A History of the Renaissance in Bengal*, by Sivanath Sastri (London: Swan Sonnenschein, 1907), Wikimedia Commons, https://commons.wikimedia.org/wiki/File:Dwarakanath_Thakur.jpg (accessed in April 2024).

European process, and under European superintendence, in India'.[92] During the economic crash of 1833, he personally took the risk for several merchant houses, accepted the risk of settling all debts of the Commercial Bank after it was already economically hit in 1828 and took steps to revive the Bengal economy.[93] He was involved in several profit-making agencies at once, and was an active and vocal member of associations such as the Landholders' Society.

Tagore also had a long-standing history of charitable and philanthropic activities, with his biographer lauding his cooperation with Ram Mohan Roy to abolish the practice of widow immolation (*sati*).[94] Tagore funded hospitals for leprosy patients, was an active member of the Native Relief Committee, was involved in the establishment and running of the Hindoo College (1817) and the Medical College (1835) in Calcutta, and funded and accompanied the first group of Bengali medical students to London, who later became the first FRCS (Fellowship of the Royal Colleges of Surgeons) doctors of Indian origin.[95] He donated 500 rupees to the Leper Asylum, 200 rupees for the relief of Indian paupers, 100,000 rupees for the relief of blind paupers in 1838, 500 rupees for relief during the Calcutta fires and 2,000 rupees in 1841 to establish an alms-house in Calcutta.[96] He was also a major donor to the Calcutta District Charitable Society. His reformist and charitable activities won him accolades from the British government, including charters of honour, a charter of citizenship of Edinburgh, the title of the 'Justice of the Peace' of Calcutta, a gold medal from the Company's Court of Directors, a medal from Queen Victoria and even an offer of knighthood (which he declined).[97]

An active supporter of 'native' press, Tagore was a shareholder in the *Bengal Hurkaru*, patronised the *Samachar Darpan*, provided financial support to establish *The Englishman*, the *Sambad Koumudi*, the *India Gazette* and the *Sambad Prabhakar*, and was involved in the maintenance of the Calcutta Public Library.[98] He actively participated in the movement for the freedom of the press following Adam's Press Ordinance of 1823, which suppressed the freedom of the English press in India. Freedom of the press, Tagore argued, strengthened the government's control over the region while also guaranteeing to the people 'that their rulers mean to govern with justice, since they are not afraid to let their subjects judge of their acts'.[99] General assemblies and meetings were not enough to ensure that all Indian subjects had the reach of the government – freedom of the press and printing presses were paramount.[100] Finally, under pressure from the likes of Tagore, the Press Act was passed in September 1835 to provide more freedom of the press. Tagore maintained that the passing of the Press Act helped remove the perceived difference between Europeans and Indians in Calcutta.[101] Similarly, when an act was passed in 1836 depriving non-official Britons of the right to appeal to the Supreme Court against judgments taken in the Company's provincial tribunals, Tagore joined the movement against it and spoke at the Town Hall about the importance of non-official Britons in bridging the gap between government servants and Indians.[102] S. R. Mehrotra argued that this movement ensured the support of the non-official British community in Indian undertakings 'almost as a quid pro quo'.[103]

Tagore's interest in labour migration was not just confined to indentured labourers. He maintained close relations with the Committee of the Edinburgh Emigration and Aborigines Protection Society, which had a strong abolitionist and anti-indenture stance.[104] He corresponded with British abolitionist George Thompson, whom he met in England in 1842 and brought to Calcutta in 1843 to deliver a series of lectures to members of the Society for the Acquisition of General Knowledge (SAGK).[105] Tagore's testimony for the Calcutta investigative committee was one of the few testimonies from Calcuttans who were not directly involved in the trade but were included as trustworthy citizen-witnesses. He was thus a prominent presence in the urban sphere of Calcutta, actively engaged in several issues of public interest. He was also close to the British ruling class – winning accolades, attending and throwing parties with Europeans, dining with Queen Victoria and Prince Albert and even once inviting the Queen to India to taste 'such a curry as has never been on [Her] Majesty's table'.[106] William Prinsep, founding partner of Carr, Tagore & Company wrote that Tagore 'launches into the full swing of London life' and enjoyed the occasional 'impudent joke which no one but himself would have dared to utter'.[107]

A contemporary of Tagore, Rustomjee Cowasjee (1792–1852) was a notable Parsi merchant and insurance and shipping magnate from Bombay, who moved base to Calcutta in 1817 (Figure 6.2).[108] Among other commercial ventures, he held shares in the Laudable Society, Sun Insurance Company, New Oriental Life Insurance Company, Universal Life Assurance Company and Union River Insurance Company.[109] Ships built in his docks at Kidderpore and Salkia near Calcutta carried mail and passengers to and from Singapore and China, and he was secretary to the Hooghly Docking Company and director of the Indian General Steam Navigation Company.[110] Partner in the shipping agency Rustomjee, Cowasjee & Company, he was involved in shipping to Mauritius from as early as 1839.[111] The company also emigrated domestic servants and *ayah*s from India to England on their ships and had a working relationship with Carr, Tagore & Company.[112] Besides commercial enterprises, Cowasjee built the Parsee Fire Temple on Ezra Street (Calcutta) in 1839 and financially contributed to the establishment of the Metcalfe Hall and the Asiatic Society of Bengal.[113] He was an annual subscriber and vice president of the Calcutta District Charitable Society and involved in trading with China in close conjunction with Carr, Tagore & Company.[114]

Figure 6.2 Rustomjee Cowasjee

Source: *A Series of Miscellaneous Rough Sketches of Oriental Heads* (Calcutta: Colesworthey Grant, 1844), p. 31, Wikimedia Commons, https://commons.wikimedia.org/wiki/File:ORIENTAL_ HEADS_p031_Rustomjee_Cowasjee,_Parsee,_Merchant_of_Bombay.jpg (accessed in April 2024). Original held and digitised by the British Library.

If Tagore held considerable interest in trading, shipping and insurance and Cowasjee had commercial interest in shipping labourers to Mauritius and England, they were both in positions to profit from a burgeoning trade in Indian indentured labourers. In fact, as contemporary shippers, both had a working relationship with Gillanders Arbuthnot & Company. A letter from 1837 mentioned the trade of goods between Gillanders Arbuthnot & Company, Tagore and Cowasjee, to be shipped on the latter's ships.[115] Why, then, were they opposed to the indenture trade? Instead of finding the answer for this discrepancy in their commercial activities, it can be found in seeing them not just as merchants, but as 'merchant-reformers'. Tagore and Cowasjee's role in contemporary Calcutta society was not confined to the commercial sphere but involved considerable philanthropic activities. It was possible for someone like Tagore to discuss *zamindari* rights and rent-free tenures in areas of the public sphere earmarked for landholders' issues and simultaneously weigh in on the rights of indentured labourers in other spaces.

As prominent entrepreneurs and philanthropists, indenture was one of many issues that Cowasjee and Tagore weighed in on. In 1842, when Bengal boasted six joint-stock companies, four were managed by Carr, Tagore & Company and one by Cowasjee.[116] As joint directors of the Indian Laudable and Mutual Assurance Society, Eastern Steam Navigation Company and the Union Bank, Tagore and Cowasjee enjoyed a close relationship, and it was not uncommon for them to engage in friendly rivalry.[117] Blair Kling noted:

> The populace of Calcutta laid their wagers and watched with excitement as Rustomjee and Dwarkanath raced their barques to and from Canton. In 1838 the *Waterwitch* [owned by Tagore] proved her superiority by beating out all rivals on a voyage from Canton to Calcutta in the record time of twenty-five days.[118]

After Tagore's death, Cowasjee became the trustee of the 'Dwarkanath Tagore Endowment', which raised funds to enable Indian students to receive education at University College, London.[119]

Tagore and Cowasjee also contributed to the spatial reform of Calcutta by financially supporting the Hindoo College and the Medical College, by improving and remodelling the Native Hospital in Durumtullah and by helping establish the Fever Hospital.[120] In 1836, Cowasjee, Tagore and Rosomoy Dutt joined the committee to endorse the opening of a fever hospital 'in a central part of the Native Town of Calcutta' to tackle tropical diseases.[121] As the committee raised 55,000 rupees (including from Tagore), secured land donated by Baboo Motilal Seal and submitted their report on the sanitary conditions of Calcutta, they put into motion early deliberations on public health that emphasised diet, cleanliness and municipal improvements alongside medical intervention.[122] This report was discussed in England as a bill on sanitation in large towns was brought to the parliament, ultimately leading to a detailed discussion on the need for public drains, better sewerage, pipe-water supply and well-ventilated houses in Calcutta.[123] In the aftermath of several fire outbreaks in 1837, Cowasjee excavated four water tanks along

Upper Circular Road as a fire prevention measure, and along with Tagore, he advocated for the building of tiled-roof huts to replace the destroyed straw- or thatched-roof huts that aided the spread of fire.[124]

Besides merchant-reformers like Tagore and Cowasjee, men from diverse professions weighed in on the indenture question. This included *zamindar*, court-pleader and educationist Prasanna Coomar Tagore; social reformer Reverend James Charles; educator, proselytiser and reformer Reverend Krishna Mohan Banerjee; judge and educationist Rosomoy Dutt; barrister Longueville Clarke; and Scottish watchmaker, educationist and philanthropist David Hare.[125] Many of them attended public meetings together, joined the same associations (like the Landholders' Society, the BIS and the SAGK) and sat on the same boards of education committees and charitable societies.[126] The resultant public sphere lent itself perfectly to the emergence of the indenture debates as it saw the coming together of a small but active community of Calcuttans to debate social issues and question colonial policy, the emergence of public meetings and petitions as a means of bringing such issues to the attention of government, the development of an intricate fabric of personal and professional networks and the coalescing of Indian reformist ideals with post-slavery humanitarianism.

The negotiation of subjecthood, citizenship and labour rights that took place in Calcutta cemented its political and intellectual position within global indenture networks. Ultimately, then, the indentured labourer had rights that the colonial state bestowed upon him and was responsible for upholding. At the same time, the labourer was the means by which Indians and Europeans in Calcutta could achieve their own claims to citizenship. Calcuttans not only advocated on behalf of indentured Indians but also used the indenture question to clarify their own position in the empire. By actively vocalising their thoughts about the rights of fellow subjects and expecting that their voices will not only be heard but will in fact shape policy, spokesmen in Calcutta asserted their position as citizens of the empire. In doing so, they redefined subjecthood questions by exploring what happened when subjects travelled beyond the geographical boundaries of the British Empire and tested the extent to which the colonial metropole was responsive to criticism and feedback from its subjects and citizens. Imperial subjecthood applied to the labourer through his right of being protected under law, and imperial citizenship applied to the spokesman through his participation in negotiating said rights. The responsiveness of metropolitan Britain to the concerns of such 'imperial citizens' was in a way completely beside the point; there was a clear expectation and demand on the part of the spokesmen to be heard and be legally recognised as part of the wider political community. Through these debates, the relationship between Calcutta's citizen-spokesmen, the imperial state and its migrating labouring population was imagined, negotiated, performed and consolidated.

Notes

1. C. A. Bayly, *Recovering Liberties: Indian Thought in the Age of Liberalism and Empire* (Cambridge, UK: Cambridge University Press, 2011), p. 31.
2. Ibid.
3. Rachel Sturman, 'Indian Indentured Labor and the History of International Rights Regimes', *American Historical Review* 119, no. 5 (2014): 1439–1465.
4. Ibid., p. 1440.
5. 'Meeting for Preventing the Exportation of Coolies', *Calcutta Review* 44 (July 1838), pp. 311, 315.
6. Letter to Alexander Ross (President of the Council of India and Deputy Governor of the President of Fort William) from James Young (Sheriff of Calcutta), [Petition] on Behalf of Those Assembled at the Town Hall Meeting in Calcutta, dated 10 July 1838, 1 August 1838, no. 1, General Department (General) Proceedings, WBSA (henceforth 'Calcutta Town Hall Petition') (emphasis mine).
7. 'Meeting for Preventing the Exportation of Coolies', p. 315 (emphasis mine).
8. *Calcutta Courier*, 11 July 1838, n.p. (emphasis in original). Charles references prominent British abolitionists William Wilberforce and Henry Brougham, who played a key role in the parliamentary campaigns to abolish British slavery.
9. 'Petition of Messers Henley, Dowson & Bestel and Others, or the Respectful Representation of the Merchants of Calcutta, Who Are Connected with the Trade of the Mauritius, in a Memorial Addressed to the President in Council of India in Council', dated 23 July 1838, Calcutta, General Department (General) Proceedings, 1 August 1838, no. 2, WBSA (henceforth 'Calcutta Merchant Petition').
10. Letter to the editor, 'The Cooley Question', *Calcutta Courier*, 21 July 1838, n.p.
11. Ibid. (translations mine).

12. *Calcutta Star*, 9 October 1843, p. 1923.

13. 'Meeting for Preventing the Exportation of Coolies', p. 314.

14. Ibid.

15. 'Copy of Mr. J. P. Grant's Minute on the Abuses Alleged to Exist in the Export of Coolies', dated 1 March 1841, in *Hill Coolies: Copy of Papers Respecting the Exportation of Hill Coolies* (ordered by the House of Commons to be printed, 21 June 1841), pp. 1–42 (henceforth 'Grant's Minute'), p. 1.

16. 'Meeting for Preventing the Exportation of Coolies', p. 311.

17. Ibid., p. 314.

18. Testimony of Sheik Manick, 1 October 1838, in 'Proceedings of the [Calcutta Investigative] Committee, from 22 August 1838 to 14 January 1839', in *Letter from Secretary to Government of India, to Committee on Exportation of Hill Coolies: Report of Committee and Evidence* (East India House, ordered by the House of Commons to be printed, 12 February 1841), Parliamentary Papers (House of Commons) 16, no. 45 (henceforth, 'Proceedings of the Calcutta Committee').

19. Ibid.

20. Testimony of Manick, vide Captain Finniss's Memorandum of 1 August 1838, in 'Statement of Coolies Returned from the Mauritius', exhibit No. 11, appendix to: *Letter from Secretary to Government of India, to Committee on Exportation of Hill Coolies: Report of Committee and Evidence* (East India House, ordered by the House of Commons to be printed, 12 February 1841), Parliamentary Papers (House of Commons) 16, no. 45 (henceforth 'Report of the Calcutta Committee').

21. Testimony of Bibee Zuhoorun, 20 September 1838, in 'Proceedings of the Calcutta Committee'.

22. Ibid.

23. Testimony of W. F. Dowson, 27 November 1838, in 'Proceedings of the Calcutta Committee'.

24. Ibid.

25. 'Report of the Calcutta Committee', p. 9.

26. See letters between W. D. Davis, Collector in charge of the Special Agents Department, and the Governor of French establishments in India, dated December 1848–June 1849, Home Department, Public Branch, 28 July 1849, progs no. 7, NAI; 'Rules for Observance in the Operations Connected with the Recruiting and Dispatch of Emigrants to the Island of Reunion under Act XLVI of 1860', Home Department, Public Branch, 19 February 1862, no. 43–49, NAI. For the French context, see Kate Marsh,

"'Rights of the Individual", Indentured Labour and Indian Workers: The French Antilles and the Rhetoric of Slavery Post 1848', *Slavery and Abolition* 33, no. 2 (2012): 221–231.

27. 'Meeting for Preventing the Exportation of Coolies', p. 315.

28. Ibid., p. 311.

29. 'Calcutta Town Hall Petition'.

30. Ibid.

31. See James Heartfield, *The Aborigines Protection Society: Humanitarian Imperialism in Australia, New Zealand, Fiji, Canada, South Africa, and the Congo, 1837–1909* (New York, NY: Columbia University Press, 2011); Zoë Laidlaw, '"Justice to India–Prosperity to England–Freedom to the Slave!" Humanitarian and Moral Reform Campaigns on India, Aborigines and American Slavery', *Journal of the Royal Asiatic Society* 22, no. 2 (2012): 299–324; Charles Swaisland, 'The Aborigines Protection Society, 1837–1909', *Slavery and Abolition* 21, no. 2 (2000): 265–280; James Heartfield, *The British and Foreign Anti-Slavery Society, 1838–1956: A History* (New York, NY: Oxford University Press, 2016); Madhavi Kale, *Fragments of Empire: Capital, Slavery, and Indian Indentured Labor in the British Caribbean* (Philadelphia, PA: University of Pennsylvania Press, 1998), esp. chs. 4 and 5; Roderick Mitcham, 'The Geographies of Global Humanitarianism: The Anti-Slavery Society and Aborigines Protection Society, 1884–1933', unpublished doctoral dissertation, Royal Holloway, University of London, 2002.

32. Michael Barnett, *Empire of Humanity: A History of Humanitarianism* (Ithaca, NY: Cornell University Press, 2011), p. 10. Other key works on imperial humanitarianism include Catherine Hall, 'The Lords of Humankind Re-Visited', *Bulletin of the School of Oriental and African Studies* 66, no. 3 (2003): 472–485; David Lambert and Alan Lester, 'Geographies of Colonial Philanthropy', *Progress in Human Geography* 28, no. 3 (2004): 320–341; Rob Skinner and Alan Lester, 'Humanitarianism and Empire: New Research Agendas', *Journal of Imperial and Commonwealth History* 40, no. 5 (2012): 729–747; Maeve Ryan, *Humanitarian Governance and the British Antislavery World System* (New Haven, CT: Yale University Press, 2022); Andrew Porter, 'Trusteeship, Anti-Slavery, and Humanitarianism', in *The Oxford History of the British Empire*: vol. 3: *The Nineteenth Century*, ed. Andrew Porter, pp. 198–221 (Oxford: Oxford University Press, 1999); Andrea Major, 'British Humanitarian Political Economy and Famine in India, 1838–1842', *Journal of British Studies* 59, no. 2 (2020): 221–244; and Zoë Laidlaw, 'Investigating Empire: Humanitarians, Reform and the

Commission of Eastern Inquiry', *Journal of Imperial and Commonwealth History* 40, no. 5 (2012): 749–768.

33. Barnett, *Empire of Humanity*, p. 55.

34. Ibid.

35. Ibid., p. 63.

36. Laidlaw, 'Investigating Empire', p. 749.

37. Ibid., p. 751. Richard Huzzey, however, contends that the Victorian opposition to slavery defied simple classification as universal humanitarianism or imperial reform. See Richard Huzzey, 'Minding Civilisation and Humanity in 1867: A Case Study in British Imperial Culture and Victorian Anti-Slavery', *Journal of Imperial and Commonwealth History* 40, no. 5 (2012): 807–825.

38. See Alan Lester and Fae Dussart, *Colonization and the Origins of Humanitarian Governance: Protecting Aborigines across the Nineteenth-Century British Empire* (Cambridge, UK: Cambridge University Press, 2014), p. 1.

39. William Green, 'Emancipation to Indenture: A Question of Imperial Morality', *Journal of British Studies* 22, no. 2 (1983): 98–121, p. 99.

40. Kate Boehme, Peter Mitchell and Alan Lester, 'Reforming Everywhere and All at Once: Transitioning to Free Labor across the British Empire, 1837–1838', *Comparative Studies in Society and History* 60, no. 3 (2018): 688–718, p. 708.

41. Peter J. Marshall, 'The Moral Swing to the East: British Humanitarianism, India and the West Indies', in *'A Free though Conquering People': Eighteenth-Century Britain and its Empire*, ed. P. J. Marshall, pp. 69–95 (Aldershot: Ashgate, 2003).

42. Ibid., p. 83.

43. 'Report of the Calcutta Committee', p. 12.

44. 'Calcutta Town Hall Petition'.

45. 'Letter from Hardinge to Stanley: The Coolie Emigration Act', V/6, IOR Neg 11691/6, dated 23 November 1844, in 'Papers of Field Marshal 1st Viscount Hardinge, Governor-General of India 1844–48' (1830–1848), IOR Neg 11691–94, BL.

46. Quoted in 'Baboo Dwarkanath Tagore', *Asiatic Journal*, November 1842, pp. 339–341.

47. *The Bengalee* 27, no. 41, dated 23 October 1886, p. 485, republished in *Dwarkanath Ganguli: Slavery in British Dominion*, ed. Kanailal Chattopadhyay and Sris Kumar Kunda (Calcutta: Jijnasa, 1959), p. 12.

48. *The Bengalee* 27, no. 42, dated 30 October 1886, p. 497, republished in *Dwarkanath Ganguli*, p. 16.

49. *The Bengalee* 27, no. 44, 13 November 1886, p. 522, republished in *Dwarkanath Ganguli*, p. 24.

50. Key works include David Zaret, *Origins of Democratic Culture: Printing, Petitions, and the Public Sphere in Early Modern England* (Princeton, NJ: Princeton University Press, 2000); Elizabeth Read Foster, 'Petitions and the Petition of Right', *Journal of British Studies* 14, no. 1 (1974): 21–45; David Zaret, 'Petitions and the "Invention" of Public Opinion in the English Revolution', *American Journal of Sociology* 101, no. 6 (May 1996): 1497–1555; Derek Hirst, 'Making Contact: Petitions and the English Republic', *Journal of British Studies* 45, no. 1 (January 2006): 26–50; Peter Fraser, 'Public Petitioning and Parliament before 1832', *History* 46, no. 158 (1961): 195–211; Mark Knights, '"The Lowest Degree of Freedom": The Right to Petition Parliament, 1640–1800', *Parliamentary History* 37 (2018): 18–34; and Philip Loft, 'Involving the Public: Parliament, Petitioning, and the Language of Interest, 1688–1720', *Journal of British Studies* 55, no. 1 (2016): 1–23. See also Brodie Waddell and Jason Peacey (eds.), *The Power of Petitioning in Early Modern Britain* (London: UCL Press, 2024).

51. Foster, 'Petitions and the Petition of Right'.

52. Zaret, 'Petitions and the "Invention" of Public Opinion'.

53. Ibid., p. 1498.

54. Rohit De and Robert Travers (eds.), 'Petitioning and Political Cultures in South Asia', *Modern Asian Studies* 53, special issue no. 1 (January 2019).

55. Rohit De and Robert Travers, 'Petitioning and Political Cultures in South Asia: Introduction', *Modern Asian Studies* 53, no. 1 (2019): 1–20, p. 3.

56. See De and Travers (eds.), 'Petitioning and Political Cultures'.

57. Prashant Kidambi, 'The Petition as Event: Colonial Bombay, circa 1889–1914', *Modern Asian Studies* 53, no. 1 (2019): 203–239, p. 207.

58. Bhavani Raman, *Document Raj: Writing and Scribes in Early Colonial South India* (Chicago: University of Chicago Press, 2012), p. 191.

59. Robert Travers, 'Indian Petitioning and Colonial State-Formation in Eighteenth-Century Bengal', *Modern Asian Studies* 53, no. 1 (2019): 89–122, p. 89.

60. Ibid., p. 121.

61. Majid Hayat Siddiqi, *The British Historical Context and Petitioning in Colonial India (M. A. Ansari Lecture)* (New Delhi: Aakar Books, 2005).

62. Daniel Carpenter and Doris Brossard, 'L'éruption patriote: The Revolt against Dalhousie and the Petitioning Explosion in Nineteenth-Century French Canada', *Social Science History* 43, no. 3 (2019): 453–485.

63. Richard Huzzey and Henry Miller, 'Colonial Petitions, Colonial Petitioners, and the Imperial Parliament, ca. 1780–1918', *Journal of British Studies* 61, no. 2 (2022): 261–289; Richard Huzzey and Henry Miller, 'Petitions, Parliament, and Political Culture: Petitioning the House of Commons, 1780–1918', *Past and Present* 248, no. 1 (2020): 123–164.

64. David Lambert, 'The Counter-Revolutionary Atlantic: White West Indian Petitions and Proslavery Networks', *Social and Cultural Geography* 6, no. 3 (2005): 405–420, p. 411.

65. Daniel Gorman, *Imperial Citizenship: Empire and the Question of Belonging* (Oxford: Oxford University Press, 2010), p. 1.

66. Ibid.

67. Sukanya Banerjee, *Becoming Imperial Citizens: Indians in the Late-Victorian Empire* (Durham, NC: Duke University Press, 2010), p. 9.

68. Ibid., p. 15.

69. Joya Chatterji, 'South Asian Histories of Citizenship, 1946–1970', *Historical Journal* 55, no. 4 (2012): 1049–1071.

70. Ibid.

71. Aihwa Ong, *Flexible Citizenship: The Cultural Logics of Transnationality* (Durham, NC: Duke University Press, 1999).

72. Frederick Cooper, *Citizenship between Empire and Nation: Remaking France and French Africa, 1945–1960* (Princeton and Oxford: Princeton University Press, 2014). Other works on negotiating colonial subjecthood and citizenship include Elizabeth Thompson, *Colonial Citizens: Republican Rights, Paternal Privilege, and Gender in French Syria and Lebanon* (New York, NY: Columbia University Press, 2000); Frederick Cooper, 'Citizenship and the Politics of Difference in French Africa, 1946–1960' in *Empires and Boundaries: Race, Class, and Gender in Colonial Settings*, ed. Harald Fischer-Tiné and Susanne Gehrmann, pp. 107–128 (New York, NY: Routledge, 2008); Hannah Weiss Muller, *Subjects and Sovereign: Bonds of Belonging in the Eighteenth-Century British Empire* (New York, NY: Oxford University Press, 2017); Emma Hunter (ed.), *Citizenship, Belonging, and Political Community in Africa: Dialogues Between Past and Present* (Athens, OH: Ohio University Press, 2016).

73. See Taylor Sherman, William Gould and Sarah Ansari, *From Subjects to Citizens: Society and the Everyday State in India and Pakistan, 1947–1970*

(Cambridge, UK: Cambridge University Press, 2014); Sandip Hazareesingh, 'The Quest for Urban Citizenship: Civic Rights, Public Opinion, and Colonial Resistance in Early Twentieth-Century Bombay', *Modern Asian Studies* 34, no. 4 (2000): 797–829; Gunnel Cederlöf and Sanjukta Das Gupta (eds.), *Subjects, Citizens and Law: Colonial and Independent India* (Abingdon and New York: Routledge, 2017); and Darren C. Zook, 'Developing the Rural Citizen: Southern India, 1900–47', *South Asia: Journal of South Asian Studies* 23, no. 1 (2000): 65–86. Global cosmopolitanism in South Asia has been explored in Kris Manjapra and Sugata Bose, *Cosmopolitan Thought Zones: South Asia and the Global Circulation of Ideas* (Basingstoke and New York: Palgrave Macmillan, 2010); Rosalind Parr, *Citizens of Everywhere: Indian Women, Nationalism and Cosmopolitanism, 1920–1952* (Cambridge, UK: Cambridge University Press, 2022).

74. Taylor Sherman, William Gould and Sarah Ansari, 'Introduction', in *From Subjects to Citizens: Society and the Everyday State in India and Pakistan, 1947–1970*, ed. Taylor Sherman, William Gould and Sarah Ansari, pp. 1–9 (Cambridge, UK: Cambridge University Press, 2014), p. 6; S. Banerjee, *Becoming Imperial Citizens*, p. 23.

75. T. H. Marshall, 'Citizenship and Social Class, 1950', in *The Anthropology of Citizenship: A Reader*, ed. Sian Lazar, pp. 52–60 (Chichester: John Wiley & Sons, 2013); Chatterji, 'South Asian Histories of Citizenship'.

76. Gunnel Cederlöf, 'Becoming and Being a Subject: An Introduction', in *Subjects, Citizens and Law: Colonial and Independent India*, ed. Gunnel Cederlöf and Sanjukta Das Gupta, pp. 1–17 (Abingdon and New York: Routledge, 2017), pp. 2–3.

77. Benedict Anderson, *Imagined Communities: Reflections on the Origin and Spread of Nationalism* (London: Verso, 2016 [1983]).

78. Huzzey and Miller, 'Colonial Petitions', pp. 287–288.

79. Crispin Bates and Marina Carter, 'Tribal and Indentured Migrants in Colonial India: Modes of Recruitment and Forms of Incorporation', in *Dalit Movements and the Meanings of Labour in India*, ed. Peter Robb, pp. 159–185 (Oxford: Oxford University Press, 1993), pp. 173–174.

80. 'Meeting for Preventing the Exportation of Coolies', p. 315.

81. Brian Hatcher argues that philanthropic behaviour in early colonial Calcutta arose from processes of colonial imitation, acknowledging that South Asia, much like Britain, did not have hermetically sealed or singular traditions of benevolence shaping the articulation of giving, kindness and public good. Brian A. Hatcher, 'Imitation, Then and Now: On the

Emergence of Philanthropy in Early Colonial Calcutta', *Modern Asian Studies* 52, no. 1 (2018): 62–98.

82. A recent lecture by Sumathi Ramaswamy demonstrates how private Indian philanthropic capital was invested into education – the popularly perceived British 'gift' of education thus critically supplemented by native monetary contributions. Sumathi Ramaswamy, 'A Strange Kindness: Largesse and Learning in the Age of Colonial Capital', Kingsley Martin memorial lecture delivered at the Centre for South Asian Studies, University of Cambridge, 19 October 2022.

83. Letter to the editor, 'The Cooly Question', *Calcutta Courier*, 21 July 1838, n.p. (translations mine).

84. Sturman, 'Indian Indentured Labor', p. 1457.

85. The employment of 'coolies' or manual labourers in Tagore's indigo plantations and coal mines are attested to in 'Memoirs of William Prinsep', vol. 3, 1838–42, MSS Eur D/1160/3, BL.

86. Key biographical works on Dwarkanath Tagore include Krishna Kripalani, *Dwarkanath Tagore: A Forgotten Pioneer, A Life* (New Delhi: National Book Trust, 1981); Hiranmay Banerjee, *The House of the Tagores* (Calcutta: Rabindra Bharati Press, 1985); Kissory Chand Mittra, *Memoir of Dwarkanath Tagore* (Calcutta: Thacker, Spink & Company, 1870); Kshitindranath Thakur, *Dwarkanath Thakurer Jiboni* (A Biography of Dwarkanath Tagore) (Calcutta: Rabindra Bharati University Press, 1969); and Debabrata Palit, *Dwarkanath Thakur* (Calcutta: Abinash Art Press, 1995). His commercial enterprises are explored in Blair Kling, *Partner in Empire: Dwarkanath Tagore and the Age of Enterprise in Eastern India* (Berkeley, CA: University of California Press, 1976); Blair Kling, 'The Origin of the Managing Agency System in India', *Journal of Asian Studies* 26, no. 1 (1966): 37–47; Farhat Hasan, 'Indigenous Cooperation and the Birth of a Colonial City: Calcutta, c. 1698–1750', *Modern Asian Studies* 26, no. 1 (1992): 65–82.

87. See letters between Carr, Tagore & Company and H. T. Prinsep, in General Department, General Branch Proceedings, 8 March 1837, nos. 50–51, WBSA. The establishment of Carr, Tagore & Company as the first Anglo-Indian business was declared in *Samachar Darpan*, 4 October 1834.

88. Tagore was part owner of the opium clipper *Water Witch* and owned two other opium clippers: *Ariel* and *Mavis*. 'Memoirs of William Prinsep', vol. 2, 1822–38, MSS Eur D/1160/2, BL; Kling, *Partner in Empire*, pp. 90–91.

89. Kripalani, *Dwarkanath Tagore*, pp. 75–77.

90. K. Mittra, *Memoir of Dwarkanath Tagore*.

91. Jogeshchandra Bagal, *Unabingsha Shataker Bangla* (Nineteenth-Century Bengal) (Calcutta: Ranjana Publishing House, 1963), pp. 28–33. See also 'Memoirs of William Prinsep', vol. 2.

92. Testimony of Dwarkanath Tagore, 9 November 1838, in 'Proceedings of the Calcutta Committee'.

93. *Samachar Darpan*, dated 23 July 1831, reported: 'Commercial bank: Mr. Dwarkanath Tagore lets everyone know that he will fulfil all debts on behalf of the bank.' Accessed in Rabindra Bharati Museum Collections, Kolkata, Acc. No. 00/3107/1. See also Kripalani, *Dwarkanath Tagore*, ch. 6; Brajendranath Bandyopadhyay, *Sambadpatre Sekaler Katha* (Representation of Past Times in Newspapers) (Calcutta: Bangiya Sahitya Parishad, 1996), p. 337.

94. K. Mittra, *Memoir of Dwarkanath Tagore*, pp. 23–29.

95. Ibid., pp. 23–28; *Samachar Darpan*, 1 June 1833, accessed in Rabindra Bharati Museum Collections, Kolkata, Acc. No. 00/3107/1.

96. *Bengal Hurkaru*, 4 February 1847, accessed in Rabindra Bharati Museum Collections, Kolkata, Acc. No. 00/3107/1; 'Calcutta Commercial Directory', in *The Bengal and Agra Annual Guide and Gazetteer* (Calcutta: William Rushton & Company, 1841), p. 360.

97. 'The grant of armorial ensigns to Prince Dwarkanath by Queen Victoria', 2000/8003/1, no. 1401; 'A Charter of Honour Presented to Dwarkanath Tagore at Town Hall in 1842 before His Departure to Europe', 2000/8004/1, no. 1402; 'A Charter of Honour Presented to Dwarkanath Tagore by the Edinburgh Emancipation and Aborigines Protection Society', 2000/8005/1, no. 1403; 'Charter of Citizenship of Edinburgh awarded to Dwarkanath Tagore', 2000/8007/1, no. 1405, accessed in Rabindra Bharati Museum Collections, Kolkata. See also 'Baboo Dwarkanath Tagore', *Asiatic Journal*, November 1842, pp. 339–341; *Bengal Hurkaru*, 25 October 1842; K. Mittra, *Memoir of Dwarkanath Tagore*, p. 63.

98. 'Manuscript on Dwarkanath Tagore's Life', file 8, no. 3, serial no. 320, Rabindra Bharati Museum Collections, Kolkata.

99. Quoted in Bagal, *Unabingsha Shataker Bangla*, p. 36.

100. 'Manuscript on Dwarkanath Tagore's Life'.

101. Ibid., p. 317.

102. S. R. Mehrotra, 'The Landholders' Society, 1838–44', *Indian Economic and Social History Review* 3, no. 4 (1966): 358–375, p. 364.

103. Ibid., p. 365.

104. K. Mittra, *Memoir of Dwarkanath Tagore*, pp. 97–100.

105. Letters between Dwarkanath Tagore and George Thompson, in 'Correspondence of Dwarkanath Tagore', 73/3676/1, no. 595, Rabindra Bharati Museum Collections, Kolkata; George Thompson, *Addresses Delivered at Meetings of the Native Community of Calcutta and on Other Occasions* (Calcutta: Thacker & Company, 1843). Crossing the *kala pani* had different connotations for Calcutta's elite. Dwarkanath Tagore's voyage to England was publicly celebrated and Kissory Chand Mittra hailed it as a move against social prejudice: 'stimulated by an earnest desire to expand his mind …, he determined to defy the prejudices of his age and country, and to cross the "kalla panee"'. K. Mittra, *Memoir of Dwarkanath Tagore*, p. 74. Similarly, Rustomjee Cowasjee's decision to cross the much shorter ocean between Bombay and Calcutta with his family was celebrated as a bold but welcome move: 'The ladies among the Parsis have the same aversion to going on board ships which the Hindu and Mohommedan [*sic*] ladies feel. This, therefore, is the first instance in which the tyranny of custom has been overcome.' *Samachar Darpan*, 18 August 1838, quoted in Prochy N. Mehta, *Pioneering Parsis of Calcutta* (New Delhi: Niyogi Books, 2020), p. 26.

106. The *Calcutta Monthly Journal*, dated December 1823, mentioned parties he threw, attended by the likes of Emily Eden. Accessed in Rabindra Bharati Museum Collections, Kolkata, Acc. No. 2001/9584; 'Memoirs of William Prinsep', vol. 3. See also Kripalani, *Dwarkanath Tagore*, p. 105.

107. 'Memoirs of William Prinsep', vol. 3.

108. See Mehta, *Pioneering Parsis of Calcutta*, esp. ch. 3.

109. 'Calcutta Commercial Directory', p. 205.

110. P. Thankappan Nair, *A History of Calcutta's Streets* (Calcutta: Firma KLM, 1987).

111. For his involvement in the firm, see 'Calcutta Commercial Directory' and 'Merchants, Agents and Companies', in *The Bengal and Agra Annual Guide and Gazetteer* (Calcutta: William Rushton & Company, 1841), p. 209. The following records show ships of his firm and ships belonging to his family emigrating labourers to Mauritius: 'Despatches to India and Bengal', Record Department, dated 25 September 1839, no. 13, p. 691, IOR/E/4/760, BL; letter from Messers Rustomjee, Cowasjee and Co., dated 27 February 1843, 1 March 1843, no. 6; letter to the Colonial Secretary, dated 28 February 1843, 1 March 1843, no. 21; letter from Messers Rustomjee, Cowasjee and Co., dated 28 February 1843, 1 March 1843, no. 7; letter from the Emigration Agent, dated 2 March 1843, 8

March 1843, no. 4; letter from M/s Rustomjee, Cowasjee and Co., dated 26 November 1844, 27 November 1844, nos. 9–11, General Department (General) Proceedings, WBSA.

112. For Rustomjee, Cowasjee & Company emigrating servants from India to England, see letters between Rustomjee Cowasjee & Company and H. T. Prinsep, dated 22 January 1840, 5 February 1840, nos. 41–43, General Department (General) Proceedings, WBSA.

113. Nair, *Calcutta's Streets*; Mehta, *Pioneering Parsis*.

114. *Samachar Darpan*, 1 June 1833, accessed in Rabindra Bharati Museum Collections, Kolkata, Acc. No. 00/3107/1; 'Memoirs of William Prinsep', vol. 2; 'Calcutta Commercial Directory', p. 361.

115. Letter from Dwarkanath Tagore to Gillanders Arbuthnot & Company, dated 30 March 1837, in 'Correspondence of Dwarkanath Tagore', 73/3675/1, no. 594, p. 166, Rabindra Bharati Museum Collections, Kolkata.

116. Kling, *Partner in Empire*, p. 245.

117. 'Calcutta Commercial Directory', pp. 150, 179, 187, 192.

118. Kling, *Partner in Empire*, p. 91.

119. 'Meeting Held in Commemoration of the Memory of Dwarkanath Tagore', *Bengal Hurkaru*, 4 December 1846, in K. Mittra, *Memoir of Dwarkanath Tagore*, app. C, pp. xlvii-lviii, esp. p. liii.

120. 'Calcutta Commercial Directory', p. 358; 'Proposed Fever Hospital, in Connection with the Medical College, Calcutta, by Fred. J. Mouat', in 'Miscellaneous Notices', *Calcutta Review* 2, no. 3 (October 1844).

121. 'Proposed Fever Hospital', p. 278.

122. 'Report of the Committee Appointed by the Right Hon'ble the Governor of Bengal for the Establishment of a Fever Hospital and for Inquiring into Local Management and Taxation in Calcutta, with Its Appendices, Calcutta 1839', *Calcutta Review* 5, no. 10 (April 1846): 373–395.

123. Ibid.

124. 'Prevention of Fires', *Calcutta Monthly Journal*, 28 June 1837, in *The Calcutta Monthly Journal and General Register of Occurrences throughout the British Dominions in the East forming an Epitome of the Indian Press for the Year 1837* (Calcutta: Samuel Smith & Company, 1838), pp. 338–342.

125. Bagal, *Unabingsha Shataker Bangla*; Anjali Bose (ed.), *Samsad Bangla Charitabhidhan* (A Dictionary of Bengali Biographies) (Calcutta: Sahitya Samsad, 1998); Peary Chand Mittra, *Biographical Sketch of David Hare* (Calcutta: W. Newman & Company, 1877).

126. K. M. Banerjee was a member of the Bengal branch of the BIS, while Dwarkanath Tagore, Prasanna Coomar Tagore and Theodore Dickens were members of the Landholders' Society. For details, see Mehrotra, 'The Landholders' Society'; S. R. Mehrotra, 'The British India Society and Its Bengal Branch, 1839–46', *Indian Economic and Social History Review* 4, no. 2 (1967): 131–154. For membership of boards of education and charitable societies of the time, see *The Bengal and Agra Annual Guide and Gazetteer* (Calcutta: William Rushton & Company, 1841).

Conclusion

City, Spaces, Encounters

Scholarship on Indian indenture has seen several historiographical turns over the years – from the overarching migration histories of the 1950s and the administrative histories of the 1960s and 1970s to the colony-focused histories that emerged in the 1980s and 1990s. The end of the century saw an increasing focus on migrants' experience of recruitment, passage and plantation, and the publication of Hugh Tinker's *A New System of Slavery* encouraged reflection on the vestiges of slavery while also prompting works that emphasised the autonomous agency of labourers in shaping their own economic futures.[1] The last two decades have seen an exciting shift in the field, as scholars are rejecting plantation colonies as the natural boundaries for framing indenture research and moving outside the 'indenture bubble' to draw links with other labour systems and wider imperial processes. Historians are increasingly framing indenture within the overseas movements of convicts, labourers, *lascar*s and servants, interrogating the implications of indenture research on understandings of colonial power and labour rights, and exploring the interplay of race and the body in the Indian indenture trade.[2] Increasingly, works have foregrounded connections between plantation colonies and explored spaces beyond the sugar colonies.[3] Yet others have flipped the narrative of indentured migrants as producers to explore their role as consumers, discussing how sale, taxation and consumption (of opium and cannabis, for instance) were ways of maintaining control over indentured Indians.[4] Indeed, the future of indenture research seems to be moving towards bringing indenture out of the slavery–indenture dichotomy and out of siloed colony-focused studies.

Voices from Calcutta fits squarely within this new, exciting turn in research. As indenture was criticised, investigated and defended in Calcutta, voices from Calcutta played an indispensable role in negotiating indenture regulations and shaping the contours of post-slavery labour migration. The movement of indentured labourers overseas was not just instigated by economic push and pull factors but was intricately woven into a complex set of social, political and economic factors tied to Calcutta and Calcuttans. Instead of seeing the indenture trade as precipitated by concerns in the imperial metropole and its sugar-producing colonies alone, this book shows that the collective voice of elite spokesmen in Calcutta made a dent in the legal and moral discourse and successfully stalled, and later shaped, indenture. In many ways, the indenture trade continued precisely because in its early years it had been questioned, criticised, investigated and then exonerated. As a result, Indian indenture continued for over 80 years and shaped migrant lives and histories of plantation colonies for decades to come.

The indenture debates reveal a Calcutta that was vocal, collaborative and negotiating its own position within the empire. The transition in the empire from a dependence on bonded and enslaved labour to nominally free labour offered an opportunity for planters, merchants and spokesmen opposed to the idea of a renewed system of slavery to weigh in on the indenture trade. The resultant debates influenced lived experience on ships and in the plantation colonies, and shaped the negotiation of subjecthood and labour rights for the empire's peripatetic labourers. The debates influenced Calcutta's position within the empire, becoming a means by which elite Calcuttans capitalised on the movement of indentured Indians to consolidate their own position. Thus, although power and authority continued to flow from the metropole to the colony, this authority was not as unqualified as previously held; Indians were active in contributing to colonial structures of power and global economic processes. With discussions in public spaces about the need to protect indentured Indians in faraway colonies, the plantation spaces in Guiana and Mauritius entered the imagination of the Calcutta elite as an extension of the British world. This connected South Asia to what Reshaad Durgahee has termed the 'indentured archipelago'.[5]

As the post-slavery empire required migrants to be free in their decision to migrate and free from modes of exploitation that had come to define the slave regime, and as planters, parliamentarians and anti-indenture petitioners discussed the legal freedom of indentured migrants (or lack thereof), indentured Indians were in many ways considered in charge of their own productive labour and able to sign their own contracts. Indentured labourers needed to be certified as free labourers – whether in the system as it then existed or by instituting critical changes in labour legislation – since only free migrants could inherit the plantation complex. At the same time, indentured labourers were imagined as primitive, ignorant, docile and outside the restrictions of traditional caste society, even as migrants came from different regions and walks of life. Such racialised understandings of indentured Indians shaped labour policy, food and leisure provisions and fuelled spokesmanship in Calcutta. As Calcuttans participated in creating this image of indentured Indians as primitive, docile and ignorant, they tested the limits of migrant subjecthood while also entrenching migrants further into the hierarchical structures of the empire.

Calcutta joined the indenture debates in the age of Abolition. This was a time that saw the rise of the British India Society (BIS), the Aborigines Protection Society (APS) and the British and Foreign Anti-Slavery Society (BFASS), which helped place India within a wider transnational context and put humanitarian concerns at the top of the imperial agenda. In the colonial metropole, petitions from abolitionists, local anti-slavery societies and parliamentarians like Lord Brougham and Lord Ellenborough lobbied for an end to indenture. John Scoble, a member of the Anti-Slavery Society and later the BFASS, wrote on the condition of indentured Indians in *Hill Coolies* (1840).[6] British newspapers were rife with descriptions of the deplorable conditions of indentured Indians and criticised the government for allowing indenture to continue. *Kendal Mercury* argued that the mere appointment of protective officers was not enough to curb abuses since these officers received remunerations from planters and were likely to be biased against the migrants.[7] The *British Emancipator* wrote in 1839 that 'the British Public has been deceived with the Idea that the Coolies are doing "well;" such is not the fact; the poor friendless Creatures are miserably treated', going on to say that in a conversation with an indentured Indian from the Bellevue estate, the migrant stated that 'Calcutta [was] better'.[8] *Liverpool Mercury* saw in indenture 'the re-establishment of the British slave-trade, and the perpetuation of slavery'.[9]

In this age of Abolition, the indenture debates in Calcutta upheld the juxtaposition to slavery and exemplified the obsession with indenture contracts. As a result, the Calcutta debates remain indispensable for understanding why the early indenture debates revolved around questions of legality, why it was pervaded by the language of freedom and unfreedom, and how rejection of slavery became the driving principle for how indenture was negotiated, legalised and valorised. As this book demonstrates that the legacies of slavery were located not in structural continuities on ships and plantations but in the very ways in which the indenture regime was framed, criticised, defended and regulated, it helps illuminate the 1830s and 1840s as a watershed moment in the protracted discussion on unfree labour and, indeed, the history of the colonial world.

The period of publicly debating indenture and negotiating labour legislation was short-lived in Calcutta, and it was not until the early twentieth century that the indenture question was taken up again. Once Act XV of 1842 was passed, allowing for the resumption of the indenture trade, the indenture debates receded into the background in Calcutta. As newspapers moved on to more pressing news and the 'coolie question' lost public interest, indenture discussions became firmly tethered to the official realm, with changing regulations in response to periodic commissions of inquiry, the publication of annual emigration reports and continued negotiation with other colonial powers on emigration to and from French and Dutch colonies.[10]

The turn of the century coincided with a turn towards indenture, with nationalist leaders like M. K. Gandhi, Gopal Krishna Gokhale and Madan Mohan Malviya, the Calcutta Marwari community, and ex-indentured labourers like Totaram Sanadhya becoming involved in discussing indenture and its abolition. As the indenture question re-entered the political sphere in British India, it became enmeshed in the anti-colonial movement, partly instigated by the experiences of Indians in South Africa. On his return from South Africa in 1896, Gandhi declared:

> A general feeling throughout South Africa is that of hatred towards Indian.... Every Indian, without exception, is a coolie in the estimation of the general body of the Europeans. Storekeepers are 'coolie storekeepers'. Indian clerks and schoolmasters are 'coolie clerks' and 'coolie schoolmasters'. Naturally, neither the traders nor the English-educated Indians are treated with any degree of respect.[11]

Consequently, a series of events helped bring the matter to government attention. As political groups discussed indenture and newspapers wrote on it, the abolition movement was carried out simultaneously in official and public circles.[12] The press coverage of indenture in the *Swarajya*, *Abhyudaya* and *Indian People* based in Allahabad, the *Advocate* based in Lucknow and the *Bharat Mitra* of Calcutta offered vivid, and at times sensationalist, accounts of the lives of indentured Indians.[13] Migrants' own accounts added to this: the harrowing story of Kunti's life in Fiji was published in the *Bharat Mitra* in 1913 and Totaram Sanadhya's autobiography *Fiji Dwip Me Mere Ikkis Varsh* (My 21 Years in the Fiji Islands) was published in 1914.[14] In the official sphere, Gokhale's 1912 resolution in the Imperial Legislative Council recommending the prohibition of the recruitment of indentured Indians was rejected.[15] However, as C. F. Andrews and W. W. Pearson's report on Fiji in 1916 resurfaced concerns about poor living and working conditions on plantations, Malviya successfully moved a resolution to abolish Indian indentured labour.[16] In 1917, the Government of India announced the termination of indentured recruitment for overseas plantations. Indenture contracts gradually ceased by 1920, and the post-war Indian Emigration Act of 1922 brought an official and authoritative end to decades of indentured emigration.[17]

The early indenture debates in Calcutta and the movement for the abolition of indenture in the twentieth century bookended the discussion on indenture as the language of resistance kept evolving from one of loyalty and negotiation to criticism to vehement protests calling for an end to indenture. Despite its changing aims, language, approach and modes of expressing dissent, anti-indenture activism continued to focus on deceptive recruitment, poor working conditions, and stereotypes of the ignorant labourer, the evil *arkatti*, the profit-driven planter and the complicit government. Almost a century after indenture was first negotiated in Calcutta, questions of subjecthood and belonging were reframed in the context of nationhood and repatriation as the Indian indenture trade was abolished. As migration continues to be a charged issue, as John Gladstone's descendants offer official apologies for their family's role in enslavement in Guiana, and as the indenture memorial near the Surinam Ghat in Calcutta stands testimony to the braided history of Calcutta and indenture and is increasingly visited by tourists and Calcuttans, the events of this book seem more relevant than ever.[18]

Notes

1. For an assessment of Tinker's position within indenture historiography, see Richard Allen, 'Re-Conceptualizing the "New System of Slavery"', *Man in India* 92, no. 2 (2012): 225–245; Doug Munro, 'The Tinker–Gillion Controversy in Indo-Fijian Indenture Historiography', *Slavery and Abolition* 42, no. 2 (2021): 363–381.

2. Clare Anderson, 'Convicts and Coolies: Rethinking Indentured Labour in the Nineteenth Century', *Slavery and Abolition* 30, no. 1 (2009): 93–109; Crispin Bates, 'Courts, Ship-Rolls and Letters: Reflections on the Indian Labour Diaspora', in *Creating an Archive Today*, ed. Toshie Awaya, pp. 131–158 (Tokyo: Centre for Documentation and Area-Transcultural Studies, Tokyo University of Foreign Studies, 2005); Nishant Batsha, 'The Currents of Restless Toil: Colonial Rule and Indian Indentured Labor in Trinidad and Fiji', unpublished doctoral dissertation, University of Columbia, 2017; Radhika Mongia, *Indian Migration and Empire: A Colonial Genealogy of the Modern State* (Durham, NC: Duke University Press, 2018); Rachel Sturman, 'Indian Indentured Labor and the History of International Rights Regimes', *American Historical Review* 119, no. 5 (2014): 1439–1465; Yoshina Hurgobin, 'Making Medical Ideologies: Indentured Labour in Mauritius', in *Histories of Medicine in the Indian Ocean World*, vol. 2: *The Modern Period*, ed. Anna Winterbottom and Facil Tesfaye, pp. 1–26 (New York, NY: Palgrave Macmillan, 2016).

3. Arunima Datta's study of indenture in Malayan rubber plantations pushed scholarly focus beyond sugar colonies and Reshaad Durgahee reimagined the indenture network to be composed of the indentured archipelago. Arunima Datta, *Fleeting Agencies: A Social History of Indian Coolie Women in British Malaya* (Cambridge, UK: Cambridge University Press, 2021); Reshaad Durgahee, *The Indentured Archipelago: Experiences of Indian Labour in Mauritius and Fiji, 1871–1916* (Cambridge, UK: Cambridge University Press, 2022).

4. Jamie Banks, 'Ganja Madness: Cannabis, Insanity, and Indentured Labor in British Guiana and Trinidad, 1881–1912', in *Cannabis: Global Histories*, ed. Lucas Richert and James H. Mills, pp. 57–80 (Cambridge, MA: MIT Press, 2021); Jamie Banks, '"Sterile Citizens" and "Excellent Disbursers": Opium and the Representations of Indentured Migrant Consumption in British Guiana and Trinidad', *Slavery and Abolition* 45, no. 2 (2024): 325–341.

5. Durgahee, *The Indentured Archipelago*.

6. John Scoble, *Hill Coolies: A Brief Exposition of the Deplorable Condition of the Hill Coolies in British Guiana and Mauritius, and of the Nefarious Means by Which They Were Induced to Resort to These Colonies* (London: Harvey & Darton, 1840).

7. 'The Trade in Hill Coolies', *Kendal Mercury*, 14 July 1838.

8. Extract from *British Emancipator*, dated 9 January 1839, in Appendix to 'Correspondence from Governor Light to the Marquess of Normanby,

dated 13 April 1839', Enclosure in No. 8, in *Correspondence Relative to the Condition of the Hill Coolies and of Other Labourers Who Have Been Introduced into British Guiana* (ordered to be printed 26 July and 12 August 1839), in *The Sessional Papers Printed by Order of the House of Lords or Presented by Royal Command in the Session 1839*, vol. 7, p. 79.

9. 'Alleged Revival of the Slave-Trade', *Liverpool Mercury*, 2 March 1838, p. 70.

10. Jonathan Connolly has explored the transition from indenture being denounced as a covert revival of slavery in the late 1830s and early 1840s to its normalisation later in the century, writing: 'Initially seen as a betrayal, indentured labour was gradually legitimized – as a means of civilizing primitive workers, and of correcting the supposed failures of emancipation.' Jonathan Connolly, 'Indentured Labour Migration and the Meaning of Emancipation: Free Trade, Race, and Labour in British Public Debate, 1838–1860', *Past and Present* 238, no. 1 (2018): 85–119, p. 89.

11. 'Speech at Public Meeting, Bombay', dated 26 September 1896, in *The Collected Works of Mahatma Gandhi*, by M. K. Gandhi, vol. 1 (New Delhi: Publications Division, Ministry of Information and Broadcasting, Government of India, 1958).

12. Recent works argue that the abolition of indenture owed more to public participation in its condemnation, like the activities of the Marwari Sahayak Samiti and the Anti-Indenture League of Calcutta, than to the interventions of elite leaders of the Indian National Congress. See Karen A. Ray, 'Kunti, Lakshmibhai and the "Ladies": Women's Labour and the Abolition of Indentured Emigration from India', *Labour, Capital and Society* 29, nos. 1–2 (1996): 126–152; Mrinalini Sinha, 'Anatomy of a Politics of the People', in *Political Imaginaries in Twentieth-Century India*, ed. Mrinalini Sinha and Manu Goswami, pp. 31–50 (London: Bloomsbury Academic, 2022).

13. Ashutosh Kumar, *Coolies of the Empire: Indentured Indians in the Sugar Colonies, 1830–1920* (Cambridge, UK: Cambridge University Press, 2017), pp. 209–210, 214–216.

14. Mrinalini Sinha, 'Totaram Sanadhya's *Fiji Mein Mere Ekkis Varsh*: A History of Empire and Nation in a Minor Key', in *Ten Books That Shaped the British Empire: Creating an Imperial Commons*, ed. Antoinette Burton and Isabel Hofmeyr, pp. 168–188 (Durham, NC: Duke University Press, 2014).

15. 'Prohibition of Indentured Labour', dated 4 March 1912, in *Speeches and Writings of Gopal Krishna Gokhale*, vol. 1: *Economic*, ed. R. P. Patwardhan and D. V. Ambekar, pp. 347–366 (Poona: Asia Publishing House, 1962).

16. C. F. Andrews and W. W. Pearson, *Report on Indentured Labour in Fiji: An Independent Enquiry* (Calcutta: Star Printing Works, 1916); 'The Abolition of Indentured Labour', dated 20 March 1916, in *Speeches and Writings of Pandit Madan Mohan Malaviya*, pp. 323–347 (Madras: G.A. Natesan & Co., n.d.).

17. M. Sinha, 'Anatomy of a Politics of the People', p. 31.

18. 'William Gladstone's Family Apologises for Role in Slave Trade', BBC News, 25 August 2023, https://www.bbc.com/news/uk-wales-66621480 (accessed 4 April 2024). For indenture memorials in Calcutta and histories of return, see Nalini Mohabir, 'Port of Departure, Port of Return: Mapping Indentured Returns to Calcutta', *Small Axe: A Caribbean Journal of Criticism* 18, no. 2 (2014): 108–122.

Glossary

arkotti / arkatti	middleman or local labour recruiting agent
ayah	female domestic servant, often a nanny or a nursemaid
bhistee	water carrier and supplier
chakor	servant, normally a domestic servant
chakri	job or profession
chini	sugar
chittack	a measure of weight
Company	English East India Company
coolie / cooly	Indian indentured labourer
darwaza	gate
dhangar / dhangur	caste designation, often used to refer to labourers with menial jobs
dhooti / dhoti	an unstitched lower-body garment worn by men
diwani	right to collect land revenue
dohai / dohye	a plea for help
duffadar	agent or middleman in labour recruitment
ghat	pier, or a flight of stairs leading down to a river
haat	local and temporary market, often weekly or biweekly
hukum	order

janau	sacred thread worn by Brahmin men as a marker of caste status
kagaz	paper or document
kala pani	lit., the dark waters; refers to caste taboo on crossing the seas
khidmutgar	servant, generally a domestic servant similar to a butler
kol / cole	a caste/ethnographic designation
lascar	Indian sailor or militiaman employed on ships
lota	water vessel, often spouted, used variously for drinking, pouring, cleansing, ritual purposes and bathing
mojurgiri	wage labour
mojuri	wages
para	neighbourhood
perwannah / *parwana*	an official or royal order, a letter of authority or a license
sahib	sir or Englishman
sati	lit., a virtuous woman; the Hindu practice of immolation of a widow in the pyre of her deceased husband
sepoy	Indian soldier
serang	seaman, often the head or captain of *lascars*
sirdar	foreman
syce	horse keeper or groomer
tapu	island
zamindar	landowner or landholder

Bibliography

Archival and Manuscript Sources

British Library, London

European Manuscripts Collection

'Memoirs of William Prinsep', vol. 2, 1822–1838, MSS Eur D/1160/2.
'Memoirs of William Prinsep', vol. 3, 1838–1842, MSS Eur D/1160/3.

India Office Records E Series

'Despatches to India and Bengal', Record Department, dated 25 September 1839, No. 13, IOR/E/4/760.

India Office Records F Series

Papers Regarding the Emigration of Indian Labourers to the British Colonies, vol. 2: *Hill Coolies: Report of the Committee, Minutes of Council*, dated 22 April 1841–12 May 1842. Board's Collections, 1840–1841, vol. 1909, no. 81645. IOR/F/4/1909/81645.

Papers Regarding the Emigration of Indian Labourers to the British Colonies, vol. 2: *Correspondence of two Calcutta Houses of Agency, viz. Messrs Colville, Gilmore and Co. and Messrs Saunders, May, Sarkies*, dated March 1841–May 1841. Board's Collections, 1840–1841, vol. 1909, no. 81646. IOR/F/4/1909/81646.

Papers Regarding the Employment of Indian Indentured Labourers Overseas, vol. 6:
   *Report on the Condition of the Labourers on 24 of the Principal Plantations in the
   Savanne District, Mauritius*, dated July 1839. Board's Collections, 1840–1841,
   vol 1847, no. 77646. Legislative Department, IOR/F/4/1847/77646.

Papers Regarding the Employment of Indian Indentured Labourers Overseas, vol. 7:
   *Report on the Condition of the Labourers on 24 Estates in the Plaines Wilhelms
   District, Mauritius*, dated June–July 1839. Board's Collections, 1840–1841,
   vol. 1847, no. 77647. IOR/F/4/1847/77647.

Papers Regarding the Employment of Indian Indentured Labourers Overseas,
   vol. 10: *Report on the Condition of the Labourers on 22 Estates in the Flacq
   District, Mauritius (Includes Answers to Questionnaires, by Both Employers and
   Labourers)*, dated February 1839–March 1839. Board's Collections, 1840–
   1841, vol. 1847, no. 77650. IOR/F/4/1847/77650.

India Office Records P Series

'Major Pitcher's Report on the Result of His Inquiry into the System of
   Recruiting Labourers for the Colonies'. Proceedings of the Revenue and
   Agricultural Department, February 1883, Proceedings no. 2. IOR/P/2057.

India Office Records V Series:

Examination of [Six] Coolies Returned from Mauritius per Gilbert Munro (Calcutta:
   Bengal Military Orphan Press, 1841). IOR/V/27/820/23.

India Office Records X Series:

Smart, R. B. 'Detail of Garden Reach'. Sheet 7 [Garden Reach] of the Hooghly
   Survey, 1887. IOR/X/9126/7.

India Office Records Neg Series:

'Papers of Field Marshal 1st Viscount Hardinge, Governor-General of India
   1844–48' (1830–1848). IOR Neg 11691–94.

Published Books and Manuscripts

Chattopadhyay, Dakshinacharan. *The Mirror of a Tea Planter, or Cha-Kar Darpan*
   (Calcutta: Jodunath Mandal, 1875).

Chattopadhyay, Jogendranath. *Cha-Coolie-r Atmakahini* [Memoirs of a Tea Labourer] (Calcutta: Bengal Medical Library, 1308 BS [1901–1902]).

Grierson, George Abraham. *Report on Colonial Emigration from the Bengal Presidency* (with diary) (Calcutta: n.p., 1883).

Vidyaratna, Ramkumar. *Kuli Kahini: Sketches from Cooly Life* (originally published anonymously) (Calcutta: Victoria Press, 1888).

———. *Udasin Satyasrabar Assam Bhraman* (The Indifferent Truth-Seeker's Travels in Assam) (originally published anonymously) (Calcutta: n.p., 1879).

Glynne-Gladstone Manuscript Collections, Gladstone's Library, Hawarden (Wales)

'A Statement of Facts Connected with the Present State of Slavery ... Together with a View of the Present Situation of the Lower Classes in the United Kingdom, Contained in a Letter Addressed to ... Sir Robert Peel, Bart. by John Gladstone'. 1830. GG/2868.

'Correspondence with Lord Glenelg, Relating Mainly to the Sending of Coolies from India to British Guiana, Incl. Copy Correspondence between Lord Glenelg and Major-General Sir J. C. Smyth (Governor of British Guiana)'. 1820–1838. GG/348.

'Correspondence, etc. on the Taking of Coolies to British Guiana, Incl. Letters from Andrew Colville, George C. Arbuthnot and Sir George Grey, and Copy Letters to the Duke of Wellington'. 1838. GG/358.

'Extract from a Despatch from Lord Bathurst to Major-General Sir B. D'Urban (Governor of British Guiana) with Resolutions of Demerara Planters, and Speeches in the Court of Policy, Concerning the Manumission of Slaves'. 1826. GG/2865.

'Letters from Andrew Colville (from London)'. 1831–1849. GG/100.

'Letters from John Moss (of Otterspool), Liverpool Merchant and Demerara Planter'. 1834–1839. GG/297.

'Miscellaneous Correspondence'. 1806–1849. GG/2768.

National Archives of India, New Delhi

Home Department, Public Branch Consultations, 1832–1862.

Index of the Home Department, Public Branch, 1835–1843.

Index of the Military Department, Military Branch, 1835–1843.

Ministry of Home Affairs, Government of India, Home Department, Public Branch, 1950.

National Library of India, Kolkata

Act XV of 1842, Colonial Emigration Acts (Bombay Education Society Press, 1842). Home Department, Public Branch, Annex Building.

Emigration Act V of 1837. Passed by the Governor-General in Council on 1 May 1837, Home Department, Public Branch, Annex Building.

Emigration Act XXXII of 1837. Passed by the President of Council of India in Council on 15 December 1837, Home Department, Public Branch, Annex Building.

Emigration Act XIV of 1839. Passed by the Honourable the President of the Council of India in Council on 27 May 1839, Home Department, Public Branch, Annex Building.

Rabindra Bharati Museum, Kolkata

'A Charter of Honour Presented to Dwarkanath Tagore at Town Hall in 1842 before His Departure to Europe', 2000/8004/1, no. 1402.

'A Charter of Honour Presented to Dwarkanath Tagore by the Edinburgh Emancipation and Aborigines Protection Society', 2000/8005/1, no. 1403.

Bengal Hurkaru (1847), acc. no. 00/3107/1.

Calcutta Monthly Journal (1823), acc. no. 2001/9584.

'Charter of Citizenship of Edinburgh Awarded to Dwarkanath Tagore', 2000/8007/1, no. 1405.

'Correspondence of Dwarkanath Tagore', 73/3675/1, no. 594.

'Correspondence of Dwarkanath Tagore', 73/3676/1, no. 595.

'Manuscript on Dwarkanath Tagore's Life', File 8, No. 3, Serial No. 320.

Samachar Darpan (1831–1833), acc. no. 00/3107/1.

'The Grant of Armorial Ensigns to Prince Dwarkanath by Queen Victoria', 2000/8003/1, no. 1401.

West Bengal State Archives, Kolkata

General Department (General) Proceedings (General Department, General Branch Proceedings), 1834–1844.

Index to General Department (General) Proceedings, 1835–1842.

Judicial (Criminal) Index, 1838–1843.

Judicial (Criminal) Proceedings, 1838–1843.

News Sources and Periodicals

Asiatic Journal, 1842.

Asiatic Journal and Monthly Miscellany, 1839.

Asiatic Journal and Monthly Register for British and Foreign India, China, and Australasia, 1832–1842.

BBC News, 2023.

Bengal Hurkaru, 1838–1842.

British Emancipator, 1839.

Calcutta Christian Observer, 1832.

Calcutta Courier, 1838–1840.

Calcutta Monthly Journal, 1838.

Calcutta Monthly Journal and General Register, 1836.

Calcutta Review, 1838–1874.

Calcutta Star, 1843–1844.

Friend of India, 1837–1842.

Kendal Mercury, 1838.

Leeds Mercury, 1836.

Leicester Chronicle, 1841.

Liverpool Mercury, 1838.

Samachar Darpan, 1831–1834.

Taunton Courier and Western Advertiser, 1838.

The Englishman, 1838–1842.

Unpublished Papers and Dissertations

Batsha, Nishant. 'The Currents of Restless Toil: Colonial Rule and Indian Indentured Labor in Trinidad and Fiji'. Unpublished doctoral dissertation, University of Columbia, 2017.

Martin, Janette. 'Popular Political Oratory and Itinerant Lecturing in Yorkshire and the North East in the Age of Chartism, 1837–60'. Unpublished doctoral dissertation, University of York, 2010.

Mitcham, Roderick. 'The Geographies of Global Humanitarianism: The Anti-Slavery Society and Aborigines Protection Society, 1884–1933'. Unpublished doctoral dissertation, Royal Holloway, University of London, 2002.

Ramaswamy, Sumathi. 'A Strange Kindness: Largesse and Learning in the Age of Colonial Capital'. Kingsley Martin Memorial lecture delivered at the Centre for South Asian Studies, University of Cambridge, 19 October 2022.

Official Reports and Publications

British Guiana: Copies or Extracts of Any Correspondence between the Secretary of State for the Colonies and the Governor of British Guiana, Respecting the Immigration of Labourers into that Colony (ordered by the House of Commons to be printed, 24 March 1840).

Burbank, Captain C. *Annual Report on Emigration from the Port of Calcutta to British and Foreign Colonies for 1864–65*. Dated 23 May 1865, No. 299 (Calcutta: Bengal Secretariat Press, 1865).

Copies of All Orders in Council, or Colonial Ordinances, for the Better Regulations and Enforcement of the Relative Duties of Masters and Employers, and Articled Servants, Tradesmen and Labourers, in the Colonies of British Guiana and Mauritius and of Correspondence Relating Thereof (ordered by the House of Commons to be printed, 2 March 1838).

Correspondence Relative to the Condition of the Hill Coolies and of Other Labourers Who Have Been Introduced into British Guiana (ordered to be printed by the House of Lords, 26 July and 12 August 1839).

Correspondence Respecting the Employment of Indian Labourers in the Mauritius (printed by the House of Commons, 7 February 1840).

Geoghegan, John. *Note on Emigration from India* (Calcutta: Superintendent of Government Printing, 1873).

Grant, J. G. *Annual Report on Emigration from the Port of Calcutta to British and Foreign Colonies for 1873–74*. No. 609/A (Calcutta: Bengal Secretariat Press, 1874).

Hill Coolies: Copy of Papers Respecting the Exportation of Hill Coolies (ordered by the House of Commons to be printed, 21 June 1841).

Letter from Secretary to Government of India, to Committee on Exportation of Hill Coolies: Report of Committee and Evidence (East India House, ordered by the House of Commons to be printed, 12 February 1841).

Mauritius: Copies of Correspondence Addressed to the Secretary of State for the Colonial Department, Relative to the Introduction of Indian Labourers into the Mauritius (ordered by the House of Commons to be printed, 28 May 1840).

Mauritius: Copies of Despatches from Sir William Nicolay on the Subject of Free Labour in the Mauritius (ordered by the House of Commons to be printed, 7 February 1840).

Papers Respecting the East-India Labourers Bill (London: Printed by order of the General Court, by J. L. Cox & Sons, 1838).

Report from the Select Committee on Transportation (Communicated by the Commons to the Lords) (ordered by the House of Commons to be printed, 16 August 1838).

Published Primary Sources

Andrews, C. F., and W. W. Pearson. *Report on Indentured Labour in Fiji: An Independent Enquiry* (Calcutta: Star Printing Works, 1916).

Autobiography of an Indian Indentured Labourer Munshi Rahman Khan (1874–1972), Jeevan Prakash. Translated by Kathinka Sinha-Kerkhoff, Ellen Bal and Alok Deo Singh (New Delhi: Shipra Publications, 2005).

Barlow, Nora (ed.). *Charles Darwin's Diary of the Voyage of H.M.S. 'Beagle'* (New York: Macmillan Company; Cambridge, UK: Cambridge University Press, 1933 [1845]).

Blackie, Walker Graham (ed.). *The Imperial Gazetteer; a General Dictionary of Geography, Physical, Political, Statistical and Descriptive*, vol. 1 (Edinburgh and London: Blackie & Son, 1856).

Campbell, George. *The Ethnology of India* (Calcutta: C.B. Lewis, 1866).

Carlile, James (ed.). *Journal of a Voyage with Coolie Emigrants, from Calcutta to Trinidad, by Captain and Mrs. Swinton, late of the ship 'Salsette'* (London: Alfred W. Bennett, 1859).

Chattopadhyay, Kanailal, and Sris Kumar Kunda (eds.). *Dwarkanath Ganguli: Slavery in British Dominion* (Calcutta: Jijnasa, 1959).

Crooke, William. *The Tribes and Castes of the North-Western Provinces and Oudh*, vol. 2 (Calcutta: Office of the Superintendent of Government Printing, 1906).

Dabydeen, David, Jonathan Morley, Brinsley Samaroo, Amar Wahab and Brigid Wells (eds.). *The First Crossing Being the Diary of Theophilus Richmond, Ship's Surgeon aboard the Hesperus, 1837–8* (Guyana: Caribbean Press, 2010).

Dalton, Edward Tuite. 'The Kols of Chota Nagpore'. *Journal of the Asiatic Society of Bengal* 35, no. 2 (1866): 153–200.

Dalton, Edward Tuite. *Descriptive Ethnology of Bengal* (Calcutta: Office of the Superintendent of Government Printing, 1872).

Das Gupta, Anil Chandra (ed.). *The Days of John Company: Selections from Calcutta Gazette, 1824–1832* (Calcutta: Superintendent Government Printing, 1959).

Gandhi, M. K. *The Collected Works of Mahatma Gandhi*, vol. 1 (New Delhi: Publications Division, Ministry of Information and Broadcasting, Government of India, 1958).

Ghose, Benoy. *Selections from English Periodicals of Nineteenth Century Bengal, 1815–33* (Calcutta: Papyrus, 1978).

Hamilton, Walter. *Description of Hindostan and the Adjacent Countries*, vol. 1 (Delhi: Oriental Publishers, 1820).

Justice Murdered in India: The Papers of the Webb Case Recording the Sacrifice of a Daughter of India to the Lust of an Anglo-Indian (Calcutta: Sadharon Brahmo Samaj Press, 1884), reprinted in Kanailal Chattopadhyay and Sris Kumar Kunda (eds.), *Dwarkanath Ganguli: Slavery in British Dominion* (Calcutta: Jijnasa, 1959).

Long, James. 'Calcutta in the Olden Time: Its Localities'. *Calcutta Review* 18 (July–December 1852).

Mangru, Basdeo (ed.). *Colonial Emigration from the Bengal Presidency* (Hertford: Hansib Publishers, 2014).

'Meeting for Preventing the Exportation of Coolies'. *Calcutta Review* 44 (July 1838).

Patwardhan, R. P., and D. V. Ambekar (eds.). *Speeches and Writings of Gopal Krishna Gokhale*, vol. 1: *Economic* (Poona: Asia Publishing House, 1962).

'Proposed Fever Hospital, in Connection with the Medical College, Calcutta, by Fred. J. Mouat', in 'Miscellaneous Notices', *Calcutta Review* 2, no. 3 (October 1844).

'Report of the Committee Appointed by the Right Hon'ble the Governor of Bengal for the Establishment of a Fever Hospital and for Inquiring into Local Management and Taxation in Calcutta, with Its Appendices, Calcutta 1839'. *Calcutta Review* 5, no. 10 (April 1846): 373–395.

Risley, H. H. *The Tribes and Castes of Bengal: Ethnographic Glossary*, vol. 1 (Calcutta: Bengal Secretariat Press, 1892).

Russell, R. V. *Tribes and Castes of the Central Provinces of India* (London: Macmillan & Company Limited, 1916).

Sanadhya, Totaram. *My Twenty-One Years in the Fiji Islands and The Story of the Haunted Line*. Edited by John D. Kelly and Uttra Kumari Singh (Suva: Fiji Museum, 1991).

Scoble, John. *Hill Coolies: A Brief Exposition of the Deplorable Condition of the Hill Coolies in British Guiana and Mauritius, and of the Nefarious Means by Which They Were Induced to Resort to These Colonies* (London: Harvey & Darton, 1840).

Sherring, Matthew Atmore. *Hindu Tribes and Castes* (Calcutta: Thacker, Spink & Company, 1872).

Speeches and Writings of Pandit Madan Mohan Malaviya (Madras: G.A. Natesan & Company, n.d.).

The Bengal and Agra Annual Guide and Gazetteer (Calcutta: William Rushton & Company, 1841).

The Calcutta Monthly Journal and General Register of Occurrences throughout the British Dominions in the East Forming an Epitome of the Indian Press for the Year 1837 (Calcutta: Samuel Smith & Company, 1838).

Thompson, George. *Addresses Delivered at Meetings of the Native Community of Calcutta and on Other Occasions* (Calcutta: Thacker & Company, 1843).

Yule, Henry. *Hobson-Jobson: A Glossary of Colloquial Anglo-Indian Words and Phrases, and of Kindred Terms, Etymological, Historical, Geographical and Discursive*. New edition edited by William Crooke (London: J. Murray, 1903 [1886]).

Secondary Works

Ahuja, Ravi. 'Mobility and Containment: The Voyages of South Asian Seamen, c. 1900–1960'. *International Review of Social History* 51, no. 14 (2006): 111–141.

———. 'Networks of Subordination: Networks of the Subordinated – The Ordered Spaces of South Asian Maritime Labour in an Age of Imperialism (c. 1890–1947)'. In *The Limits of British Colonial Control in South Asia: Spaces of Disorder in the Indian Ocean Region*, edited by Ashwini Tambe and Harald Fischer Tiné, pp. 23–58 (London: Routledge, 2008).

Akurang-Parry, K. O. '"A Smattering of Education" and Petitions as Sources: A Study of African Slaveholders' Responses to Abolition in the Gold Coast Colony, 1874–1875'. *History in Africa* 27 (2000): 39–60.

Alatas, Syed Hussein. *The Myth of the Lazy Native: A Study of the Image of the Malays, Filipinos and Javanese from the 16th to the 20th Century and Its Function in the Ideology of Colonial Capitalism* (London: Frank Cass, 1977).

Allen, Richard. 'Re-Conceptualizing the "New System of Slavery"'. *Man in India* 92, no. 2 (2012): 225–245.

———. 'Slaves, Convicts, Abolitionism and the Global Origins of the Post-Emancipation Indentured Labor System'. *Slavery and Abolition* 35, no. 2 (2014): 328–348.

———. *Slaves, Freedmen and Indentured Laborers in Colonial Mauritius* (Cambridge: Cambridge University Press, 1999).

Altink, Henrice. *Representations of Slave Women in Discourses on Slavery and Abolition, 1780–1838* (New York, NY: Routledge, 2007).

Amrith, Sunil. *Crossing the Bay of Bengal: The Furies of Nature and the Fortunes of Migrants* (Cambridge, MA: Harvard University Press, 2013).

Anderson, Benedict. *Imagined Communities: Reflections on the Origin and Spread of Nationalism* (London: Verso, 2016 [1983]).

Anderson, Clare. 'After Emancipation: Empires and Imperial Formations'. In *Emancipation and the Remaking of the British Imperial World*, edited by Catherine Hall, Nicholas Draper and Keith McClelland, pp. 113–127 (Manchester: Manchester University Press, 2014).

——— (ed.). *A Global History of Convicts and Penal Colonies* (London: Bloomsbury Publishing, 2018).

———. 'Convicts and Coolies: Rethinking Indentured Labour in the Nineteenth Century'. *Slavery and Abolition* 30, no. 1 (2009): 93–109.

———. *Convicts in the Indian Ocean: Transportation from South Asia to Mauritius, 1815–53* (London: Palgrave Macmillan, 2000).

———. *Legible Bodies: Race, Criminality and Colonialism in South Asia* (Oxford and New York: Berg Publishers, 2004).

———. 'The Andaman Islands Penal Colony: Race, Class, Criminality, and the British Empire'. *International Review of Social History* 63, no. S26 (2018): 25–43.

———. 'Transnational Histories of Penal Transportation: Punishment, Labour and Governance in the British Imperial World, 1788–1939'. *Australian Historical Studies* 47, no. 3 (2016): 381–397.

Archer, John. 'Paras, Palaces, Pathogens: Frameworks for the Growth of Calcutta, 1800–1850'. *City and Society* 12, no. 1 (2000): 19–54.

Ashforth, Adam. 'Reckoning Schemes of Legitimation: On Commissions of Inquiry as Power/Knowledge Forms'. *Journal of Historical Sociology* 3, no. 1 (1990): 1–22.

Bagal, Jogeshchandra. *Unabingsha Shataker Bangla* (Nineteenth-Century Bengal) (Calcutta: Ranjana Publishing House, 1963).

Balachandran, Gopalan. 'Conflicts in the International Maritime Labour Market: British and Indian Seamen, Employers, and the State, 1890–1939'. *Indian Economic and Social History Review* 39, no. 1 (2002): 71–100.

Ballantyne, Tony. 'Rereading the Archive and Opening up the Nation-State: Colonial Knowledge in South Asia (and Beyond)'. In *After the Imperial Turn:*

Thinking with and through the Nation, edited by Antoinette Burton, pp. 102–121 (Durham, NC: Duke University Press, 2003).

Bandyopadhyay, Brajendranath. *Sambadpatre Sekaler Katha* (Representation of Past Times in Newspapers) (Calcutta: Bangiya Sahitya Parishad, 1996).

Banerjee, Hiranmay. *The House of the Tagores* (Calcutta: Rabindra Bharati Press, 1985).

Banerjee, Sukanya. *Becoming Imperial Citizens: Indians in the Late-Victorian Empire* (Durham, NC: Duke University Press, 2010).

Banks, Jamie. 'Ganja Madness: Cannabis, Insanity, and Indentured Labor in British Guiana and Trinidad, 1881–1912'. In *Cannabis: Global Histories*, edited by Lucas Richert and James H. Mills, pp. 57–80 (Cambridge, MA: MIT Press, 2021).

———. '"Sterile Citizens" and "Excellent Disbursers": Opium and the Representations of Indentured Migrant Consumption in British Guiana and Trinidad'. *Slavery and Abolition* 45, no. 2 (2024): 325–341.

Barnett, Michael. *Empire of Humanity: A History of Humanitarianism* (Ithaca: Cornell University Press, 2011).

Bates, Crispin. 'Coerced and Migrant Labourers in India: The Colonial Experience'. *Edinburgh Papers in South Asian Studies* 13 (2000): 1–33.

———. 'Courts, Ship-Rolls and Letters: Reflections on the Indian Labour Diaspora'. In *Creating an Archive Today*, edited by Toshie Awaya, pp. 131–158 (Tokyo: Centre for Documentation and Area-Transcultural Studies, Tokyo University of Foreign Studies, 2005).

———. 'Some Thoughts on the Representation and Misrepresentation of the Colonial South Asian Labour Diaspora'. *South Asian Studies* 33, no. 1 (2017): 7–22.

Bates, Crispin, and Marina Carter. 'Enslaved Lives, Enslaving Labels: A New Approach to the Colonial Indian Labor Diaspora'. In *New Routes for Diaspora Studies*, edited by Sukanya Banerjee, Aims McGuinness and Steven McKay, pp. 67–92 (Bloomington, IN: Indiana University Press, 2012).

———. 'Kala Pani Revisited: Indian labour migrants and the sea crossing'. *Journal of Indentureship and Its Legacies* 1, no. 1 (2021): 36–62.

———. 'Sirdars as Intermediaries in Nineteenth-Century Indian Ocean Indentured Labour Migration'. *Modern Asian Studies* 51, no. 2 (2017): 462–484.

———. 'Tribal and Indentured Migrants in Colonial India: Modes of Recruitment and Forms of Incorporation'. In *Dalit Movements and the*

Meanings of Labour in India, edited by Peter Robb, pp. 159–185 (New Delhi: Oxford University Press, 1993).

Bayly, C. A. *Recovering Liberties: Indian Thought in the Age of Liberalism and Empire* (Cambridge, UK: Cambridge University Press, 2011).

Bayly, Martin J. 'Imperial Ontological (In)Security: "Buffer States", International Relations and the Case of Anglo-Afghan Relations, 1808–1878'. *European Journal of International Relations* 21, no. 4 (2015): 816–840.

———. *Taming the Imperial Imagination* (Cambridge, UK: Cambridge University Press, 2016).

Bayly, Susan. 'Caste and "Race" in the Colonial Ethnography of India'. In *The Concept of Race in South Asia*, edited by Peter Robb, pp. 165–218 (New Delhi: Oxford University Press, 1995).

Bhana, Surendra. *Indentured Indian Emigrants to Natal, 1860–1902: A Study Based on Ships' Lists* (New Delhi: Promilla & Company, 1991).

Bhattacharya, Bhabani. *Socio-Political Currents in Bengal: A Nineteenth Century Perspective* (New Delhi: Vikas Publications, 1980).

Boehme, Kate, Peter Mitchell and Alan Lester. 'Reforming Everywhere and All at Once: Transitioning to Free Labor across the British Empire, 1837–1838'. *Comparative Studies in Society and History* 60, no. 3 (2018): 688–718.

Bose, Anjali (ed.). *Samsad Bangla Charitabhidhan* (A Dictionary of Bengali Biographies) (Calcutta: Sahitya Samsad, 1998).

Bose, Sugata. *Peasant Labour and Colonial Capital: Rural Bengal since 1770* (Cambridge, UK: Cambridge University Press, 1993).

Brown, Mark. 'Ethnology and Colonial Administration in Nineteenth-Century British India: The Question of Native Crime and Criminality'. *British Journal for the History of Science* 36, no. 2 (2003): 201–219.

Burnard, Trevor, and Kit Candlin. 'Sir John Gladstone and the Debate over the Amelioration of Slavery in the British West Indies in the 1820s'. *Journal of British Studies* 57, no. 4 (2018): 760–782.

Burton, Antoinette. 'Introduction: Archive Fever, Archive Stories'. In *Archive Stories: Facts, Fictions, and the Writing of History*, edited by Antoinette Burton, pp. 1–24 (Durham, NC: Duke University Press, 2006).

Carpenter, Daniel, and Doris Brossard. 'L'éruption patriote: The Revolt against Dalhousie and the Petitioning Explosion in Nineteenth-Century French Canada'. *Social Science History* 43, no. 3 (2019): 453–485.

Carter, Marina. *Servants, Sirdars and Settlers: Indians in Mauritius, 1834–1874* (New Delhi and New York: Oxford University Press, 1995).

———. 'Strategies of Labour Mobilisation in Colonial India: The Recruitment of Indentured Workers for Mauritius'. *Journal of Peasant Studies* 19, nos. 3–4 (1992): 229–245.

———. *Voices from Indenture: Experiences of Indian Migrants in the British Empire* (London: Burns & Oates, 1996).

Carter, Marina, and Khal Torabully. *Coolitude: An Anthology of the Indian Labour Diaspora* (London: Anthem Press, 2002).

Cederlöf, Gunnel, and Sanjukta Das Gupta (eds.). *Subjects, Citizens and Law: Colonial and Independent India* (Abingdon and New York: Routledge, 2017).

Chakravorty Spivak, Gayatri. 'Can the Subaltern Speak?' In *Marxism and the Interpretation of Culture*, edited by Cary Nelson and Lawrence Grossberg, pp. 271–314 (Urbana and Chicago, IL: University of Illinois Press, 1988).

Chandra, Uday. 'Kol, Coolie and Colonial Subject: A Hidden History of Caste and the Making of Modern Bengal'. In *The Politics of Caste in West Bengal*, edited by Uday Chandra, Geir Heierstad and Kenneth Bo Nielsen, pp. 19–34 (Oxon and New York: Routledge, 2015).

———. 'Liberalism and Its Other: The Politics of Primitivism in Colonial and Postcolonial Indian Law'. *Law and Society Review* 47, no. 1 (2013): 135–168.

Chapman, S. D. 'The Agency Houses: British Mercantile Enterprise in the Far East c. 1780–1920'. *Textile History* 19, no. 2 (1988): 239–254.

Chatterji, Joya. 'South Asian Histories of Citizenship, 1946–1970'. *Historical Journal* 55, no. 4 (2012): 1049–1071.

Chattopadhyay, Basudeb. *The Town Hall of Calcutta: A Brief History* (Calcutta: Homage Trust, 1998).

Chattopadhyay, Swati. *Representing Calcutta: Modernity, Nationalism and the Colonial Uncanny* (London: Routledge, 2005).

Chaudhuri, Sukanta. *Calcutta, the Living City*, vol. 1: *The Past* (Calcutta: Oxford University Press, 1990).

Chaudhuri, Sukanta. *Calcutta, the Living City*, vol. 2: *The Present and Future* (Calcutta: Oxford University Press, 1995).

Checkland, Sydney George. 'John Gladstone as Trader and Planter'. *Economic History Review* 7, no. 2 (1954): 216–229.

———. *The Gladstones: A Family Biography 1764–1851* (London and New York: Cambridge University Press, 1971).

Connolly, Jonathan. 'Indentured Labour Migration and the Meaning of Emancipation: Free Trade, Race, and Labour in British Public Debate, 1838–1860'. *Past and Present* 238, no. 1 (2018): 85–119.

Cooper, Frederick. 'Citizenship and the Politics of Difference in French Africa, 1946–1960'. In *Empires and Boundaries: Race, Class, and Gender in Colonial Settings*, edited by Harald Fischer-Tiné and Susanne Gehrmann, pp. 107–128 (New York, NY: Routledge, 2008).

———. *Citizenship between Empire and Nation: Remaking France and French Africa, 1945–1960* (Princeton and Oxford: Princeton University Press, 2014).

Dasgupta, Keya. *Mapping Calcutta: The Collection of Maps at the Visual Archives of the Centre for Studies in Social Sciences* (Kolkata: Centre for Studies in Social Sciences, 2009).

Dasgupta, Sangeeta. '"Heathen Aboriginals", "Christian Tribes", and "Animistic Races": Missionary Narratives on the Oraons of Chhotanagpur in Colonial India'. *Modern Asian Studies* 50, no. 2 (2016): 437–478.

Datta, Arunima. *Fleeting Agencies: A Social History of Indian Coolie Women in British Malaya* (Cambridge, UK: Cambridge University Press, 2021).

———. '"Immorality", Nationalism and the Colonial State in British Malaya: Indian "Coolie" Women's Intimate Lives as Ideological Battleground'. *Women's History Review* 25, no. 4 (2016): 584–601.

Datta, Partho. *Planning the City: Urbanization and Reform in Calcutta, c. 1800–1940* (New Delhi: Tulika Books, 2012).

Datta, Partho. 'Review Essay: Celebrating Calcutta'. *Urban History* 19, no. 1 (1992): 84–98.

De, Rohit, and Robert Travers. 'Petitioning and Political Cultures in South Asia: Introduction'. *Modern Asian Studies* 53, no. 1 (2019): 1–20.

Doherty, Stephen, Lisa Ford, Kirsten McKenzie, Naomi Parkinson, David Roberts, Paul Halliday, Zoë Laidlaw, Alan Lester and Philip Stern. 'Inquiring into the Corpus of Empire'. *Journal of World History* 32, no. 2 (June 2021): 219–240.

Draper, Nicholas. 'The Rise of a New Planter Class? Some Countercurrents from British Guiana and Trinidad, 1807–33'. *Atlantic Studies* 9, no. 1 (2012): 65–83.

Drescher, Seymour. 'Whose Abolition? Popular Pressure and the Ending of the British Slave Trade'. *Past and Present* 143 (1994): 136–166.

Drescher, Seymour, and Christine Bolt. *Capitalism and Antislavery: British Mobilization in Comparative Perspective* (New York and Oxford: Oxford University Press, 1987).

Dumas, Paula. *Proslavery Britain: Fighting for Slavery in an Era of Abolition* (New York, NY: Palgrave Macmillan, 2016).

Durgahee, Reshaad. *The Indentured Archipelago: Experiences of Indian Labour in Mauritius and Fiji, 1871–1916* (Cambridge, UK: Cambridge University Press, 2022).

Emmer, P. C. *Colonialism and Migration: Indentured Labour Before and After Slavery* (Leiden: Martinus Nijhoff Publishers, 1986).

Engerman, Stanley L. 'Contract Labor, Sugar, and Technology in the Nineteenth Century'. *Journal of Economic History* 43, no. 3 (1983): 635–659.

Fisher, Michael. *Counterflows to Colonialism: Indian Travellers and Settlers in Britain, 1600–1857* (New Delhi: Permanent Black, 2004).

———. 'Working Across the Seas: Indian Maritime Labourers in India, Britain, and in between, 1600–1857'. *International Review of Social History* 51, no. S14 (2006): 21–45.

Fokken, Margriet. *Beyond Being Koelies and Kantráki: Constructing Hindostani Identities in Suriname in the Era of Indenture, 1873–1921* (Hilversum: Verloren, 2018).

Foster, Elizabeth Read. 'Petitions and the Petition of Right'. *Journal of British Studies* 14, no. 1 (1974): 21–45.

Frankel, Oz. 'Scenes of Commission: Royal Commissions of Inquiry and the Culture of Social Investigation in Early Victorian Britain'. *European Legacy* 4, no. 6 (1999): 20–41.

———. *States of Inquiry: Social Investigations and Print Culture in Nineteenth-Century Britain and the United States* (Baltimore, MD: Johns Hopkins University Press, 2006).

Fraser, Peter. 'Public Petitioning and Parliament before 1832'. *History* 46, no. 158 (1961): 195–211.

Ghosh, Anindita. *Power in Print: Popular Publishing and the Politics of Language and Culture in a Colonial Society, 1778–1905* (New York, NY: Oxford University Press, 2006).

Ghosh, Kaushik. 'A Market for Aboriginality: Primitivism and Race Classification in the Indentured Labour Market of Colonial India'. In *Subaltern Studies X: Writings on South Asian History and Society*, edited by Gautam Bhadra, Gyan Prakash, and Susie Tharu, pp. 8–48 (New Delhi: Oxford University Press, 1999).

Gorman, Daniel. *Imperial Citizenship: Empire and the Question of Belonging* (Oxford: Oxford University Press, 2010).

Green, William A. 'Emancipation to Indenture: A Question of Imperial Morality'. *Journal of British Studies* 22, no. 2 (1983): 98–121.

Grewal, J. S. (ed.). *Calcutta: Foundation and Development of a Colonial Metropolis* (Chandigarh: Urban History Association of India, 1991).

Hall, Catherine. 'The Lords of Humankind Re-Visited'. *Bulletin of the School of Oriental and African Studies* 66, no. 3 (2003): 472–485.

Hangloo, Rattan Lal. *Indian Diaspora in the Caribbean: History, Culture, and Identity* (New Delhi: Primus Books, 2012).

Hasan, Farhat. 'Indigenous Cooperation and the Birth of a Colonial City: Calcutta, c. 1698–1750'. *Modern Asian Studies* 26, no. 1 (1992): 65–82.

Hassankhan, Maurits, Brij V. Lal and Doug Munro (eds.). *Resistance and the Indian Indenture Experience: Comparative Perspectives* (New Delhi: Manohar Publishers, 2014).

Hatcher, Brian A. 'Imitation, Then and Now: On the Emergence of Philanthropy in Early Colonial Calcutta'. *Modern Asian Studies* 52, no. 1 (2018): 62–98.

Hay, Douglas, and Paul Craven (ed.). *Masters, Servants, and Magistrates in Britain and the Empire, 1562–1955* (Chapel Hill, NC: University of North Carolina Press, 2005).

Hazareesingh, Sandip. 'The Quest for Urban Citizenship: Civic Rights, Public Opinion, and Colonial Resistance in Early Twentieth-Century Bombay'. *Modern Asian Studies* 34, no. 4 (2000): 797–829.

Heartfield, James. *The Aborigines Protection Society: Humanitarian Imperialism in Australia, New Zealand, Fiji, Canada, South Africa, and the Congo, 1837–1909* (New York, NY: Columbia University Press, 2011).

———. *The British and Foreign Anti-Slavery Society, 1838–1956: A History* (New York, NY: Oxford University Press, 2016).

Hirst, Derek. 'Making Contact: Petitions and the English Republic'. *Journal of British Studies* 45, no. 1 (January 2006): 26–50.

Hoefte, Rosemarijn. *In Place of Slavery: A Social History of British Indian and Javanese Laborers in Suriname* (Gainesville, FL: University Press of Florida, 1998).

Hossain, Purba. "'A Matter of Doubt and Uncertainty': John Gladstone and the Post-Slavery Framework of Labour in the British Empire'. *Journal of Imperial and Commonwealth History* 50, no. 1 (2022): 52–80.

———. "'Docile, Quiet, Orderly': Indian Indenture Trade and the Ideal Labourer'. In *Across Colonial Lines: Commodities, Networks, and Empire Building*, edited by Devyani Gupta and Purba Hossain, pp. 179–198 (London: Bloomsbury Publishing, 2023).

———. 'Protests at the Colonial Capital: Calcutta and the Global Debates on Indenture, 1836-42'. *South Asian Studies* 33, no. 1 (2017): 37–51.

Hunter, Emma (ed.). *Citizenship, Belonging, and Political Community in Africa: Dialogues Between Past and Present* (Athens, OH: Ohio University Press, 2016).

Hurgobin, Yoshina. 'Making Medical Ideologies: Indentured Labour in Mauritius'. In *Histories of Medicine in the Indian Ocean World*, vol. 2: *The Modern Period*, edited by Anna Winterbottom and Facil Tesfaye, pp. 1–26 (New York, NY: Palgrave Macmillan, 2016).

Huzzey, Richard, and Henry Miller. 'Colonial Petitions, Colonial Petitioners, and the Imperial Parliament, ca. 1780–1918'. *Journal of British Studies* 61, no. 2 (2022): 261–289.

———. 'Petitions, Parliament, and Political Culture: Petitioning the House of Commons, 1780–1918'. *Past and Present* 248, no. 1 (2020): 123–164.

Huzzey, Richard. 'Minding Civilisation and Humanity in 1867: A Case Study in British Imperial Culture and Victorian Anti-Slavery'. *Journal of Imperial and Commonwealth History* 40, no. 5 (2012): 807–825.

Ivermee, Robert. *Hooghly: The Global History of a River* (London: Hurst Publishers, 2020).

Jones, Stephanie. *Merchants of the Raj: British Managing Agency Houses in Calcutta Yesterday and Today* (London: Macmillan Press, 1992).

Kale, Madhavi. *Fragments of Empire: Capital, Slavery, and Indian Indentured Labor Migration in the British Caribbean* (Philadelphia, PA: University of Pennsylvania Press, 1998).

Kerr, Ian. 'On the Move: Circulating Labor in Pre-Colonial, Colonial, and Post-Colonial India'. *International Review of Social History* 51, no. S14 (2006): 85–109.

Kidambi, Prashant. 'The Petition as Event: Colonial Bombay, circa 1889–1914'. *Modern Asian Studies* 53, no. 1 (2019): 203–239.

Kling, Blair. *Partner in Empire: Dwarkanath Tagore and the Age of Enterprise in Eastern India* (Berkeley, CA: University of California Press, 1976).

———. 'The Origin of the Managing Agency System in India'. *The Journal of Asian Studies* 26, no. 1 (1966): 37–47.

Knights, Mark. '"The Lowest Degree of Freedom": The Right to Petition Parliament, 1640–1800'. *Parliamentary History* 37 (2018): 18–34.

Kolff, D. H. A. *Naukar, Rajput and Sepoy: The Ethnohistory of the Military Labour Market in Hindustan, 1450–1850* (Cambridge, UK: Cambridge University Press, 1990).

Kolsky, Elizabeth. *Colonial Justice in British India: White Violence and the Rule of Law* (Cambridge, UK: Cambridge University Press, 2010).

Kosambi, Meera, and John E. Brush. 'Three Colonial Port Cities in India'. *Geographical Review* 78, no. 1 (1988): 32–47.

Kripalani, Krishna. *Dwarkanath Tagore: A Forgotten Pioneer, A Life* (New Delhi: National Book Trust, 1981).

Kumar, Ashutosh. *Coolies of the Empire: Indentured Indians in the Sugar Colonies, 1830–1920* (Cambridge, UK: Cambridge University Press, 2017).

Laidlaw, Zoë. 'Investigating Empire: Humanitarians, Reform and the Commission of Eastern Inquiry'. *Journal of Imperial and Commonwealth History* 40, no. 5 (2012): 749–768.

———. '"Justice to India–Prosperity to England–Freedom to the Slave!" Humanitarian and Moral Reform Campaigns on India, Aborigines and American Slavery'. *Journal of the Royal Asiatic Society* 22, no. 2 (2012): 299–324.

Lal, Brij V. *Chalo Jahaji: On a Journey through Indenture in Fiji* (Acton: Australian National University Press, 2012).

———. *Girmitiyas: The Origins of the Fiji Indians* (Lautoka: Fiji Institute of Applied Studies, 2004 [1983]).

Lambert, David. 'The Counter-Revolutionary Atlantic: White West Indian Petitions and Proslavery Networks'. *Social and Cultural Geography* 6, no. 3 (2005): 405–420.

Lambert, David, and Alan Lester. 'Geographies of Colonial Philanthropy'. *Progress in Human Geography* 28, no. 3 (2004): 320–341.

Laurence, K. O. *A Question of Labour: Indentured Immigration into Trinidad and British Guiana, 1875–1917* (London: Ian Randle Publishers, 1994).

Lester, Alan. 'Imperial Circuits and Networks: Geographies of the British Empire'. *History Compass* 4, no. 1 (2006): 124–141.

Lester, Alan, and Fae Dussart. *Colonization and the Origins of Humanitarian Governance: Protecting Aborigines across the Nineteenth-Century British Empire* (Cambridge, UK: Cambridge University Press, 2014).

Loft, Philip. 'Involving the Public: Parliament, Petitioning, and the Language of Interest, 1688–1720'. *Journal of British Studies* 55, no. 1 (2016): 1–23.

Look Lai, Walton. *Indentured Labor, Caribbean Sugar: Chinese and Indian Migrants to the British West Indies, 1838–1918* (Baltimore, MD: Johns Hopkins Press, 1993).

Losty, Jeremiah P. *Calcutta: City of Palaces. A Survey of the City in the Days of the East India Company (1690–1858)* (London: British Library, 1990).

Major, Andrea. 'British Humanitarian Political Economy and Famine in India, 1838–1842'. *Journal of British Studies* 59, no. 2 (2020): 221–244.

———. '"Hill Coolies": Indian Indentured Labour and the Colonial Imagination, 1836–38'. *South Asian Studies* 33, no. 1 (2017): 23–36.

———. *Reimagining Empire in India: George Thompson, Anti-Slavery Activism, and the Global Networks of British Colonial Reform, 1831–1858* (London: Bloomsbury Publishing, 2025).

Mamun, Muntasir. *Unish Shatake Bangladesher Sambad-Samayikpatra, 1847–1905* (Nineteenth-Century Newspapers and Periodicals of Bangladesh) (Dhaka: Bangla Akademi, 1985).

Manjapra, Kris, and Sugata Bose. *Cosmopolitan Thought Zones: South Asia and the Global Circulation of Ideas* (Basingstoke and New York: Palgrave Macmillan, 2010).

Mann, Michael. *A British Rome in India: Calcutta – Capital for an Empire* (Worms: Wernersche Verlagsgesellschaft, 2022).

Marsh, Kate. '"Rights of the Individual", Indentured Labour and Indian Workers: The French Antilles and the Rhetoric of Slavery Post 1848'. *Slavery and Abolition* 33, no. 2 (2012): 221–231.

Marshall, Peter J. 'British Society in India under the East India Company'. *Modern Asian Studies* 31, no. 1 (1997): 89–108.

———. 'Eighteenth Century Calcutta'. In *Colonial Cities: Essays on Urbanism in a Colonial Context*, edited by R. J. Ross and G. Telkamp, pp. 87–104 (Dordrecht: Martinus Nijhoff Publishers, 1985).

———. 'The Company and the Coolies: Labour in Early Calcutta'. In *The Urban Experience, Calcutta: Essays in Honour of Professor Nisith R. Ray*, edited by Pradip Sinha, pp. 23–38 (Calcutta: Riddhi-India, 1987).

———. 'The Moral Swing to the East: British Humanitarianism, India and the West Indies'. In *'A Free though Conquering People': Eighteenth-Century Britain and Its Empire*, edited by P. J. Marshall, pp. 69–95 (Aldershot: Ashgate, 2003).

Marshall, T. H. 'Citizenship and Social Class, 1950'. In *The Anthropology of Citizenship: A Reader*, edited by Sian Lazar, pp. 52–60 (Chichester: John Wiley & Sons, 2013).

Mayer, Adrian C. *Indians in Fiji* (London: Oxford University Press, 1963).

Mbembe, Achille. 'The Power of the Archive and Its Limits'. In *Refiguring the Archive*, edited by Carolyn Hamilton, Verne Harris, Jane Taylor, Michele Pickover, Graeme Reid and Razia Saleh, pp. 19–27 (Dordrecht: Springer, 2002).

Mehrotra, S. R. 'The British India Society and Its Bengal Branch, 1839–46'. *Indian Economic and Social History Review* 4, no. 2 (1967): 131–154.

———. 'The Landholders' Society, 1838–44'. *Indian Economic and Social History Review* 3, no. 4 (1966): 358–375.

Mehta, Prochy N. *Pioneering Parsis of Calcutta* (New Delhi: Niyogi Books, 2020).

Metcalf, Thomas. '"Hard Hands and Sound Healthy Bodies": Recruiting "Coolies" for Natal, 1860–1911'. *Journal of Imperial and Commonwealth History* 30, no. 3 (2002): 1–26.

———. *Ideologies of the Raj* (Cambridge, UK: Cambridge University Press, 1994).

———. *Imperial Connections: India in the Indian Ocean Arena, 1860–1920* (Berkeley, CA: University of California Press, 2007).

Mishra, Amit Kumar. 'Sardars, Kanganies and Maistries: Intermediaries in the Indian Labour Diaspora During the Colonial Period'. In *The History of Labour Intermediation: Institutions and Finding Employment in the Nineteenth and Early Twentieth Centuries*, edited by Sigrid Wadauer, Thomas Buchner and Alexander Mejstrik, pp. 368–387 (New York and Oxford: Berghahn Books, 2015).

Mishra, Saurabh. 'Violence, Resilience and the "Coolie" Identity: Life and Survival on Ships to the Caribbean, 1834–1917'. *Journal of Imperial and Commonwealth History* 50, no. 2 (2022): 241–263.

Misra, A. M. '"Business Culture" and Entrepreneurship in British India, 1860–1950'. *Modern Asian Studies* 34, no. 2 (2000): 333–348.

Misra, Maria. *Business, Race, and Politics in British India, c. 1850–1960* (Oxford: Clarendon Press, 1999).

Mittra, Kissory Chand. *Memoir of Dwarkanath Tagore* (Calcutta: Thacker, Spink & Company, 1870).

Mittra, Peary Chand. *Biographical Sketch of David Hare* (Calcutta: W. Newman & Company, 1877).

Mohabir, Nalini. 'Port of Departure, Port of Return: Mapping Indentured Returns to Calcutta'. *Small Axe: A Caribbean Journal of Criticism* 18, no. 2 (2014): 108–122.

Moir, Martin. 'Kaghazi Raj: Notes on the Documentary Basis of Company Rule: 1783–1858'. *Indo-British Review* 21, no. 2 (1993): 185–193.

Mongia, Radhika. 'Impartial Regimes of Truth: Indentured Indian Labour and the Status of the Inquiry'. *Cultural Studies* 18, no. 5 (2004): 749–768.

———. *Indian Migration and Empire: A Colonial Genealogy of the Modern State* (Durham, NC: Duke University Press, 2018).

Mookherji, S. B. *The Indenture System in Mauritius, 1837–1915* (Calcutta: Firma KLM, 1962).

Mukherjee, S. N. *Calcutta, Myths and History* (Calcutta: Subarnarekha, 1977).

Munro, Doug. 'The Tinker–Gillion Controversy in Indo-Fijian Indenture Historiography'. *Slavery and Abolition* 42, no. 2 (2021): 363–381.

Naidu, Suresh, and Noam Yuchtman. 'Coercive Contract Enforcement: Law and the Labor Market in Nineteenth Century Industrial Britain'. *American Economic Review* 103, no. 1 (2013): 107–144.

Nair, P. Thankappan. *A History of Calcutta's Streets* (Calcutta: Firma KLM, 1987).

———. *Calcutta in the 18th Century: Impressions of Travellers* (Calcutta: Firma KLM, 1984).

——— (ed.). *Calcutta in the 19th Century: Company's Days* (Calcutta: Firma KLM, 1989).

Nath, Dwarka. *A History of Indians in British Guyana* (London: Thomas Nelson & Sons, 1950).

Neal, Stan. 'Imperial Connections and Colonial Improvement: Scotland, Ceylon, and the China Coast, 1837–1841'. *Journal of World History* 29, no. 2 (June 2018): 213–238.

———. *Singapore, Chinese Migration and the Making of the British Empire, 1819–67* (Woodbridge: Boydell Press, 2019).

North-Coombs, M. D. 'From Slavery to Indenture: Forced Labour in the Political Economy of Mauritius, 1834–1867'. In *Indentured Labour in the British Empire, 1834–1920*, edited by Kay Saunders, pp. 78–125 (London and Canberra: Croom Helm, 1984).

Northrup, David. *Indentured Labour in the Age of Imperialism, 1834–1922* (New York, NY: Cambridge University Press, 1995).

O'Shaughnessy, Andrew Jackson. *An Empire Divided: The American Revolution and the British Caribbean* (Philadelphia, PA: University of Pennsylvania Press, 2000).

Ong, Aihwa. *Flexible Citizenship: The Cultural Logics of Transnationality* (Durham, NC: Duke University Press, 1999).

Orsini, Francesca. *The Hindi Public Sphere 1920–1940: Language and Literature in the Age of Nationalism* (Oxford: Oxford University Press, 2002).

Palit, Debabrata. *Dwarkanath Thakur* (Calcutta: Abinash Art Press, 1995).

Pandey, Gyanendra (ed.). *Unarchived Histories: The 'Mad' and the 'Trifling' in the Colonial and Postcolonial World* (Oxon and New York: Routledge, 2013).

Parr, Rosalind. *Citizens of Everywhere: Indian Women, Nationalism and Cosmopolitanism, 1920–1952* (Cambridge, UK: Cambridge University Press, 2022).

Petley, Christer. '"Devoted Islands" and "That Madman Wilberforce": British Proslavery Patriotism during the Age of Abolition'. *Journal of Imperial and Commonwealth History* 39, no. 3 (2011): 393–415.

———. 'Gluttony, Excess, and the Fall of the Planter Class in the British Caribbean'. *Atlantic Studies* 9, no. 1 (2012): 85–106.

———. 'Rethinking the Fall of the Planter Class'. *Atlantic Studies* 9, no. 1 (2012): 1–17.

Porter, Andrew. 'Trusteeship, Anti-Slavery, and Humanitarianism'. In *The Oxford History of the British Empire*: vol. 3: *The Nineteenth Century*, edited by Andrew Porter, pp. 198–221 (Oxford: Oxford University Press, 1999).

Prakash, Gyan. *Bonded Histories: Genealogies of Labor Servitude in Colonial India* (Cambridge: Cambridge University Press, 2003).

Ragatz, Lowell Joseph. *Fall of the Planter Class in the British Caribbean, 1763–1833: A Study in Social and Economic History* (New York, NY: Century Company, 1928).

Raman, Bhavani. *Document Raj: Writing and Scribes in Early Colonial South India* (Chicago, IL: University of Chicago Press, 2012).

Rand, Gavin, and Kim Wagner. 'Recruiting the "Martial Races": Identities and Military Service in Colonial India'. *Patterns of Prejudice* 46, nos. 3–4, (2012): 232–254.

Ray, Karen A. 'Kunti, Lakshmibhai and the "Ladies": Women's Labour and the Abolition of Indentured Emigration from India'. *Labour, Capital and Society* 29, nos. 1–2 (1996): 126–152.

Ray, Nisith Ranjan. *Calcutta: Profile of a City* (Calcutta: K. P. Bagchi & Company, 1986).

Robb, Peter. 'Introduction: South Asia and the Concept of Race'. In *The Concept of Race in South Asia*, edited by Peter Robb, pp. 1–76 (New Delhi: Oxford University Press, 1995).

Roopnarine, Lomarsh. *Indo-Caribbean Indenture: Resistance and Accommodation, 1838–1920* (Kingston: University of the West Indies Press, 2007).

———. 'Review of Coolies of the Empire: Indentured Indians in the Sugar Colonies, 1830–1920 by Ashutosh Kumar'. *Labor History* 60, no. 5 (2019): 590–591.

———. 'The First and Only Crossing: Indian Indentured Servitude on Danish St. Croix, 1863–1868'. *South Asian Diaspora* 1, no. 2 (2009): 113–140.

Roy, Tirthankar. 'Sardars, Jobbers, Kanganies: The Labour Contractor and Indian Economic History'. *Modern Asian Studies* 42, no. 5 (2008): 971–998.

Ryan, Maeve. *Humanitarian Governance and the British Antislavery World System* (New Haven, CT: Yale University Press, 2022).

Ryden, David Beck. 'Sugar, Spirits, and Fodder: The London West India Interest and the Glut of 1807–15'. *Atlantic Studies* 9, no. 1 (2012): 41–64.

Saha, Panchanan. *Emigration of Indian Labour 1834–1900* (New Delhi: People's Publishing House, 1970).

Samaroo, Brinsley. 'The Caribbean Consequences of the Indian Revolt of 1857'. In *Indian Diaspora in the Caribbean: History, Culture, and Identity*, edited by Rattan Lal Hangloo, pp. 71–93 (New Delhi: Primus Books, 2012).

Sarup, Leela Gujadhur. *Colonial Emigration, 19th–20th Century: Annual Reports from the Port of Calcutta to British and Foreign Colonies* (Kolkata: Aldrich International, 2007).

Schwartz, Joan, and Terry Cook. 'Archives, Records, and Power: The Making of Modern Memory'. *Archival Science* 2, no. 2 (2002): 1–19.

Sengupta, Kaustubh Mani. 'The New Fort William and the Dockyard: Constructing Company's Calcutta in the Late Eighteenth Century'. *Studies in History* 32, no. 2 (2016): 231–256.

Sheridan, Richard. 'The Condition of the Slaves on the Sugar Plantations of Sir John Gladstone in the Colony of Demerara, 1812–49'. *New West Indian Guide* 76, nos. 3–4 (2002): 243–269.

Sherman, Taylor, William Gould and Sarah Ansari. *From Subjects to Citizens: Society and the Everyday State in India and Pakistan, 1947–1970* (Cambridge, UK: Cambridge University Press, 2014).

Siddiqi, Majid Hayat. *The British Historical Context and Petitioning in Colonial India (M.A. Ansari Lecture)* (New Delhi: Aakar Books, 2005).

Singh, S. B. *European Agency Houses in Bengal: 1783–1833* (Calcutta: Firma KLM, 1966).

Sinha, Mrinalini. 'Anatomy of a Politics of the People'. In *Political Imaginaries in Twentieth-Century India*, edited by Mrinalini Sinha and Manu Goswami, pp. 31–50 (London: Bloomsbury Academic, 2022).

———. 'Totaram Sanadhya's *Fiji Mein Mere Ekkis Varsh*: A History of Empire and Nation in a Minor Key'. In *Ten Books That Shaped the British Empire: Creating an Imperial Commons*, edited by Antoinette Burton and Isabel Hofmeyr, pp. 168–188 (Durham, NC: Duke University Press, 2014).

Sinha, Nitin. 'Domestic Servants and Master–Servant Regulations in Colonial Calcutta, 1750s–1810s'. *Past and Present* 255, no. 1 (2022): 141–188.

Sinha, Nitin, and Nitin Varma (ed.). *Servants' Pasts: Late-Eighteenth to Twentieth Century South Asia*, vol. 2 (New Delhi: Orient Blackswan, 2019).

Sinha, Nitin, Nitin Varma and Pankaj Jha (eds.). *Servants' Pasts: Sixteenth to Eighteenth Century South Asia*, vol. 1 (New Delhi: Orient Blackswan, 2019).

Sinha, Pradip. *Calcutta in Urban History* (Calcutta: Firma KLM, 1978).

——— (ed.). *The Urban Experience: Calcutta, Essays in Honour of N. R. Ray* (Calcutta: Riddhi-India, 1986).

Skinner, Rob, and Alan Lester. 'Humanitarianism and Empire: New Research Agendas'. *Journal of Imperial and Commonwealth History* 40, no. 5 (2012): 729–747.

Stanziani, Alessandro. 'Local Bondage in Global Economies: Servants, Wage Earners, and Indentured Migrants in Nineteenth-Century France, Great Britain, and the Mascarene Islands'. *Modern Asian Studies* 47, no. 4 (2013): 1218–1251.

Stark, Ulrike. *An Empire of Books: The Naval Kishore Press and the Diffusion of the Printed Word in Colonial India* (New Delhi: Permanent Black, 2007).

Steele, Ian. *The English Atlantic, 1675–1740: An Exploration of Communication and Community* (New York and Oxford: Oxford University Press, 1986).

Stoler, Ann Laura. *Along the Archival Grain: Epistemic Anxieties and Colonial Common Sense* (Princeton, NJ: Princeton University Press, 2009).

———. 'Colonial Archives and the Arts of Governance'. *Archival Science* 2, nos. 1–2 (2002): 87–109.

———. '"In Cold Blood": Hierarchies of Credibility and the Politics of Colonial Narratives'. *Representations* 37 (January 1992): 151–189.

Sturman, Rachel. 'Indian Indentured Labor and the History of International Rights Regimes'. *The American Historical Review* 119, no. 5 (2014): 1439–1465.

Swaisland, Charles. 'The Aborigines Protection Society, 1837–1909'. *Slavery and Abolition* 21, no. 2 (2000): 265–280.

Swaminathan, Srividhya. 'Developing the West Indian Proslavery Position after the Somerset Decision'. *Slavery and Abolition* 24, no. 3 (2003): 40–60.

Tan, Tai-Yong. 'Port Cities and Hinterlands: A Comparative Study of Singapore and Calcutta'. *Political Geography* 26, no. 7 (2007): 851–865.

Taylor, Michael. 'British Proslavery Arguments and the Bible, 1823–1833'. *Slavery and Abolition* 37, no. 1 (2016): 139–158.

Thakur, Kshitindranath. *Dwarkanath Thakurer Jiboni* (A Biography of Dwarkanath Tagore) (Calcutta: Rabindra Bharati University Press, 1969).

Thompson, Elizabeth. *Colonial Citizens: Republican Rights, Paternal Privilege, and Gender in French Syria and Lebanon* (New York, NY: Columbia University Press, 2000).

Tinker, Hugh. *A New System of Slavery: The Export of Indian Labour Overseas 1830–1920* (London: Oxford University Press, 1974).

Tomlinson, B. R. *The Economy of Modern India: From 1860 to the Twenty-First Century* (Cambridge, UK: Cambridge University Press, 2013).

Tomlinson, Tom. 'The Empire of Enterprise: Scottish Business Networks in Asian Trade, 1793–1810'. *KIU Journal of Economics and Business Studies* 8 (2001): 67–83.

Travers, Robert. 'Indian Petitioning and Colonial State-Formation in Eighteenth-Century Bengal'. *Modern Asian Studies* 53, no. 1 (2019): 89–122.

Trouillot, Michel-Rolph. *Silencing the Past: Power and the Production of History* (Boston, MA: Beacon Press, 1995).

Waddell, Brodie, and Jason Peacey (eds.). *The Power of Petitioning in Early Modern Britain* (London: UCL Press, 2024).

Weiss Muller, Hannah. *Subjects and Sovereign: Bonds of Belonging in the Eighteenth-Century British Empire* (New York, NY: Oxford University Press, 2017).

Yang, Anand. 'Peasants on the Move: A Study of Internal Migration in India'. *Journal of Interdisciplinary History* 10, no. 1 (1979): 37–58.

———. *The Limited Raj: Agrarian Relations in Colonial India, Saran District, 1793–1920* (Berkeley, CA: University of California Press, 1989).

Zaret, David. *Origins of Democratic Culture: Printing, Petitions, and the Public Sphere in Early Modern England* (Princeton, NJ: Princeton University Press, 2000).

———. 'Petitions and the "Invention" of Public Opinion in the English Revolution'. *American Journal of Sociology* 101, no. 6 (May 1996): 1497–1555.

Zehmisch, Philipp. 'The Invisible Architects of Andaman: Manifestations of Aboriginal Migration from Ranchi'. In *Manifestations of History: Time, Space, and Community in the Andaman Islands*, edited by Frank Heidemann and Philipp Zehmisch, pp. 122–138 (New Delhi: Primus Books, 2016).

Zook, Darren C. 'Developing the Rural Citizen: Southern India, 1900–47'. *South Asia: Journal of South Asian Studies* 23, no. 1 (2000): 65–86.

Index